Texts in Philosophy
Volume 19

History and Philosophy of Physics in the South Cone

Volume 10
The Socratic Tradition. Questioning as Philosophy and as Method
Matti Sintonen, ed.

Volume 11
PhiMSAMP. Philosophy of Mathematics: Sociological Aspects and Mathematical Practice
Benedikt Löwe and Thomas Müller, eds.

Volume 12
Philosophical Perspectives on Mathematical Practice
Bart Van Kerkhove, Jonas De Vuyst, and Jean Paul Van Bendegem, eds.

Volume 13
Beyond Description: Naturalism and Normativity
Marcin Miłkowski and Konrad Talmont-Kaminski, eds.

Volume 14
Corroborations and Criticisms. Forays with the Philosophy of Karl Popper
Ivor Grattan-Guinness

Volume 15
Knowledge, Value, Evolution.
Tomáš Hříbek and Juraj Hvorecký, eds.

Volume 16
Hao Wang. Logician and Philosopher
Charles Parsons and Montgomery Link, eds.

Volume 17
Mimesis: Metaphysics, Cognition, Pragmatics
Gregory Currie, Petr Koťátko, Martin Pokorný

Volume 18
Contemporary Problems of Epistemology in the Light of Phenomenology. Temporal Consciousness and the Limits of Formal Theories
Stathis Livadas

Volume 19
History and Philosophy of Physics in the South Cone
Roberto de Andrade Martins, Guillermo Boido, and Víctor Rodríguez, eds.

Volume 20
History and Philosophy of the Life Sciences in the South Cone
Pablo Lorenzano, Lilian Al-Chueyr Pereira Martins, and Anna Carolina K. P. Regner, eds.

Texts in Philosophy Series Editors
Vincent F. Hendriks   vincent@hum.ku.dk
John Symons   jsymons@utep.edu
Dov Gabbay   dov.gabbay@kcl.ac.uk

History and Philosophy of Physics in the South Cone

Edited by
Roberto de Andrade Martins,
Guillermo Boido,
and
Víctor Rodríguez

© Individual author and College Publications 2013.
All rights reserved.

ISBN 978-1-84890-105-6

College Publications
Scientific Director: Dov Gabbay
Managing Director: Jane Spurr
Department of Computer Science
King's College London, Strand, London WC2R 2LS, UK

http://www.collegepublications.co.uk

Original cover design by orchid creative   www.orchidcreative.co.uk

Printed by Lightning Source, Milton Keynes, UK

All rights reserved. No part of this publication may be reproduced, stored in a retrieval system or transmitted in any form, or by any means, electronic, mechanical, photocopying, recording or otherwise without prior permission, in writing, from the publisher.

TABLE OF CONTENTS

Presentation IX
    Pablo Lorenzano
Introduction XI
    Roberto A. Martins, Guillermo Boido, and Víctor Rodríguez
Science and Music in the Works of Vincenzo Galilei (*ca*. 1520-1591) 1
    Guillermo Boido and Eduardo Kastika
    1. Introduction 1
    2. Stages of the science of music: from the Middle Ages to the Renaissance 3
    3. The points of view of Zarlino 6
    4. Galilei: a dissident disciple 8
    5. Galilei on the threshold of acoustics 11
    6. Did Galilei carry out real experiments? 12
    7. Vincenzo Galilei and Galileo 13
    8. Some notes about acoustics after Galilei 16
    9. Conclusions: Galilei and a second line team 17
    References 18

William Crookes' Researches on Radiometric Effect *versus* His Methodological Concerns on Residual Phenomena 21
    Juliana M. Hidalgo Ferreira
    1. First comments 21
    2. The atomic weight of thallium 24
    3. Investigations on the radiometric effect 25
    4. The radiometer 33
    5. William Crookes' methodological concerns 38
    6. Crookes' researches on radiometric effect viewed in the light of his methodological concerns 39
    7. Final comments 42
    References 43

The Guiding Hypothesis of the Curies' Radioactivity Research: Secondary X-rays and the Sagnac Connection 45
    Roberto de Andrade Martins
    Conclusions 61
    References 61

Galileo's Matter-Theory: *resolutio* and Infinite Indivisibles 67
    Fernando Tula Molina
    1. Introduction 67
    2. Conflicting traditions at the back of Galileo's science 68
        2.1. Sunspots and atomism 68

2.2. Hydrostatic and atomism..70
　　　2.3 The evaluation of the Aristotle-Democritus controversy:
　　　　　specific weight as characteristic ratio of elementary units.............73
　3. Fluids cohesion and Galilean matter-theory...78
　4. Mathematical or physical atomism?...82
　5. Resolutio as key concept in Galileo's atomism.......................................87
　6. Concluding remarks...90
　References...91

T-Invariance, Irreversibility, Arrow of Time: Similar But Different 93
Olimpia Lombardi
　1. Introduction..93
　2. T-invariance..94
　3. Irreversibility..96
　4. Relationship between t-invariance and irreversibility.......................98
　5. The problem of irreversibility: Boltzmann versus Gibbs..................99
　　　5.1. The approach of Boltzmann..101
　　　5.2. The approach of Gibbs...102
　　　5.3. Boltzmann versus Gibbs..104
　6. The problem of the arrow of time...107
　7. Arrow of time and thermodynamics...110
　8. Topological conditions for defining the arrow of time...................113
　　　8.1. T-orientability..114
　　　8.2. Cosmic time...115
　9. T-asymmetry...117
　10. T-invariance and the arrow of time...121
　11. Concluding remarks..122
　References...123

Principles in Cosmology 127
Antonio Augusto Passos Videira
　References...141

Geometrical and Epistemological Aspects of the Schrödinger's Unified Field Theory 145
Víctor Rodríguez and Pedro W. Lamberti
　1. Introduction..145
　2. The epistemology of Schrödinger...146
　3. The evolution of his geometrical ideas..151
　　　3.1. Background...152
　　　3.2. The contributions of Schrödinger...154
　4. Conclusions...155
　References...156

Map of Interpretations of Quantum Theory 159
Osvaldo Pessoa Jr.

1. General considerations 159
2. Four broad interpretative groups 162
3. Key questions for distinguishing the interpretations................ 164
   3.1. Two slit experiment... 165
   3.2. Mach-Zehnder interferometer 166
   3.3. Anti-correlation experiment..................................... 167
   3.4. The quantum-mechanical state 168
   3.5. Measurements in quantum physics 169
   3.6. Interpretations of the uncertainty principle 171
4. The main interpretations of quantum theory 172
   4.1. The first semi-classical theories 173
   4.2. The complementarity interpretation 174
   4.3 Hidden variable theories 176
   4.4. Stochastic interpretations... 177
   4.5. Statistical ensemble interpretation........................... 178
   4.6. Potentiality interpretations 179
   4.7. The orthodox interpretations................................... 179
   4.8. Wave interpretations 182
   4.9. Interpretations that question classical logic 185
5. Map of the interpretations 187
6. Conclusion 188
References 188

Randomness vs. Arbitrariness in Classical Statistical Mechanics or Statistical Mechanics? 193
Eduardo H. Flichman

1. Purposes 193
2. Introduction... 195
   2.1. About what this paper will not treat 196
      2.1.1. The epistemic problem.................................. 196
      2.1.2. Evolution equations....................................... 196
   2.2. About what this paper will indeed treat 197
3. First difficulty 197
   3.1. Terminology and something more........................... 198
   3.2. An example 200
   3.3. The questions 201
   3.4. First explanatory assumption.................................. 202
   3.5. Second explanatory supposition.............................. 203
   3.6. Articulation of the first and second suppositions.... 205
   3.7. Third explanatory supposition................................. 205
   3.8. Conclusion 207
4. Second problem and my conjecture..................................... 207
   4.1. The problem 207
   4.2. The conjecture.. 208
5. Complementary note: two ontological notions of probability........... 209

References 209

Presentation

The *Association of Philosophy and History of Science in the South Cone* (AFHIC) is a non-profit academic association, founded on May 5th, 2000, in Quilmes, Argentina, at the closing ceremony of the *2nd Meeting of Philosophy and History of Science in the South Cone*.

The creation of this Association was the result of the interest to deepen and strengthen the exchange between the researchers in Philosophy and History of Science from the countries of the South Cone, from the two first meetings that took place in Porto Alegre (Brazil, 1998) and Quilmes (Argentine, 2000) onwards. Since then, there have been biennial meetings organized as its responsibility.

The main aim of AFHIC is to contribute to a better understanding of science from a philosophical as well as a historical point of view in the Spanish- and Portuguese-speaking countries, especially in those which belong to the American South Cone, promoting a space for reflection, exchange, discussion, communication, and dissemination of such an understanding.

This volume is – with minor changes – the English version of *Física: Estudos Filosóficos e Históricos*. It is composed of refereed and, in some cases, opportunely modified contributions made by members of the *Association of Philosophy and History of Science in the South Cone*, some of them who are unfortunately no longer among us. It is an integral part of AFHIC's Book Series.

Its publication has been possible thanks to two men and their willingness to cooperate in this way with AFHIC's Book Series, and thus help us in achieving the main aim of our Association. Such men are the Editors of the Series "Philosophy", Vincent F. Hendricks and John Symons, to whom I wish to express my deep gratitude.

Pablo Lorenzano
Director of AFHIC's Book Series

Introduction

This book – *Philosophy and History of Physics* – constitutes the first volume of the series *Philosophy and History of Science in the South Cone*. The articles published here, on different aspects of the philosophy and the history of physics, present significant contributions to the study on this area. Besides the authors' work, the elaboration of this book counted on help from those researchers who were anonymous referees, contributing to the selection, and making suggestions for improving the works here published. The editors thank the invaluable collaboration of all those researchers.

Two of the articles of this book address issues on the history of physics at the beginning of the Modern Age. Guillermo Boido and Eduardo Kastika analyze the contribution of Vincenzo Galilei (the father of Galileo Galilei) to the science of music, in a period in which the theory of music had important relationships not just with mathematics (its oldest connection to science), but also with astronomy and with the study of emotions – among other aspects –, before it was transformed into the cold science of acoustics. Fernando Tula Molina, on his side, studies an aspect of Galileo's physics: his matter-theory. The concern about the existence of atoms, which goes through several phases in Galileo's work, has an impact on his understanding of the bodies cohesion, the nature of the solids and fluids, the surface tension, and some considerations on geometry and the indivisibles.

In her article, Olimpia Lombardi discusses the fundamental problem of the "arrow of time", clarifying the important differences among concepts that are often confused by dealing with this topic: the concept of invariance in relation to the substitution of t by $-t$ (a property of the physical laws), the concept of reversibility (a property of the physical processes), and the concept of symmetry in relation to time (a property of the models).

Antonio Augusto Passos Videira's contribution refers to the nature of the principles used in cosmology. The modern theory on the origin and the structure of the universe demands the utilization of certain fundamental principles that open a discussion in what extent cosmology has the same scientific *status* as other studies in physics, or whether it has peculiarities and limitations that would turn it into a metaphysical study.

Schrödinger's unified field theory is the theme of the work by Víctor Rodríguez and Pedro W. Lamberti. They analyze the epistemological point of view underlying the work of Schrödinger as well as the geometric vision that influenced in the formulation of that unified field theory in the 1940's.

Osvaldo Pessoa Jr. presents a vast overview of the dozens of different interpretations that were successively proposed for quantum mechanics. He compares and classifies the different interpretations, especially using the ontological and epistemological criteria for analyzing and differentiating the distinct approaches.

Finally, this volume contains a work by the late Professor Eduardo Héctor Flichman (Mendoza, 19.12.1932 – Buenos Aires, 13.06.2005) on the foundations of statistical mechanics. Flichman shows the difficulty of understanding certain aspects of classical statistical mechanics, by particularly discussing the probability distribution of initial conditions, from the ontological point of view. After clarifying some less discussed problems, he proposes the introduction of certain additional initial conditions that are not usually taken into account.

With a wide variety of topics and approaches, but always with reliability and depth, the present book constitutes an important contribution to the study of the philosophy and the history of physics.

The editors

Science and Music in the Works of Vincenzo Galilei (*ca*. 1520-1591)[*]

Guillermo Boido

Faculty of Exact and Natural Sciences, University of Buenos Aires (UBA)

Eduardo Kastika

Faculty of Economical Sciences, University of Buenos Aires (UBA)

1. Introduction

We have held in a previous paper that in times of the rise of modern science scholars accorded music an important role as a means for their inquiries about the universe or simply about certain natural phenomena that needed explanation for the needs of musical composition and interpretation. It was considered that *music* and *knowledge*

---

[*] Parts of this paper were read in the *XIII Jornadas de Epistemología e Historia de la Ciencia*, Facultad de Filosofía y Humanidades, Universidad Nacional de Córdoba, La Falda, Córdoba, Argentina (November 28-30, 2002) The considerations in the introduction are a development of ideas in Boido & Kastika (2002). We are grateful to Professor Ramiro Albino for several observations related to the history of music which have enabled us to clarify important points of this paper, and to Professor Horacio Abeledo, who read a preliminary version and made several appropriate suggestions that led to us to modify some passages. The original Spanish version was translated into English by Horacio Abeledo.

were strongly connected (Boido & Kastika 2002, pp. 60-61). In terms of what we consider the "science" of the period, we believe it necessary to understand *musical science* as the combination of studies, reflections and experimentation connected with music as it was understood from the point of view of its association to knowledge. This discipline, at present nonexistent, received the contributions of various dissimilar personalities and modes of thought: natural philosophers, astronomers, mathematicians, composers and performers of music, manufacturers of instruments. In particular in the 16th and 17th centuries music could be considered variously as a science dealing with "unheard sounds", as a means to decipher the harmony of the world, as a field of pre-scientific and scientific experimentation, as an autonomous art, or as an art necessarily bound to rhetoric. The science of music during this period was a disciplinary universe that comprised those (many sided and changing) points of view about music and its relation to the sciences and to knowledge in general.[1]

The position occupied by science of music during the Scientific Revolution can be analyzed on the basis of recognizing three points of view that coexisted in permanent tension at the time: (a) the point of view implied in the ideas of thinkers that theorized about music from a perspective (of mathematical slant and Pythagorean origins) that placed it among the disciplines of the *quadrivium*; (b) the ideas of those who, on the basis of the new music of the late 16th and early 17th century ("First Baroque" in Manfred Bukofzer's terms), inaugurated a theoretical perspective which tried to relate different types of music with the effects they produced on the emotional states of the hearer; and (c) the viewpoint included in the considerations of those

---

[1] In order to avoid misinterpretations, we must point out that "science of music" is here a historiographic category of analysis, constructed from the consideration of ideas, studies, and practices of various natures that were *in use during the historic period considered*. For our purposes it would be anachronistic to use the expression in relation to present day scientific research about, say, the psychological effects of different kinds of music on children or on persons affected by illness and to use that knowledge with educational or therapeutic aims. Such contemporary studies could be referred to as "science of music", but the meaning of the expression will be different from the meaning with which it is used in this paper. The former refers to science and music as we understand them in the present time. We thank Dr. Eduardo Rabossi for pointing out to us the need to emphasize this distinction.

who (entertaining a conception of music that depended much less on academic traditions) used it as a field of experimentation of the new science that was being born at the time.

As we have said the three viewpoints were in conflict during the 16th and 17th centuries. The emphasis on music understood as the discipline of the sonorous numbers or as a reflection of the harmony of the spheres gradually decreased in favor of music conceived as an emotion-generating factor on the basis of its rhetoric power. Music slowly transformed into an art, hence to be judged by means of esthetic criteria, while the science of music was disappearing and a new discipline – acoustics – was developing as one of the branches of modern physical science.

Aspects of all these transformations converge in Vincenzo Galilei (*circa* 1520-1591), Galileo Galilei's father. An analysis of his work, from the perspective of the history of the science of music is the object of the present work, in which we shall consider the role of Galilei in three aspects in which he had a decisive role: the conformation of music as an art and gradual vanishing of the science of music, the rise of the Baroque style, and the birth of the *new science*.

2. Stages of the science of music: from the Middle Ages to the Renaissance

In the 6th century Roman philosopher Boethius (circa 480-524) set down in his treatise *De Institutione musica* the complete musical theory of his time. Boethius was the guide and authority through the Middle Ages regarding classical texts on music. His concept of *musica mundana* refers to the music of the spheres of Pythagoras, that is to say, harmony in a broad sense. This was the only music that really existed. Other kinds of music existed only as a "reflection" of *musica mundana*, insofar as they took part in, or reminded of, the harmony of the cosmos: *musica humana* referred to the psycho-physical harmony reigning in the interior of man and *musica instrumentalis* (the lowest of Boethius's categories) is audible music, the nearest to music as we understand it today.

There is no doubt that in the Middle Ages music was considered a science. The laws of this science mirrored the laws of the universe, since musical harmony was a reflection of celestial harmony. The systems of scales, the theories of harmony and rhythm, were justified by philosophic and cosmological considerations. Conversely, the orbits, positions and movements of the planets were to be explained by scales, musical modes and harmonic proportions. In this way, music linked Pythagorean conceptions and Christian mystics.

This Pythagorean-platonic style of musical thinking makes it possible to speak of a "non-real" and a "real" evolution of music during the Middle-Ages and even the Renaissance. The "real" evolution (that of audible sounds) took place from the beginning of Gregorian chant up to the first experiments in polyphony. And the "non-real" evolution refers to the ideas of the theoreticians of *musica mundana*, who progressed in their speculations about proportions, sonorous numbers, theories of consonance in relation to fractions or *ratios*, etc. These theoreticians very rarely delved into esthetic theses in relation to the sound world itself, that is to say, to instrumental music.

With the exception of Reginon of Prüm, who in the 10th century held that the strings of an instrument are comparable to those that produce celestial music, and associated each sound of the musical scale with each of the planets, there usually was no relation between mundane, human and instrumental music. The gap between the theoretical and practical planes was continually confirmed during the Middle Ages (Fubini 1999, pp. 103-104). However, Guido d'Arezzo (980-1050), already considered that the ideas of Boethius were "useful only to philosophers". After that, theoreticians increasingly addressed the *cantores* (players) rather than the *musici* (philosophers).

Ever since the 11th century, the development of polyphony and counterpoint has become of uttermost importance because of the stimulus it provided for theorizing. Now it is the musician that must face the problem of consonance with a greater number of sounds, within the counterpoint maze involved in the simultaneous melodies of polyphony. New challenges connected with musical notation and problems of rhythm have to be dealt with. Music, as we have pointed out, begins to be thought of as something "real", linked with the world of the senses.

Gradually, then, music was defined more and more as the science of the sounds produced by the human voice or the instruments of musicians. The problems generated by the new polyphonic practice brought about the gradual decadence of the theological-cosmological conception of music. New conceptions which take into account the factor of *beauty* in music appear during the 14th century. According to M. Gerbert in his book *Scriptores Ecclesiastii de Musica Sacra Potissimum* (1784), Marchetto of Padua affirms at the beginning of that century:

> *Music is the most beautiful of arts* [...]; in its nobility all things that possess life and all things that do not possess it participate. [...] Surely, nothing is more consonant to man than letting himself be relax by the sweeter modes and becoming tense with the modes opposite to those. Moreover, there is no age in which man does not experience delight upon hearing a sweet melody. (Quoted in Fubini 1999, pp. 112-113; our italics)

Ars nova appeared during the 14th century as a new musical style. This style meant a movement towards freedom from the old influences of *organum* (consisting in doubling the plainsong in octaves, fourths or fifths) and the *conductus* (adding original or secular parts – i.e. popular, profane or picaresque melodies – to an already existing melody), which brought about an increasing variety in rhythm, more harmonious melodic contours, and vocal parts of greater independence. Probably the work of troubadours and trouvères (poet-composers who wrote in Provençal and French, respectively) paved the way for this more artistic conception of music, which would become consolidated with the Italian madrigal (Scholes 1981, p. 131.)

One of the first esthetic controversies between the new theoreticians of music and philosophers is the one between the partisans of *Ars nova* and those of *Ars antiqua*. For example, Pope John XXII strongly endorsed the latter, praising its simplicity and clarity. But this is not merely a "reactionary" response to innovation. In its deeper sense it is a criticism to music considered as an end in itself, self sufficient and autonomous in what regards to its purely aural value. Music had been previously an instrument for religious edification. But now, as Fubini writes, "the *reasons* of music become gradually more overbearing and tend to affirm themselves disregarding theological, cosmological and moral motivations and justifications in an increasingly open way" (Fubini 1999, p. 116).

The cosmological-mathematical-religious structure of musical science at the start of the Renaissance began to crumble partly because of the birth of polyphony and *Ars nova*. Johannes Tinctoris (*circa*

1435-1511) expressed his opinions about music from the standpoint of Aristotelian philosophy. For this author, the only music of interest is the music of instruments, the music that can be heard, and as a consequence is analyzable through its effects. E. Coussemaker, in his book *Scriptorum de Musica Medii Aevii* (1868) quotes the following words of Tinctoris:

> I cannot remain silent in relation to the opinions of numerous philosophers, among which are Pythagoras and Plato, and those that came after them, like Cicero, Macrobius, Boethius and our Isidore, according to whom the celestial spheres spin according to harmonic modulations, or what is the same, according to the adjustment between different sounds. But when, as Boethius reports, some of them affirm that Saturn moves producing a sound of lower pitch […] whereas the Moon produces a higher one, and others hold inversely that the lower sound corresponds to the Moon and the higher sound is that of the fixed stars, I share none of these opinions. I believe instead in Aristotle and his commentators, as well as our more recent philosophers, who have shown with all evidence that in the heavens there is no sound, whether in potency or in act. For this reason, nobody can ever persuade me that musical harmonies, which cannot be produced without sounds, can be a result of the movement of celestial bodies. The harmonies of sounds and melodies, from whose sweetness, in the words of Lactantius, derives the pleasure of the ear, are produced, not by celestial bodies, but rather by earthly instruments with the aid of nature. (Quoted in Fubini 1999, pp. 123-124)

These controversies acquire new significance with the thought and works of Gioseffo Zarlino (1517-1590), teacher of Vincenzo Galilei.

3. The points of view of Zarlino

Although he studied theology and received minor orders, Zarlino stood out as a scholar in philosophy, languages, and music. Born in Chioggia, he settled in Venice in 1541, where he became chapel master of St. Mark's. The greater part of his compositions and of his theoretical works on music has been lost. His book *Institutioni harmoniche* (Venice 1558) had great influence on his contemporaries and was translated to French, German, and Dutch.

The "mathematization" of music, according to Zarlino, corresponded to the "mathematization" of nature. Although music still built on a system of numerical relations – Zarlino was essentially a

Pythagorean – the harmony of unheard sounds began with him to be *tightly linked* to the harmony of sounds that are heard. If medieval rationalism was abstract and led to the setting up of theoretical constructions in relation to music that were deprived of connections with experience, and grounded on extraneous principles, Zarlino instead tried to justify rationally the use of the musical intervals, which are made in real music.

Zarlino redefined the problem of consonance tackled by Pythagoras by means of the *scenario*, a system of numeric ratios based on the first six natural numbers (which Zarlino regarded according to tradition as "sonorous numbers"). This range, in Zarlino's view, had the capacity of generating all musical consonances. Why six numbers? Basically the reasons have to do with numerological speculation. The number six is a "perfect" number: it can be obtained by the addition of its divisors (1, 2, 3), that is, $1 + 2 + 3 = 1 \times 2 \times 3$. The number 28 has the same property of being the sum of its divisors (1, 2, 4, 7, and 14). In his *Elements*, Euclid dwells on the perfection of these numbers, and in particular the number six, not only because it is the first of the perfect numbers, but also because its divisors are consecutive numbers. Moreover, Zarlino adds that God completed Creation in *six* days, and that there exist *six* planets: The Moon, Mercury, Venus, Mars, Jupiter and Saturn (Cohen 1984, pp. 5-6).[2] To these he adds other reasons of similar kind.

But in the proportions of the Zarlino's consonances the number eight, which is not a part of the *scenario*, is included (in the minor sixth, 5:8). In this case, Zarlino makes use of an Aristotelian distinction: where the other consonances are really included in the *scenario*, the minor sixth is only *potentially* included. (Here, we would consider today, he introduces a convenient *ad hoc* hypothesis). Zarlino could have extended the range of his analysis to the first eight natural numbers, but in that case he would have had to include the number *seven*, but that would have generated problems for his conception of consonance. In terms of beauty and perfection the number seven has never been very fortunate.

---

[2] Zarlino prudently omits the Sun, which is also a planet in the geocentric system. Kepler mentions six planets, but from the heliocentric perspective: The Moon is dropped out (because it is a satellite) and the Earth is included.

But Zarlino does not explain in what way these numbers affect the human faculty of perceiving sounds and experimenting pleasure when there is consonance. In fact, the chasm between experience of the senses and abstract numbers had not been bridged. The Venetian musician does not stray very far from numerical mysticism. Whenever necessary, it resorts to Aristotelian explanations far removed from independent experimentation and from any mathematical formulation based on the quantification of natural phenomena.

Until the *Cinquecento* a musical theory was considered *true* if it followed the tradition transmitted by the more prestigious of the theorists of the Middle Ages and Antiquity, mainly Aristotle and Boethius. In his *Institutioni harmoniche*, Zarlino introduces a new criterion of truth: a mathematical order is as simple and rational as nature itself. He does not discard the Boethian concept of *musica mundane*, but interprets it in his own special way: "it is that harmony that is known to exist not only between the objects that can be seen in the heavens, but is also contained in the relations of the Elements and in the variety of times" (quoted by Fubini 1999, p. 129).

In the quest for a criterion of truth based on the mathematical order of nature, the phenomenon of *harmonics* had an essential role. Harmonics are found in nature, and because of that their sequence generated consonant chords. This is the point of departure for all theoreticians of harmony from Zarlino to Rameau. Starting from harmonics a new tonal-harmonic scheme began to be built. It slowly extended from popular song and profane music, to the musical repertory in general. This new method of musical construction (that by the late Baroque period had been fully established) unchained simpler musical forms that had logic different from that of Renaissance music. Musical theorization began to be intertwined with the activities of playing and composing music. Musical theoreticians concentrated for the first time on searches similar to those of painters, writers and other men of arts, particularly on the search for the classical essence of ancient Greece, a synonym of simplicity, clarity and rationality.

4. Galilei: a dissident disciple

Vincenzo Galilei (*circa* 1520-1591) is one of the main exponents of that search, which rummage in classical antiquity in search of "true" music. He is remembered for his contributions to musical theory and as the author of several musical compositions that are still (though seldom) played today. Born near Florence, he enjoyed the protection of Giovanni Bardi, count of Vernio, and was able to study in Venice with Zarlino. In the 14th century, the Galilei family belonged to the Florentine nobility, but two centuries later financial hardship had blurred the family glitter and Vincenzo had to alternate his musical vocation with the practice of commerce in textiles. Judging from the chronicles that have been preserved, Galilei was a prominent music teacher and a remarkable lute player.

In his *Dialogo della musica antica e della moderna* (1581) Galilei laid down, together with other members of the Camerata Fiorentina, whose patron was Bardi, the basic principles of a new musical style, the accompanied monody, based on what was then believed to be "true" Greek music. It must be borne in mind that, unlike the case of sculpture, architecture and poetry, the nature of Greek music was not known exactly, although the written texts of various scholars, philosophers, poets and essayists of antiquity could be inquired in hope of finding traces that lead us to the nature of this music. In disagreement with other musical tendencies of the time, for the Camerata Fiorentina the sources to consult were not treatises about music and harmony understood as science or philosophy, but rather those that considered music as a form of expression related with rhetoric, poetry or drama. In these last disciplines, the Camerata Fiorentina attempted to find the roots of the authentic Greek music of antiquity, which was believed to be structured in a single voice or in unison, and associated a particular musical *ethos* to each musical form: music, according to Galilei and the other theoreticians of the Camerata, should move the *affections*.

This expressive ideal (moving affections) is the common denominator of Baroque music, of which Galilei is one of the forerunners. The polyphonic music of the time was in his view absurd, because it generated linguistic and musical confusion and above all it mixed the different effects it produced on the hearer. The *Dialogo* is intended to serve as an antidote against chaotic vocal polyphony (in particular that of Venetian composers) and the excess of theoretical abstraction that curtailed the musicians' creativity. The new tonal harmony, instead, was more understandable, simple and rational according to Galilei, and it solved in a more efficient way the relation between *music and text*. This relation had been seriously jeopardized by the complicated structures of polyphonic music. For Galilei each word or group of words expressed a concept or a feeling that was in correspondence with certain melodic intervals. It was inadmissible then, that the rights of music should prevail over those of the words. The polemic with Zarlino was of course inevitable, and it could only end with the death of both men, which happened almost simultaneously.

With the new type of music, *the separation between those who reflected music and those who composed it and played it, ceased to exist*. Vincenzo Galilei theorized and wrote about musical questions but, as said before, he was also a remarkable player of the lute. The worlds of scholarship and of practice came into contact for the first time, and this brought about new polemics, new concepts, new categories, but it also caused the older problems (complexity of polyphonic texture, difficulty for the hearer in understanding the texts, fixed rules for the placing of dissonance) to lose interest. There was no relation between that music, on one hand, that expresses or imitates feelings, emotions or natural phenomena, that resounds in the ear of common mortals, and that is played by musicians (a profession that up to then had been despised), and music as thought, researched and theorized upon by philosophers on the other. The ideas of Galilei and the Camerata Fiorentina demathematize music and free it from the theoretical complexities of polyphony; but they also subordinate it to the supremacy of words. Those who endorsed the tenets of the Camerata held that the complex counterpoints of polyphonic music were inadequate to express and transmit the emotional contents of poetry. Madrigals, intermezzi (interludes of pastoral, allegoric or mythological character that were interposed between acts in Renaissance theater), and madrigal comedies – all of them, musical compositions of the late 16th century in which texts predominate – were the forerunners of opera. Two members of the Camerata, Julio Caccini and Jacopo Peri, used monody for the monologues and dialogues of a stage drama, and in 1598 Peri, with the collaboration of Caccini, presented his first opera, *Dafne*. With Galilei and the Camerata we witness the beginnings of the conception of music as an art, severed already from the philosophical speculations of the past and to be evaluated solely by reference to esthetic criteria: the Baroque is being born.

5. Galilei on the threshold of acoustics

From the point of view of modern science's birth, Galilei seems to have been, according to Stillman Drake, the first to discover a physical law that involves movement by means of measurement, obtained through experiment (Drake 1992, p. 10). In his protracted controversy with Zarlino, Galilei introduced the concept of tension from a string, which, apart from length, is relevant for musical consonance. In order to arrive to these conclusions, Galileo's father appeals to experimentation from a point of view similar to that accorded by the *new science* to the activity of experimenting: he used the monochord for his studies on the production of sound and, starting from certain preliminary tentative hypotheses, found that the pitch of the sound produced by a string varied not only inversely with its length, but also with the square of the weight of a body attached to the string (so that the octave could be produced by increasing the weight four times). By means of experimentation, he showed that equal strings produce the fifth if their tensions are in the relation 4:9. (He published this result mentioned by Drake in 1589, in a reply to Zarlino.) He also asserted (though without experimentation, as it can be assumed since the result is erroneous) that the note emitted by an organ pipe depends on its volume, and that the ratio 1:8 produces the octave. On the basis of these results, he built a mathematical scheme in order to prove Zarlino's theory incorrect. He established as a base the natural numbers between *1* and *8* as an alternative to Zarlino's *scenario* which comprised the numbers between *1* and *6*.

Musical developments produced during the second half of the 16th century, with the appearance of early Baroque, gradually brought about the need for a tempered scale. In 1578, Galilei sent Zarlino a defense of the modifications that practical musicians had made of the temperament recommended by Zarlino. (Which Zarlino attacked in his final word on musical theory, *Sopplementi armoniche*.) From the point of view of the independence of music as an art, Galilei was one of the pioneers in demathematizing music. He denied that the intervals were "natural" or that they were consonant because they could be represented by simple ratios. All sounds, in his view, were natural, but they offered pleasure to the ear in different ways. The way to prove this was through listening and not because of the adoption of this or the other numerical system. Mathematics had no power over the senses. Ultimately, the senses were the defining criterion for excellence of colors, flavors, smells and sounds. In the case of temperament, Galilei supported a system that was approximately equal to that determined by a trained ear. In his final answer to Zarlino, we can find the experimental refutation of the hypothesis that sonorous numbers are the cause of consonance. Galilei confirmed that the ratios 2:1, 3:2 and 4:3 correspond to octaves, fifths and fourths for strings made of the same material, with corresponding lengths, provided they have equal tension, and equal thickness. But if they had the same thickness and unequal tension, or the material of which they were built changed, the ratios corresponding to those intervals changed too.[3] With Galilei, the relationship between music and mathematics ceases to be aprioristic and mystical, and acquires the traits that are typical of the *new science*: mathematics, understood instrumentally, allows the formulation and testing of quantitative hypothesis about sound phenomena.

6. Did Galilei carry out real experiments?

There is a controversy regarding the experiments Galilei declares to having carried out that parallels the similar controversy affecting the experiments purportedly performed by his renowned son. Are the alleged experimental results the product of authentic experiments or do they originate from intuitive or aprioristic considerations? Just as Galileo, Galilei uses the words *sperienza* and *esperienza* (synonyms ac-

---

[3] Let us recall anachronistically that the possible frequencies of vibration of a string with both ends fixed are: $v_n = [n/2l]\sqrt{T/\mu}$, where T is the tension of the string, and $\square$ is the mass per unit of length. For $n=1$ the fundamental frequency is obtained; for $n = 2, 3, 4...$, the frequencies of the overtones. From the mathematical expression of the law it can be deduced that to duplicate the frequency of vibration of a certain string (and so obtain the octave) it is necessary to quadruple the tension. The parameter $\square$ expresses the influence of the thickness and the material on the pitch of the emitted note and hence on the musical intervals obtained, something that Galilei found qualitatively.

cording to the Accademia della Crusca, founded in 1583) in two distinct senses. When he declares, for instance, that the fifth (3:2) is an interval that is more perfect and sweeter than any other, because "I have confirmed it by means of the ear after many experiences", he obviously does not refer to any experiment but rather to the aesthetic satisfaction produced by the sensory experience of listening to the sounds. But in some other contexts, *esperienza* refers clearly to experiments. Claude Palisca quotes an example where, trying to undermine the statement attributed to Pythagoras that weights suspended from strings in the relation 2:1 necessarily produce the octave, Galilei says (in his *Discorso intorno all'opere di messer Gioseffo Zarlino da Chioggia*, 1589) that he has been able to refute this affirmation through experiments:

> Regarding the theories of Pythagoras, I wish to point out two false opinions as to which people have been persuaded through the reading of diverse texts, and which I have myself endorsed until I ascertained the truth through experiment [*esperienza*], master of all things. (Quoted in Palisca 1992, pp. 103-104)

Palisca and other historians of music have reconstructed satisfactorily the experiment we have already mentioned, in which Galilei loaded a string with bodies of different weight so as to vary the tension, and discovered that to obtain an octave it was necessary to use weights in the relation 4:1 instead of 2:1. He hardly could have obtained the relation by means other than experimentation. Moreover, in many cases the experimental setup is described painstakingly. Such amount of detail would not be justified if Galilei had not carried out real experiments. Usually he employs the lute as a laboratory instrument, using strings made of different materials and in different configurations. He performs a series of tests with these strings and establishes, by hearing, how each of the factors – which he varies one at a time – affects the pitch and the musical intervals. Some of these experiments have been reconstructed by Palisca with a XVII century lute from the Yale collection, with results that in general confirm Galilei's assertions (Palisca 1992, pp. 143-151).

7. Vincenzo Galilei and Galileo

In 1585, Galileo left the University of Pisa without finishing his medical studies as his father had wanted and lived in Florence until 1589, when he decided to return to Pisa as a professor of Mathematics. These four years were probably the years of the greatest interaction between father and son, since shortly after Galileo's departure, Galilei died. According to Drake, Galileo assisted in Vincenzo's experiments and was to adopt his father's ideas, not only about sound but also about the equilibrium between theory and experience. But the influence of the father's disdain for all that was established dogmatically seems to have been no less. Vincenzo wrote in the second page of his *Dialogo*, and the echo would resound in Galileo's *Saggiatore* (1623), the following:

> In my view those who only cite the argument of authority as a proof of any assertion whatsoever, without any supporting reasoning, act in an absurd way. On the contrary, I want to ask you questions and make replies freely, without adulation of any kind, as all those who search for the truth must do. (Quoted in Pardo de Santayana 1977, p. 16)

After Vincenzo's death in 1591, his manuscripts fell into Galileo's hands, and there is general agreement that his son used some experimental results of his father in the First Journey of his *Discorsi e dimostrazione matematiche intorno a due nuove scienze* (1638). Galileo describes experiments with tensed strings, besides other experiments in acoustics allegedly carried out by him. In the case of results obtained by Vincenzo, Galileo used them to cast doubts on the standard numerological explanation of consonance. And he used his own results to build up a new musical theory that was not centered any more on consonances and their gradation (Galileo 1638, pp. 138-150).

It is significant that Galileo, as well as his father, detached himself from the well rooted practice of attributing the properties of the musical intervals to the properties of the so called *numeri numerantes* (counting numbers) that had been used until then to express the proportions corresponding to string lengths. Galileo recurs instead to *numeri numerati* (those numbers that are obtained from measurement); in this case the number of oscillations of the string in certain circumstances, obtained through experimentation. In the book cited, Galilio will affirm that the ratios associated with musical intervals are not immediately determined by the length or the tension of the string, but rather by the frequency of vibration, that is, by the number of thrusts of air emitted by the source (per time unit), that are transmitted, hit on the eardrum and make it oscillate. An unpleasant sensation is generated, according to Galileo's assumption, by discordant vibrations of two notes that arrive to the ear out of proportion. The more the pulses that produce the vibration of each of the notes coincide, the more consonant are the notes. In the case of the octave, all of the pulses coincide. In the case of the fifth, on the other hand, the higher note vibrates with three pulses for every two of the lower note. Two of them coincide, but one does not.

The influence of Galilei on his son does not seem to end here. In his manuscript *Discorso intorno all'uso delle dissonanze*, in the Florence National Library, Vincenzo distinguishes between knowledge stemming from the senses and that obtained through the intellect and experiments:

> By means of the senses we prudently grasp differences of form, color, taste, odor and sound. They also distinguish the light from the heavy, the rough and hard from the smooth and soft, and other surface accidents. But the intrinsic qualities and virtues of things due to which they are hot or cold, dry or humid, can only be judged by means of the intellect, by means of the persuasion accorded by experiment, and not simply by the senses, immersed in the diversity of forms, colors and other accidents. (Quoted in Palisca 1992, p. 145)

This passage is remarkable because in it Galilei anticipates the distinction between primary and secondary qualities. In view of the profound musical interests of Galileo, there is no justification in supposing he did not have a detailed acquaintance with his father's writings. Thus he makes the same point in a famous fragment of the *Saggiatore*:

> As soon as I conceive a corporeal matter or substance, I feel the immediate need to conceive that it has boundaries and some shape or other, that it is, in relation to others, big or small; that it is in one place or another, in this or that other time, that it is moving or still, that it touches or not another body, that it is one or several or many. I cannot separate it from these conditions by any effort of the imagination. But my mind does not feel the compulsion to grasp it as necessarily accompanied by other conditions, such as its being white or red, bitter or sweet, mute or sonorous, of pleasant or unpleasant odor. Without the guidance of the senses, reason or imagination by themselves would perhaps never arrive to such qualities. For this reason, I think that all flavors, odors, colors and the rest are only pure

names in what regards the subject in which it appears to us that they reside; and that they reside only in the body that perceives them. Thus, if the living creature were suppressed, these qualities would disappear and would be canceled. (Galileo 1623, pp. 347-348)

This distinction between "primary" and "secondary" qualities, as John Locke shall call them, will constitute a radical break with old Aristotelianism and become one of the pillars of the mechanistic conception that will guide research from the midst of the 17th century. The subsequent history of Physics will tread that path, reaching landmarks that the author of the *Saggiatore* could not have imagined. As William Shea tells us, the devaluation of the sensible, proposed by Galileo, opened up infinite questionings about the relation between inner experience and the external world, between private reality and public truth. The fact that they are still a matter of philosophic discussion is a tribute to his daring. Was it ever surmised by Vincenzo Galilei that his brief and incidental observation would have, by way of his son, such an enormous transcendence? Not likely.

8. Some notes about acoustics after Galilei

In 1616, Isaac Beeckman created the first mechanistic corpuscular theory of sound. Any vibrating object, such as a string, as the Dutch philosopher would say, cuts the surrounding air into small spherical corpuscles of air, which are propelled in all directions by the vibrational movement of the vibrating object. Years later, Christiaan Huygens (who, like Galileo, was the son of a musician) shall deal with diverse theoretical aspects of music; in particular he shall deal with the problem of consonance, proposing a (qualitative) wave model of sound propagation, while analyzing the relationship between wavelength, frequency, and speed of propagation. Although Marin Mersenne was the first to formulate empirical laws connecting the frequency of vibration of a string with the pitch of the sound it emits, it will be French physicist Joseph Sauveur (1653-1716) who will calculate the number of vibrations corresponding to different sounds. To him we owe the terms *acoustics* and *harmonics*. He shall also establish the simultaneous presence of sounds at different frequencies, multiples of the fundamental, when a string vibrates: the harmonics.

Sauveur was the first to affirm (1702) that the quality of a sound (the *timbre*) depends on the mixture of harmonics. In his time, the problem of harmonics required the explanation of the simultaneous existence of more than one mode of vibration in one vibrating sound source. This problem, that for Mersenne was a paradox without a solution, was dealt with by Sauveur on the basis of the observation that when a string of the harpsichord is struck, it is possible to hear not only the sound (fundamental) determined by the length, thickness, and tension of the string, but also other higher sounds, due to some of its parts that in some way separate from the general vibrations to produce particular vibrations. Starting with Sauveur's works, sound waves throughout the 18th century shall be subjected to physical-mathematical treatment in the works of Taylor, D'Alembert, Daniel Bernoulli, Euler, Fourier and many others (Bensa & Zanarini 1999, pp. 81-110). But by then music, finally understood as an art and object of purely *esthetic* considerations connected with *musical styles*, had started on another road.

9. Conclusions: Galilei and a second line team

History of science and history of music have had little relevance to the thought and works of Vincenzo Galilei. But their significance is enhanced when we focus on them as belonging to a stage in the science of music as we have characterized it; and if we consider simultaneously the aspects related to the growth of music as an art, to the appearance of the Baroque style, and to the birth of the new science that originates in the Scientific Revolution. Moreover, as Stillman Drake pointed out more than three decades ago, the influence of Galilei on his son in several diverse aspects, seems to be of much greater significance that most Galileo historians have been willing to concede (Drake 1970, p. 43).

In the history of the science of music of the period in which Vincenzo Galilei lived we do not find a linear path in which a discipline "strengthens" while it develops and increases its specialization. Instead, in this case it followed an intricate path in which all kinds of events took place simultaneously: births, deaths, transformations. The protagonists were not necessarily the "heroes" of either the Scientific Revolution or the history of music. They were not great specialists in science, philosophy, or musical composition, but rather bourgeois professionals of letters, clergymen, university professors, physicians, officials and minor scientists who had a significant part in the musical-scientific thought of the age. They have names like Zarlino, Galilei, Benedetti, Stevin, Beeckman, Mersenne, and Kircher.

However, it was these men of a second-line team who made the big questions about music. They were the protagonists of the transformations that arose of the relation between the Scientific Revolution, the science of music and musical art. These transformations include the collapse of the Pythagorean perspective of music, the rejection of the theories based on the legacies of natural magic, and hermetic and neoplatonic postulates, the birth of musical acoustics as an episode in the consolidation of the mechanistic view of the world, the impact on music of the theory of the affections, the rise of Baroque as the first musical style of the West in which musical theory and practice are no more two completely separate universes. It was these which contributed with their efforts to create modern musical art and modern acoustics. In the figure of Vincenzo Galilei we have paid them the homage they deserve.

References

Bensa, E. & G. Zanarini (1999), "La fisica della musica. Nascita e sviluppo dell'acustica musicale nei secoli XVII e XVII", *Nuncius* XIV (1): 69-111.

Bianconi, L. (1999), *Music in the Seventeenth Century*, Cambridge: Cambridge University Press. (First edition in Italian, 1982.)

Boido, G. & E. Kastika (2002), "La ciencia de la música entre los siglos XVI y XVIII: de los sonidos que no se oyen a los orígenes de la acústica", in Horenstein, N., Minhot, L. & H. Severgnini (eds.), *Epistemología e Historia de la Ciencia*, Córdoba: Facultad de Filosofía y Humanidades, Universidad Nacional de Córdoba, Vol. 8, n.8, pp. 60-66.

Bukofzer, M.F. (1994), *La música en la época barroca. De Monteverdi a Bach*, Madrid: Alianza Editorial. (First edition in English, 1947.)

Coelho, V. (ed.) (1992), *Music and Science in the Age of Galileo*, Dordrecht: Kluwer.

Cohen, H.F. (1984), *Quantifying Music, The Science of Music at the First Stage of the Scientific Revolution, 1580-1650*, Dordrecht: Reidel.

Crombie, A. (1990), *Science, Optics and Music in Medieval and Early Modern Thought*, London: The Hambledon Press.

Drake, S. (1970), "Vincenzio Galilei and Galileo", in *Galileo Studies. Personality, Tradition, and Revolution*, Michigan: Ann Arbor, Ch. 2.

Drake, S. (1975), "The Role of Music in Galileo's Experiments", *Scientific American* 232: 98-104.

Drake, S. (1992), *Music and Philosophy in Early Modern Science,* in Coelho (1992), pp. 3-34.

Fubini, E. (1999), *La estética musical desde la Antigüedad hasta el siglo XX*, Madrid: Alianza Editorial. (First edition in Italian, 1976.)

Galileo Galilei (1638), *Discorsi e dimostrazioni matematiche intorno a due nuove scienze*, in *Le Opere di Galileo Galilei* (edited by Antonio Favaro), Firenze: Edizione Nazionale, 1980-1909, VIII, pp. 9-448.

Galileo Galilei (1623), *Il Saggiatore*, in *Le Opere di Galileo Galilei* (edited by Antonio Favaro), Firenze: Edizione Nazionale, 1980-1909, VI, pp. 197-372.

Gouk, P. (1999), *Music, Science and Natural Magic in Seventeenth-Century England*, London: Yale University Press.

Gozza, P. (ed.) (2000), *Number to Sound, The Musical Way to the Scientific Revolution*, Dordrecht: Kluwer.

Kastika, E. (2001), "Música, ciencia y tecnología en la Europa de los siglos XVI y XVII", unpublished thesis, Centro de Estudios Avanzados, Universidad de Buenos Aires.

Palisca, C. (1991), *Baroque Music,* New Yersey: Prentice Hall. (First edition, 1968.)

Palisca, C. (1992), "Was Galileo's Father an Experimental Scientist?", in Coelho (1992), pp. 143-151.

Pardo de Santayana, J. (1977), *Galileo Galilei*, Hernando: Madrid.

Scholes, P. (1981), *Diccionario Oxford de la música*, La Habana: Editorial Arte y Literatura. (Reprint in English: 1964.)

William Crookes' Researches on Radiometric Effect *versus* His Methodological Concerns on Residual Phenomena

Juliana M. Hidalgo Ferreira

Group of History and Theory of Science, State University of Campinas (UNICAMP)/
Science Teaching and Culture Research Group, Federal University of Rio Grande do Norte (UFRGN)

1. First comments

William Crookes (1832-1919) was an important chemist in the second half of the nineteenth and early twentieth century. Around 1870, Crookes also started his purely physical research. He conducted studies on various topics such as photography, spectroscopy, meteorology, electrical discharges in gases, radioactivity and investigation of phenomena so-called spiritual. Certainly, Crookes was a successful researcher who accomplished many contributions to applied science, and produced mainly experimental work. He obtained several important positions such as the presidency of the British Association for the Advancement of Science, and the Royal Society of London.[1]

---

[1] All the information presented here came from the biography of Crookes (*The Life of Sir William Crookes*), written in 1923 by Fournier d'Albe, from obituaries published by scientists between 1920 and 1921 (see references), and from the entry "William Crookes" in the *Dictionary of Scientific Biography*. The book written by d'Albe's is an invaluable source of information about Crookes as the biographer had access at that time to an extensive documentation now nearly all disappeared.

Fig. 1

Among the contributions which received widespread recognition in the scientific community, we can highlight the discovery of the chemical element thallium in 1861, by spectroscopic analysis of the refuse from pyrite burners.[2] This finding would have motivated him to point out, throughout his career, the importance of the study of residues obtained from manufacturing processes, to which he referred to as "the most fruitful source of novel and interesting bodies" (Crookes 1878, p. 20).

After the discovery of thallium, further investigations were necessary to add to the knowledge of its chemical and physical properties, and determination of its possible natural sources. By 1871, Crookes started an enquiry to determine the atomic weight of the new element. In 1872, he sent a paper to the Royal Society on that research. However, while conducting that investigation, William

---

[2] The name "thallium" came from the similarity between the green color of the young plant and the green line observed in the spectrum.

Crookes realized some irregularities in the weightings when the analyzed material was warmer or colder than the box containing the balance. That irregularity led Crookes to investigate forces associated with heat and light.

Initially, William Crookes thought he had discovered a new force, which he called "Force X" (D'Albe 1923, p. 245; Greenaway 1962, p. 182). Through this force, supposedly able to change the weight of bodies, Crookes hoped to elucidate some issues in celestial mechanics, including the tails of comets and solar flares. He also expected to figure out the nature of gravitation (Woodruff 1966, p. 191).[3]

Then, William Crookes produced many devices which he used to carry out a great variety of experiments aimed at exploring this effect in vacuum. As an outcome of that enterprise he further produced vacuums never before achieved.

Crookes examined the action of radiation on white and black surfaces. From that observation, he invented the radiometer which is a device that would spin under the influence of radiation, so that the speed of revolution was proportional to the intensity of the incident radiation.

The radiometer caused a sensation in the scientific *milieu*. It has become extremely popular and was found in London and several other cities during that time. However, the acceptance of William Crookes' explanation for its movement was not unanimous. The controversy went on for years until another explanation for the radiometer convinced the scientific community. Even Crookes changed his mind and accepted the new hypothesis.

In this work, we reviewed the researches carried out by Crookes on the radiometric effect, analyzing them in light of methodological concerns presented by the scientist years later on the importance of researching on residual phenomena. We also collected some interesting aspects of the polemics around the radiometer during that time period.

---

[3] This initial expectation was expressed by Crookes later in 1875 (Crookes 1875, p. 350).

2. The atomic weight of thallium

Around the year 1871, William Crookes began to dedicate himself to determine the atomic weight of thallium. Obtaining the thallium used in weightings demanded a long process. Initially, impure thallium was obtained in a spongy state from the dust of the chimneys of pyrite burners. Then, this material was solidified, dissolved in sulfuric acid, and converted to thallium sulphate "commercially pure". Only after a lengthy preparation, the scientist achieved the thallium. He then dissolved a certain amount of thallium in nitric acid, and weighed the thallium nitrate produced. Thus, the atomic weight of thallium was obtained, since the other elements of the thallium nitrate atomic weights were already known.

Many precautions were taken in an attempt to identify and minimize potential sources of errors (D'Albe 1923, pp. 241-244). The materials and devices used have been specially built for this research. Crookes was deeply concerned with the accuracy of scales and weights used. He held the weightings both in air and in vacuum.

The weights used were of pure platinum. The vacuum weighing-machine, built with a traverse of fourteen inches of agate and cleavers, was packaged in an iron box evacuated by an air pump. The iron box was wrapped in several layers of copal resin mixed with lead to prevent the air from penetrating through the holes of the box.

William Crookes also seems to have paid particular attention to overcome certain difficulties such as variations in temperature that could make the weighing-machine less sensitive due to differences in dilatation of its components. In addition, the heating of the device, which could be caused by the need to illuminate the scale and the pointer, was also considered harmful to the measurements. This last obstacle, Crookes sought to solve through the use of a small evacuated tube inserted in the box, which may have been a significant precursor of its subsequent activities related to electric lighting.

From that careful and systematic determination of the atomic weight of thallium, residual "facts" not covered by the science of that period emerged. Then William Crookes went on studying and publishing papers on the effects observed. One of these articles, published in July 1875, in the Quarterly Journal of Science, is particularly interesting. In it, the scientist described the whole process which occurred from the discovery of the effects until the time he wrote the article, when he was trying to champion its interpretation of the phenomena (Crookes 1875). The analysis of this article may shed some light on the methodology used by Crookes in his research on the radiometric effect. We highlight this analysis in the next section of the present work.

3. Investigations on the radiometric effect

In the article "The Mechanical Action of Light", in 1875, William Crookes looked back over the research that led him to conclude that radiation was a driving force. Crookes described the experimental procedures accomplished by him in these investigations. He sought to emphasize the wide variety of tests, making it clear that his conclusions were not mere speculation. According to him, they had solid experimental basis. His attitude was understandable in view of the so-emergent controversy about that subject, as we shall come to observe (Crookes 1875).

As William Crookes described, an irregularity would have been observed by him in the weightings when the analyzed material was warmer or colder than the box containing it. In the weighting of pieces of glass in a sensitive weighing-machine packaged in an iron box, he had noticed what appeared to be a change in gravitational force, when the glass was at a higher temperature than the air enveloping it (Crookes 1875, pp. 337-340; information listed below are related to these pages).

His first move was to try to eliminate possible sources of error and to perform tests to verify this effect, making use of devices increasingly sensitive. Thus, Crookes obtained similar results using an arm extremely thin and light, delicately suspended in a glass tube through a needle, and containing in each of its ends a small ball. He accomplished the tests with balls made out of different materials such as coal, glass, wood, cork, selenium, platinum, silver and other metals.

Then William Crookes assumed that this effect would disappear gradually as the box was evacuated. His assumption was that at regular conditions of pressure this fact could be attributed to air currents. He began to investigate this hypothesis, using a device even more sensitive: a stalk of straw with tiny balls of cork in the ends put in a glass tube that could be evacuated by a Sprengel pump.

First, before starting the pump, the scientist found out with a micrometer, that while putting a gas lamp just below one end of the tube, the small mass that was inside it went down slightly and then rose to a position just above the original one. This led him to believe that everything was an action of attraction of heat instantly overcome by air updrafts.

Trying to verify whether this effect only occurred with gas lamps, Crookes also made use of glass rods and heated metal pipes, hot water and a thermometer inserted in a glass tube containing water at 70 degrees Celsius, which, according to him, served for heat acting more regularly. In all those cases, the same results were obtained. Furthermore, while placing the lamp above the glass tube, the ball rose up slightly. To Crookes, this effect could be explained by the influence of air currents.

Possibly in an attempt to see what would happen in situations for which he considered impossible this explanation, William Crookes started the pump. At the beginning, the barometer scored 767 mm of mercury, and the reference index for the box scored zero. When the index reached 147 mm of mercury below the index showed by the barometer, similar results, though somewhat attenuated, were obtained using the thermometer as a heat source. According to Crookes, as long as the rarefaction increased, the intensity of the effect seemed to diminish: with 12 mm of mercury the action on the ball was little noticed, with 10 mm of mercury the effect was even smaller and, with 7 mm of mercury, neither the hot water pipe nor the rod nor the lamp-heated gas caused any movement in the ball. Regarding these results, he admitted in an 1875's article:

> The inference was almost irresistible that the rising of the pit was only due to currents of air, and that at this near approach to a vacuum the residual air was too highly rarefied to have Power in its rising to overcome the inertia of the straw beam and the pith balls. A more delicate instrument would doubtless show traces of movement at a still nearer approach to a vacuum; but it seemed evident that when the last trace of air had been removed from the tube surrounding the balance – when the balance was suspended in empty space only – the pith ball would remain motionless, wherever the hot body were applied to it (Crookes 1875, p. 340).

William Crookes, then, would have insisted on obtaining experimental evidence that while achieving the "perfect vacuum" no movement would be noticed. However, when Crookes continued to evacuate the box, he realized that when some source of heat was applied under the ball, this one amounted in a stable way, without the hesitation observed in situations where the rarefaction was lower. When the index reached 3 mm below the mercury barometer, the rise of the ball resembled the one obtained when the ball was suspended in air of normal density. Moreover, when the barometer and the index reached the same level (and hence the vacuum seemed perfect), the movements were not only sharper than those observed in the air, but they occurred in the presence of heat sources of lower intensity, such as a finger, for example.

By investigating his first hypothesis, therefore, Crookes would have been surprised. Contrary to his thoughts, the effects seemed stronger the greater the degree of exhaustion. Thus, in 1873, the scientist sent to the Royal Society the article "On the Action of Heat on Gravitating Masses". The weights of the objects appeared to be modified depending on the temperature: a body if in a higher temperature seemed lighter than the same one in a lower temperature. To Crookes, this phenomenon could not be caused by a possible condensation of air steam in the colder body, or by air currents surrounding the warmer body, because the measures were made in a vacuum. So he presented the preliminary outcomes of his investigations:

> I. When the ball is in air of ordinary density.
> (a) If the mass is colder that the ball, it repels the ball.
> (b) If the mass is hotter than the ball, it attracts the ball.
> II. When the ball is in a vacuum.
> (a) If the mass is colder than the ball, it attracts the ball.
> (b) If the mass is hotter than the ball, it repels the ball.
> […] The density of the medium surrounding the ball, the material of which the ball is made, and a very slight difference between the temperatures of the mass and the ball, exert so strong an influence over the attractive and repulsive force […] (Quoted in D'Albe 1923, pp. 245-246).

In this article from 1873, the scientist claimed that some evidence pointed out to a repulsive action of heat, and an attractive action of cold (in vacuum). These results would have been reached out in several experiments. The tests also showed that although the action was in a certain direction in the air with normal density, and in the opposite direction in vacuum, there was an intermediate pressure, the "critical pressure", where the temperature changes had little or no interference.

A new publication of these results with the title of "Attraction and Repulsion resulting from Radiation", also in 1873, and the presentation of the measuring apparatus at a meeting of the Royal Society on the evening of April 22 the following year, led to fervent criticism. Osborne Reynolds, who became one of the strongest opponents of William Crookes' hypothesis, saw him making a presentation in which the radiation acted on a stem with a small ball of cork at its ends, suspended in the vacuum. Reynolds noticed that the approaching of a candle caused the rod to swing. It seemed that a certain force was acting directly upon the little balls. However, contrary to what might be expected if the force was constant or depended only on distance from the candle, the oscillations were not damped, but rather increased in amplitude, as if the effect depended on the heating of the balls (Woodruff 1966, p. 192).

At a meeting of the Royal Society on June 18th 1874, Reynolds argued that the observed effects could be attributed to evaporation:

> When the radiated heat from the lamp falls on the pith, its temperature will rise, and any moisture on it will begin to evaporate, and to drive the pith from the lamp. The evaporation will be greatest on that ball which is nearest to the lamp, therefore this ball will be driven away until the force on the other becomes equal, after which the balls will come to rest unless momentum carries them further. On the other hand, when a piece of ice is brought near, the temperature of the pith will be reduced, and it will condense the vapour and be drawn towards the ice (Osborn, quoted in D'Albe 1923, p. 247).

To answer this, William Crookes insisted that the box was completely evacuated. If the effects observed were due to evaporation and condensation, they would disappear as long as the box was evacuated, which had not occurred. Furthermore, William Crookes argued that Reynolds' hypothesis was incorrect. To Crookes, if it was correct it would be impossible that he had found no differences in the results using evacuated boxes which initially contained as different substances as water vapor, hydrogen, air, and carbon dioxide (D'Albe 1923, p. 248).

Giving an outline of that research, in the 1875's article, William Crookes stated that from those early unexpected results, more variations were tested. Crookes allowed air to enter slowly into the device and the same effects and critical point previously observed were obtained. He also repeated the experiment using a piece of ice underneath the ball, and noticed an effect exactly opposite to that one produced by the heat source (Crookes 1875, pp. 341-343; information listed below are related to these pages).

Another experiment was designed to examine more closely the movement of the weighing-machine during the process of exhaustion and to identify more precisely the pressure corresponding to the critical point. In this case, Crookes used balls of brass, and as a source of heat, an evacuated tube containing a spiral of platinum made incandescent by electricity and placed inside the box. According to Crookes, with this equipment (shown in detail in an article sent to the Royal Society in 1874), he notice that the downward movement of the ball, when the incandescent tube was positioned underneath it, only stopped when the barometer and the index were equaled. On the other hand, leaving the vacuum pump still running one more hour, he observed that the critical point had been exceeded, and that the action on the ball had taken the opposite direction. With the pump on for a few more hours, the position of the ball was increasingly high. Thus, the spiral bulb produced an increasingly strong repulsion. The same effect was observed with a finger, a heated glass rod, a gas lamp, and a heated piece of copper.

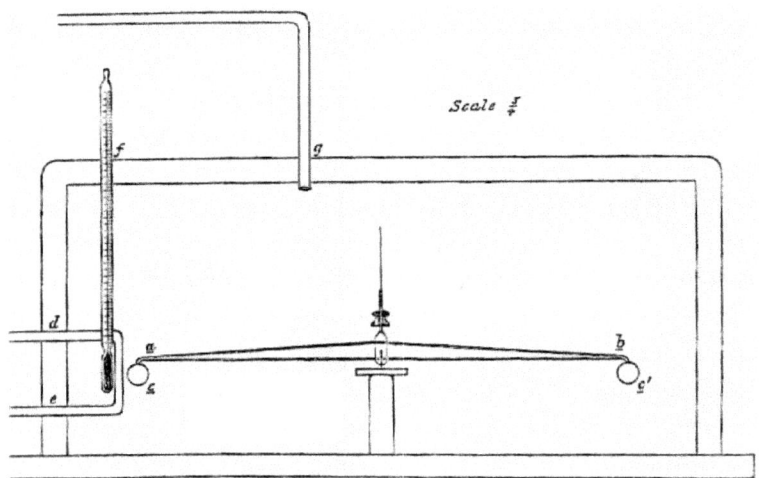

Fig. 2. Apparatus used by Crookes in 1873 (Crookes 1874, p. 506).

William Crookes was still not satisfied with even more intriguing results obtained. Then, he built a new device designed, according to him, to elucidate *definitively* whether these effects were or were not caused by air currents:

> By chemical means I obtained in an apparatus a vacuum so nearly perfect that it would not carry a current from a Ruhmkorff's coil when connected with platinum wires sealed into the tube. In such a vacuum the repulsion by heat was still found to be decided and energetic (Crookes 1875, p. 342).

Thus, in that vacuum, Crookes realized that the repulsion by heat was even more intense. He took that evidence as a strong reason to convince himself that it was not a mistake, but a real phenomenon, not explained by the action of air currents. Afterwards, as the 1875's article showed, the British scientist carried out tests with both simple devices, that produced surprising visible effects, as with more sensitive and accurate devices, with which the observation was not made only by naked eye, but through scales, and rays of light (Crookes 1875, pp. 344-346).

As an example of a simplified test, Crookes mentioned a device in which a vertical tube was connected to the vacuum pump. The bottom of the tube ended in a glass globe, inside which he put a light rod suspended by a thread of silk. Referring to the results obtained with this device, the scientist reported:

> [...] when the vacuum is perfect, is so sensitive to heat that a touch with the finger on a part of the globe near one extremity of the pith will drive the index round over 90^0 [...]. The pith bar commences to oscillate to and fro, the swing gradually increasing in amplitude until the dead centre is passed over, when several complete revolutions are made. The torsion of the suspending fibre now offers resistance to the revolutions, and the bar commences to turn in the opposite direction (Crookes 1875, p. 344).

Crookes also referred to a more sophisticated device consisting of a vertical tube attached to air pump through a side exit. From a cover sealing the top end of this tube, hung a thin glass tube[4] which ended in an aluminum stirrup, which by its turn held a concave mirror glass, and a light horizontal rod with small plates of variable material at its ends. He put all this part attached to the end of the glass tube inside a horizontal pipe welded to the bottom of the standpipe. Having made the vacuum, William Crookes put a finger near one end of the rod. He noticed that the light beam reflected by the mirror center of a graduated scale, placed in front of the instrument, moved a few inches, showing what would be repulsion. A piece of ice, on the other hand, seemed to cause a movement in the opposite direction.

Crookes said that to ensure that the light index was in zero, it was necessary to prevent any strange radiation from acting on the torsion balance. Thus, the device was covered with a six inch thick layer of raw cotton, around which he put a double row of "Winchester bottles", containing a quart of water. In those circumstances, the remaining space only allowed that radiation could reach the balance, and that the beam could reach and be reflected by the mirror.

---

[4] According to Crookes, the suspension through a glass tube was advantageous, because the rod attached to the tube always returned to its original position.

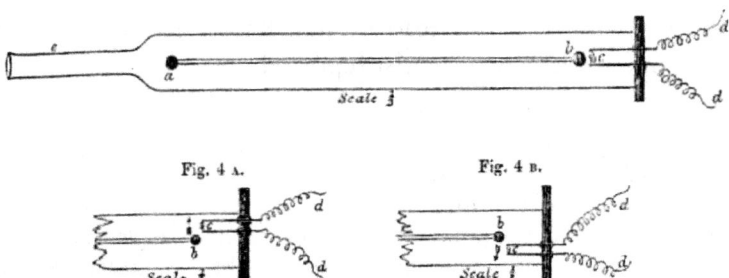

Fig. 3. Incandescent tubes used by Crookes (Crookes 1874, p. 513).

Realizing that the critical point to a thin surface was lower than the one he noticed of a moderately thick piece of platinum, Crookes would have been encouraged to come out with a two vertical tubes device. One of them went directly from the vacuum pump and the other was coupled to the first one through a horizontal pipe that extended from a point before the lower end of the first standpipe to a point just a little beyond the end of the second tube. Thus, two rods could be used, suspended horizontally from the pipes inside the vertical tubes.

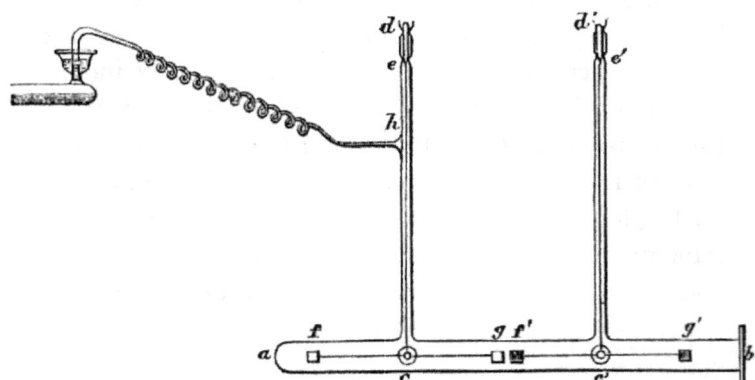

Fig. 4. Experiment accomplished by Crookes (Crookes 1875, p. 346).

At the ends of the first rod, Crookes put small sheets of platinum, and in the same position at the second rod, he put sheets of the same size, but of a lighter material. Similarly to the previous situation, each of those rods had on its center, a concave mirror supported by an aluminum bracket. Thus, rays of light that reached the center of these rods were reflected to graduated scales, and it was possible to notice different effects caused by the same type of radiation acting on the leaves at the ends of stems.

Using a torsion device, like the one already mentioned, William Crookes decided to study the action of different rays of the spectrum on colored discs. He obtained the most remarkable outcomes for rays of different regions of the spectrum acting on white and black surfaces:

> The result was to show a decided difference between the action of light and of radiant heat. At the highest exhaustions dark heat from boiling water acts almost equally on white pith and on pith coated with lamp-black, repelling either with about the same force. The action of the luminous rays, however, is different. The repel the black surface more energetically than they do the white surface, and, consequently, if in such an apparatus […] one disc of pith is white and the other is black, an exposure of both of them to light of the same intensity will cause the torsion thread to twist round, owing to the difference of repulsion exerted on the black and the white surface. If […] the halves of the pith bar are alternately white and lamp-blacked, this differential action will produce rapid rotation in one direction (Crookes 1875, p. 346).

So Crookes conducted a series of tests about that peculiar action of the radiation on those surfaces. Such enquiries led Crookes to build the radiometer. He then studied the influence of the intensity of the incident rays with the instrument.

4. The radiometer

In a supplement to the article "The Mechanical Action of Light", William Crookes described the process that would have lead to the construction of the radiometer. At that time, the instrument caused a great popular sensation extrapolating the limits of the scientific community.

According to Crookes, he further tried to examine the action of radiation on the black and white surfaces. He then noticed that the higher the vacuum reached, the heat seemed to repel much the same way that the little white balls and those shaded with black smoke did. Furthermore, using light, the effect was remarkably different. The white surfaces were repelled more intensely than the black ones. Taking advantage of this fact, William Crookes designed the instrument which he called "radiometer".

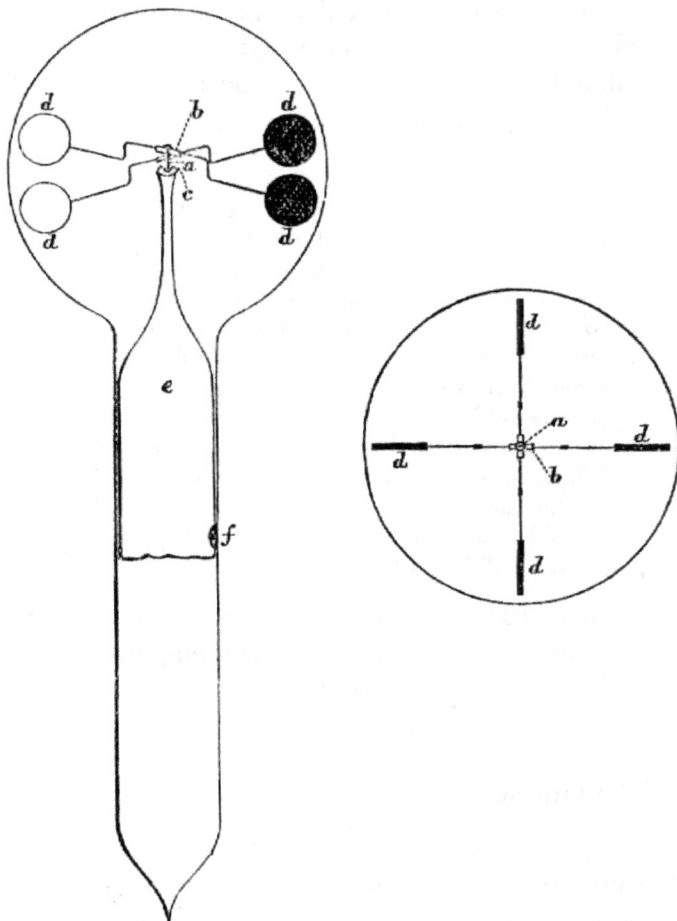

Fig. 5. The radiometer (Crookes 1875, p. 347).

The radiometer consisted of four arms suspended from a central point of steel, placed upon something firm. The arms could rotate horizontally and they had small discs attached to each one of its ends. On each disc, one side was white and the other one was darkened with carbon black smoke. The disks were attached to the arms in such a way that the black surfaces faced the same direction of rotation. Crookes put the device inside a hermetically sealed globe and evacuated as it was possible.

According to Crookes, the instrument rotated because of the influence of radiation had on it. The white surface reflected the strength of the beam incident on it, while the black surface absorbed the strength and transformed it into motion, causing that surface to retreat. The speed of revolution was proportional to the intensity of the incident beam.[5]

Thus, in that first description of the radiometer, William Crookes left explicit (as the title "The Mechanical Action of Light" given to the article pointed out) that, even after Reynolds' criticism, he had not changed his interpretation.

The article presented several tests that were performed with the radiometer (Crookes 1875, pp. 346-348). William Crookes exposed the instrument to solar radiation. The effect was so strong that the discs could not be individually distinguished. He also placed candles at varying distances from the radiometer. The mechanical action of radiation appeared to be inversely proportional to the square distance.

Performing some variation on this same test, Crookes changed the amount of candles, keeping a constant distance from the device. He concluded that the speed of rotation of the radiometer was directly proportional to the intensity of the incident. On the other hand, leaving only one candle at a fixed distance of five inches from the radiometer and changing the color of pieces of glass placed in front of the candle, the scientist reported that under the red light the radiometer was faster, while the green light seemed to be the less influential.

Crookes also tried the radiometer when the heat was prevented to pass by a thick aluminum shield. In this case, he noted that the

---

[5] However, as E. Woodruff noticed, the rotation observed by Crookes happened in a direction opposite to that one that might be expected if the effect was caused by radiation pressure. The variation in the momentum of the incident radiation on the reflecting surface, and the resulting force exerted on this surface, would be twice that of the one caused by radiation on the dark surface (Woodruff 1966, pp. 193-194).

speed seemed to diminish. Even when he let pass only the "dark heat", using a pot of boiling water, no rotation was produced.

In 1875, when Crookes presented these results, the radiometer called the attention of the general public, being exposed as a curiosity, at some window shops in London. In scientific millieu, the explanation proposed by Crookes was not accepted unanimously. As we have already mentioned in the present work, in the previous year, Reynolds had already performed experiments that suggested that the effects observed by Crookes in another device could be attached to evaporation. The debate opened by Reynolds lead to new investigations, but even so controversy was not concluded. The radiometer would then take part in that debate.

Only in 1876, performing another series of experiments, Arthur Schuster proposed a new explanation for the radiometer, which convinced the scientific community. Even Crookes changed his mind. Schuster was able to explain the movement of the radiometer through the action of the residual gas inside the tube, even when the best vacuum was reached (D'Albe 1923, p. 251). Schuster took as a starting point, the fact that the gas molecules reached (according to the kinetic theory of gases) both black and white surfaces of the blades. Ordinarily these molecules would be thrown back with equal average speeds. However, in the presence of a radiation source, the black surface would be warmer and it would repel the molecules with a higher speed. This surface would go back, and that movement would produce the observed rotation. As evidence that his hypothesis was correct, that is, the movement of the blades was not due to something outside the evacuated tube, Schuster put a radiometer to float in water. The blades rotated in one direction, while the box of glass spun in the opposite direction, although much more slowly.[6] Crookes finally accepted that this result suggested that the molecules went back, im-

---

[6] While d'Albe attributed this experiment to Schuster, Woodruff says that he did not put the radiometer into the water. According to Woodruff, Schuster suspended the radiometer in the air using two parallel fibers. This experiment suggested that the movement of the radiometer was caused by residual gas in the box, because the radiation made the blades move in the opposite direction of the box movement. This outcome indicated the existence of action and reaction inside the radiometer, which would not occur if the light produced a pressure directly on the surfaces. See D'Albe (1923, p. 252), and Woodruff (1966, p. 194).

parting movement to the walls of the box. Afterwards, he carried out new investigations seeking a full explanation for this effect.

In November of 1876, William Crookes sent a note to the Royal Society explaining the repulsion movements through the influence of radiation according to the kinetic theory of gases.[7] According to Crookes, Johnston Stoney first suggested this explanation for the movement of the radiometer, which took into account the existence of residual gas in the bulb, even in the best vacuum possible at that time.[8] Thus, Crookes accepted the existence of residual gas in the box and agreed with the interpretation that the presence of this gas could cause the movement of the radiometer:

> When the mean length of path between successive collisions of the molecules is small compared with the dimensions of the vessel, the molecules rebounding from the heated surface, and therefore moving with an extra velocity, help to keep back the more slowly moving molecules which are advancing towards the heated surface; it thus happens that though the individual kicks against the heated surface are increased in strength in consequence of the heating, yet the number of molecules struck is diminished in the same proportion, so that there is equilibrium on the two sides of the disc, even though the temperature of the faces are unequal. But when the exhaustion is carried to so high a point that the molecules are sufficiently few and the mean length path between their successive collisions is comparable with the dimensions of the vessel, the swiftly moving, rebounding molecules spend their force, in part or in whole, on the sides of the vessel, and the onward crowding, more slowly moving molecules are not kept back as before, so that the number which strike the warmer face approaches to, and in the limit equals, the number which strike the back, cooler face; and as the individual impacts are stronger on the warmer than on the cooler face, pressure is produced, causing the warmer face to retreat (Crookes, quoted in D'Albe 1923, pp. 252-253).

---

[7] D'Albe (1923, pp. 252-253). The information and quotes below relate to the same page pointed out in this note.

[8] There does not seem to be union so to to attribute this explanation to Johnston Stoney. Tilden pointed out Stoney as the author of the explanation (Tilden 1920, p. iii). Brock made the same statement in the *Dictionary of scientific biography* (Brock 1970, p. 477). However, D'Albe (1923, p. 251) and Lord Rayleigh (Strutt 1936, p. 237), mentioned that Arthur Schuster advanced on that explanation for the movement of the radiometer. Greenaway (1962, pp. 182-185), reported Schuster's researches, but said nothing about Stoney being the author of this explanation.

To Crookes, this theory explained the reason why he had observed more intense movements for white balls. It also explained why, for a while, he could not justify the fact that the dark heat and light rays produced essentially different reactions on the white and black surfaces.

Thus, the most intense rays, i.e., the light, passed through the walls of the box without warming it and then reached the white surface, being simply reflected. Moreover, reaching the black surface, the light was absorbed and increased the surface temperature. It produced disorder of the molecules and caused the movement. Rays of lower intensity (the "dark heat") did not pass through the glass surface of the box. They were absorbed by the surface, increasing its temperature. In that case, the box repelled the molecules, which bounced off at higher speeds than when they hit the box. Hence, molecular pressure flowed from the inner surface of the box and that pressure repelled whatever was in front of it, regardless of the color of its surface.

5. William Crookes' methodological concerns

The methodology used by William Crookes to deal with these unexpected effects can be better understood through his article "On Residual Phenomena", published in 1878. In this article, it is possible to notice that Crookes tried to draw attention to inconsistencies between predicted results and researches outcomes. He championed that some details generally taken by negligible, should be investigated carefully because they could generate new findings (Crookes 1878).

Crookes began this article explaining the different situations which, according to him, it could happen when a scientist investigate whether and how far a certain theory agrees with some of the facts yet to be explained:

> In the first place, the theory in question may agree exactly and completely with the facts, leaving merely such minute errors as are plainly due to the shortcomings of experiment and observation. [...]. Secondly, the theory may distinctly fail to account for the phenomena before us, and may prove utterly contradictory to facts. [...]. We are thus brought to the threshold of the third possible case: - The theory or the law may agree with or account for the facts to a certain extent, leaving, however, a margin unexplained. Such margins are the "resid-

ual phenomena" which we are about to consider: their value as a clue to further discovery will best appear from examples […] (Crookes 1878, pp. 20-22).

In the same article, Crookes came to reflect upon how the scientist could discern between inevitable errors, and residual phenomena in his researches:

[in case of residual phenomena] the correspondence between the fact and the theory cannot to certain extent be denied, but there is a margin which, though generally small, is constant, and cannot be lessened by any niceties and refinements of procedure (Crookes 1878, p. 24).

But if the residual phenomenon was identified, what should the attitude of the scientist be?

Crookes then tried to establish how the scientist should deal with the residual phenomena, advancing with patience and care, which are both essential in those circumstances. The author lamented the existence of situations where, despite the differences between predictions and outcomes, the researcher only suggests hypotheses to explain the unexpected results, but he does not investigate them. These situations, he said, would account for many really noticed residual phenomena being not surveyed. Generally, they would receive some superficial explanation, with no experimental basis.

6. Crookes' researches on radiometric effect viewed in the light of his methodological concerns

To some extent, there seems to be coherence between Crookes' methodological speech, and the way he dealt with the effect noticed during the investigation to determine the atomic weight of thallium.

First, when confronted with the irregularities produced in weighing, Crookes would not have treated this effect as a residual phenomenon. His first hypothesis seems to have been that it was some error inherent to the weightings accomplished in the air, where air currents could exert strong influence.

Therefore, to confirm his assumption that it was an intrinsic error of the experiment which could not be eliminated in weightings accomplished in the air, William Crookes decided to evacuate the box. He believed the effect would gradually disappear. And, as we have already mentioned, in the beginning the effect seemed to tend to disappear. Because of that, William Crookes said it was "almost irresistible" to assign it to air drafts.

William Crookes, however, would not have been satisfied with that assumption, and would have continued to evacuate the box. In this regard, it is interesting to notice that in the 1875's article, Crookes hinted that in stages of research similar to that one, many researchers would behave in a way which he considered incorrect. They would promptly take as true the hypothesis that it was just an effect caused by air currents.

Crookes, however, seems to have taken an attitude consistent with that one, in the article on residual phenomena as he would advance as proper to a serious researcher: he insisted on obtaining experimental evidence that in the "perfect vacuum" no movement would be noticed.

Continuing to investigate this possibility, however, William Crookes noticed a remarkable opposite outcome (i.e., the effects seemed stronger the greater the degree of exhaustion reached). Then, it is likely that in those circumstances Crookes would have changed his mind, concluding that he was indeed facing a residual phenomenon.

Thus, William Crookes kept his investigations on that phenomenon, and published his results. His findings, noticed in several experiments, pointed toward a repulsive action of the heat, and an attractive action of the cold. There was still a "critical pressure", under which variations in temperature had little or no interference.

Therefore, it is possible to say that William Crookes undertook to investigate the phenomenon residual which he had identified. Crookes did not merely justify that phenomenon with some accessory explanation, which, he said, typically would not be subject to any investigation. In this sense, it can be said that the scientist acted in accordance with the methodological concerns he expressed years later.

On the other hand, to a certain extent, one can say that a particular attitude adopted by Crookes in the controversy about the radiometric effect would not match with his methodological advices. This attitude is specifically related to his arguments used in facing Reynolds' criticism, between 1873 and 1874.

As we have already mentioned, Osborne Reynolds became one of the fiercest opponents to Crookes' hypotheses. Reynolds claimed that the effects observed could be explained by evaporation. In respond to this, William Crookes insisted that the box had been *totally* evacuated.

Up to this point, there seems to be some incompatibility with what Crookes would write years later. At that time, the chemist admitted the existence of "errors of observation and experiment that could not be avoided, even by the most careful operator"(Crookes 1878, p. 23). From this point of view, it seems unlikely that Crookes could ensure "a perfect vacuum in the box", that is, he could not guarantee that the box contained any air molecule.[9] In a way, Crookes seems to have become an advocate of the hypothesis which delegated the effects to a mechanical action of radiation. To contradict Reynolds' theory, he argued that the box was completely evacuated; something which seems that he himself would take as something impossible to be sustained.

Even if we accept that the expression "totally evacuated" simply meant that the number of molecules inside it was so small that it would not be enough to account for the observed effects, Crookes' behavior was not in accord to his own methodological advices. He still should have done some research to support that hypothesis, instead of accepting it without any investigation, which could provide

---

[9] Moreover, it appears that Crookes seemed to predict quite optimistic estimates of vacuum which supposedly could be reached by his devices. In 1871, for example, he congratulated his assistant Charles Gimingham by the conditions of "best vacuum" and "no air in the tank" provided by a Sprengel pump on which they had been working. A few days later, however, would have Crookes find that this device still left significant amounts of air in the tank (Correspondence between William Crookes and Gimingham, *Science Museum*, London, SML Archives: MS 409). Besides, in that time, there was no reliable means of detecting pressures in highly evacuated reservoirs. It was possible to observe with some accuracy, the decrease in pressure in the vessel evacuated by the Sprengel pump by comparing the mercury at the bottom of the downpipe to the height of a Torricelli barometer. However, in situations where these heights were closed to each other it was difficult to detect visually the small differences between the indexes. Then Crookes would have tried to develop best suited methods to these readings, and possibly he considered in 1874 that according to the indexes there was no residual air in the box (Dekosky 1983, pp. 4-5).

experimental basis for that assertion. Indeed, at that moment, Crookes did not enquire into whether the remaining air (if he accepted its existence) could explain those effects.

On the other side, however, it should be noticed that somehow Crookes called into question his response to Reynolds and decided to study it experimentally, by using boxes which contained different substances before being evacuated. Moreover, by Crookes' assertions on this subject we can say that at times he appeared to be a little more cautious when faced with the first attempts of refutation of his hypothesis:

> For my own part, I wish to avoid having a theory on the subject. As far as the facts have led me, I think that the repulsion accompanying radiation is directly due to the impact of the waves upon the surface of the moving mass, and not secondarily through the intervention of air-currents, electricity, or evaporation and condensation. Whether the ethereal waves actually strike the substance moved, or whether at the boundary surface separating solid from gaseous matter, there are intermediary layers of condensed gas which, taking up the blow, pass it on to the layer beneath, are problems the solution of which must be left to further research (Crookes *apud* D'Albe 1923, p. 248).

7. Final comments

William Crookes carried out an intensive investigation on the effect noticed by him in his researches to determine the atomic weight of thallium. With some exceptions, we can say that Crookes acted according to what years later he recommended to be the correct behavior of a scientist when facing residual phenomena.

Crookes improved the experimental conditions for investigating the hypothesis which he had before some error inherent to the weightings accomplished in the air. Crookes would not have been satisfied with an assumption without experimental basis. He endeavored to investigate further that issue.

Because his investigations dismissed his first hypothesis, he then thought it was a remarkable residual phenomenon. This second hypothesis proved to be incorrect with the intensification of discussions with other researchers, especially after the proposal and euphoria around the radiometer. The observed effect was still due to the residual gas contained in the experimental apparatus. But despite his failure in the assessment, it should be pointed out that Crookes' commitment to investigate the phenomenon led him to overcome relevant technical problems during that period.

He, for example, has developed mechanisms to detect pressure in high evacuations. He further obtained vacuums that were never before achieved. These technical improvements have opened paths for many other discoveries, such as the X-rays, and the electron. This could not have occurred at that time if the irregularities had been overlooked.

References

Barrett, W. (1921), "William Crookes [Obituary]", *Proceedings of the Society for Psychical Research* 31: 12-29.

Brock, W.H. (1970), "Crookes, William", in Gillispie, C.C. (ed.), *Dictionary of scientific biography*, New York: Charles Scribners Sons, Vol. 3, pp. 474-482.

Brush, S.G. & C.W.F. Everitt (1969), "Maxwell, Osborne Reynolds, and the Radiometer", *Historical Studies in the Physical Sciences* 1: 105-125.

Crookes, W. (1874), "On Attraction and Repulsion Accompanying Radiation", *Philosophical Transactions of the Royal Society* 164: 501-527.

Crookes, W. (1876), "On Attraction and Repulsion Accompanying Radiation", *Proceedings of the Physical Society of London* 1: 35-51.

Crookes, W. (1875), "The Mechanical Action of Light", *Quarterly Journal of Science* 5 (2): 337-352.

Crookes, W. (1876), "The Mechanical Action of Light", *Notices of the Proceedings at the Meeting of the Members of the Royal Institution of Great Britain* 8 (1875-1878): 44-67.

Crookes, W. (1878), "On Residual Phenomena", *Quarterly Journal of Science* 8 (2): 20-34.

D'Albe, E.E.F. (1923), *The Life of Sir William Crookes, O.M., F.R.S.*, with an introduction by Oliver Lodge, London: T. Fisher Unwin.

Dekosky, R.K. (1983), "William Crookes and the Quest for Absolute Vacuum", *Annals of Science* 40: 1-18.

Ferreira, J.M.H. (2004), *Estudando o invisível: William Crookes e a nova força*, São Paulo: EDUC/FAPESP.

Greenaway, F. (1962), "A Victorian Scientist: the Experimental Researches of Sir William Crookes (1832-1919)", *Proceedings of the Royal Institution of Great Britain* 39: 172-198.

Tilden, A. (1920), "William Crookes [Obituary]", *Proceedings of the Royal Society* 96 A: i-ix.

Woodruff, A.E. (1966), "William Crookes and the Radiometer", *Isis* 57: 188-198.

Manuscripts

Letters from William Crookes to his assistant Charles Henry Gimingham, between 1871 and 1877, Science Museum, London, SML Archives: MS 409.

The Guiding Hypothesis of the Curies' Radioactivity Research: Secondary X-rays and the Sagnac Connection[*]

Roberto de Andrade Martins

Center of Sciences and Technology, State University of Paraba (UEPB)

Pierre and Marie Sklodowska Curie's main contributions to radioactivity are usually regarded as empirical investigations, which were developed without any theoretical guidance. Their approach has been contrasted to Ernest Rutherford's, and it has been suggested that the use of concrete models and hypotheses by the later contributed to his success, where the Curies failed.

Up until 1900, the French physicists were the leaders in the study of radioactivity.[1] However, the understanding of radioactivity as a phenomenon of atomic transmutation came from abroad. How did they lose their leadership?

In 1899 the Curies discovered that an object placed near a strongly radioactive source became radioactive. Rutherford also noticed that bodies near thorium became radioactive. In both cases, it was noticed that the radioactivity of those bodies was short lived. The Curies described the phenomenon as an "induced activity", and they initially rejected Rutherford's proposal that it could be produced by a material emanation coming from the radioactive substances. Rutherford's approach led to the discovery of radon and of atomic transmutation. The Curies' approach to induced radioactivity led to a mere accumulation of facts and attempts to discuss them in a more general, abstract way.

---

[*] The author is grateful to the Brazilian National Council for Scientific and Technological Development (CNPq), and to the São Paulo State Research Foundation (FAPESP) for supporting this research.
[1] See Jauncey (1946), for a standard description of the early years of radioactivity research.

According to some historians, the Curies systematically adhered to an abstract and timid approach to radioactivity, attempting to produce generalizations from observed facts and following a thermodynamic perspective. Rutherford, on the other hand, is described as a bold researcher who framed concrete, risky hypotheses and allowed them to guide his research.

The difference between the attitudes of Rutherford and the Curies has been sometimes described as due to contrasting personalities; or to national differences (see Malley 1979, and Nye 1993, for a discussion of the French and English national styles);[2] or to the distinct research schools they belonged to (Davis 1995).

However, before attempting to *explain* a fact, it is wise to check whether the fact is true, or if it an artefact produced by the historian's analysis.

I maintain in this paper that the attitudes of the Curies and Rutherford corresponding to the use of hypotheses were not widely different as it has been claimed.

It is usually assumed that Henri Becquerel's research was also purely empirical. In a former paper I have argued that Becquerel's work was guided by a hidden hypothesis concerning the violation of Stokes' law in uranium and its compounds (Martins, 1997b). I contend that, in a similar way, the Curies' researches on radioactivity were strongly directed by a hypothesis – one that was not as concealed or secret as in the case of Becquerel's work. Indeed, the Curies' papers usually averted theoretical discussion and presented no hint of a guiding hypothesis. However, in other papers it is possible to identify plain clues of the main hypothesis that directed their work.

The hypothesis that will be discussed here appeared in print, for the first time, in Marie Sklodowska Curie's paper announcing that thorium emitted a penetrating radiation, just like uranium. She suggested that the radiation emitted by uranium and thorium compounds (and, later, by other similar substances) was produced by an unknown radiation coming from space, that was transformed inside those substances, in the same way as X-rays can be transformed into secondary

---

[2] Of course, national differences between England and France are difficult to apply in this specific case, because Rutherford was from New Zealand and Marie Sklodowska Curie was Polish.

rays. This hypothesis, together with other relevant assumptions, was suggested by Georges Sagnac's investigation on X-rays.

> *Analogy with the secondary rays of the Röntgen rays.* – The properties of the rays emitted by uranium and thorium are very similar to those of the secondary rays of the Röntgen rays, recently studied by Mr. Sagnac. Besides that, I have noticed that under the action of the Röntgen rays, uranium, pitchblende and thorium oxide emit secondary rays which, from the point of view of the discharge of electrified bodies, often produce stronger effects than the secondary rays of lead. Among the metals studied by Mr. Sagnac, uranium and thorium would be placed in the neighbourhood of lead, and beyond it.
>
> To elucidate the spontaneous radiation of uranium and thorium we could imagine that the entire space is always crossed by rays analogous to the Röntgen rays, but much more penetrating and that could only be absorbed by certain elements with a large atomic weight, such as uranium and thorium. (Sklodowska-Curie 1898a, p. 1103)

Let us first clarify the meaning of Marie Sklodowska Curie's hypothesis.

The starting point of Curie's research was, of course, Henri Becquerel's investigation of the rays emitted by uranium and its compounds, in 1896-97. Becquerel believed that those rays were similar to X-rays (or Röntgen rays). Although the nature of X-rays was not established at that time, Becquerel believed that they were high-frequency electromagnetic waves (beyond the ultraviolet). He supposed that uranium and its compounds could transform visible light into X-rays by a special phenomenon of phosphorescence violating Stokes's law. Led by his belief, Becquerel reported observations to the effect that the radiation emitted by uranium compounds decreased slowly in the darkness, and increased after they were strongly illuminated; that the radiation of uranium compounds could be reflected by a metallic mirror, could be refracted by glass and polarized by a tourmaline crystal. All of his experiments seemed to confirm that uranium radiation was a high-frequency electromagnetic radiation.

Becquerel's investigations on uranium radiation lasted from 1896 to 1897. During this period, there were very few other scientists who published any paper on this topic. The limited literature on this theme was one of the reasons that led Marie Sklodowska Curie to choose it as a research object for her PhD thesis. The decision was made at the end of 1897. Her experimental researches started on the 16th of December, 1897 (Joliot-Curie 1955, p. 106).

Georges Sagnac (1869-1928), a close friend of the Curies at that time, was one of the very few people who had carefully studied Becquerel's work before 1898 and published a review paper on that phenomenon (Sagnac 1896). It is possible that Sagnac influenced Marie Sklodowska Curie's choice of uranium radiation as a research topic.

Both Georges Sagnac and Jean Perrin (1870-1942) – another friend of the Curies – were working on their PhD theses on X-rays. Perrin studied the discharge of electricity produced by X-rays. Sagnac studied the secondary radiation emitted by metals hit by X-rays. It is likely that Perrin and Sagnac discussed their researches with the Curies.

Becquerel had shown that the uranium rays were also able to discharge electrified bodies. Marie Sklodowska Curie's first experiments, as shown in her laboratory notebook, were aimed at the study of the conductivity of air produced by uranium radiation. It is likely that she initially accepted all the conclusions published by Becquerel, and that she intended to develop a research similar to that of Jean Perrin, making a detailed study of all circumstances involved in the production of electric conduction by the uranium rays. Indeed, if the uranium rays were similar to X-rays, it was natural to use the researches on X-rays of her friends, as a model for her own investigation. This circumstance could be the motivation for the specific decision Marie Curie made at the beginning of her research.

Some early experiments led Marie Sklodowska Curie to conclude (as Becquerel had already noticed) that chemical reactions or temperature changes do not modify the intensity of the radiation emitted by uranium compounds (Joliot-Curie 1955, pp. 106-108). The emission of the radiation only depended on the amount of uranium in a sample. Subsequently Curie noticed that all thorium compounds also emitted a similar radiation. As the emission was not influenced by external changes, it seemed an *atomic property* – and, of course, at that time, it was customary to regard atoms as unchangeable particles.[3]

---

[3] Some years later, Frederick Soddy remarked: "The view that radioactivity is an atomic property necessitates, on the older view of the unchangeability of the atom,

This was one of the explicit hypotheses presented by the Curies. It is well known that this hypothesis – that the emission of radiation was an atomic property – guided their successful search for new elements in pitchblende. The *atomic property hypothesis* was also confirmed when Marie Sklodowska Curie noticed that the amount of radiation emitted by uranium compounds is approximately proportional to their uranium contents, independent of the presence of other non-active elements in the substance.

Those facts did not conflict with Becquerel's initial conclusions. However, one of her early findings was that the radiation emitted by uranium and its compounds, carefully measured with an ionization chamber, did not decrease in darkness and did not increase under strong illumination (Joliot-Curie 1955, p. 106). Therefore, it did not behave as a phosphorescence phenomenon, as was supposed by Becquerel.

This discovery commanded a reflection on the source of energy behind the radiation phenomenon. Of course, for Becquerel the problem did not exist – the uranium radiation was just a form of energy that had been absorbed by the uranium compounds from light, and was slowly released under the form of penetrating radiation. However, since that interpretation was not correct, it became imperative to find out the energy source behind the emission of radiation by uranium and thorium. This was probably the motive that led the Curies to formulate their second hypothesis (the penetrating radiation hypothesis), that has already been pointed out.

On April 12, Marie Sklodowska Curie's first paper on the radiation of thorium was read by Gabriel Lippman at the French Academy of Science. In the period of less than 4 months, besides obtaining several relevant experimental results, the Curies had also framed the hypotheses that would guide their future research, abandoning Becquerel's perspective concerning the uranium phenomenon.[4]

---

that the activity should be in all cases a permanent property of the matter exhibiting it." (Soddy 1905, p. 256)

[4] One may wonder why it was Gabriel Lippman, not Henri Becquerel, who was asked by the Curies to report Marie's first paper to the Paris Academy of Science. Perhaps the reason was just that Marie had already worked with Lippman for some

Marie Sklodowska Curie's initial experiments were probably guided by Becquerel's ideas and by her own experimental results. When did Georges Sagnac's influence start?

This happened probably in the second half of March. The laboratory notebooks of Marie and Pierre Curie show that on the 16th of March most of the measurements required by the thorium paper had already been completed (Joliot-Curie 1955, p. 109). Pierre was beginning to help Marie, and on that day they both wrote a summary of the previous work, probably as a draft for a future paper. They were probably excited with the new results, and it is likely that they would discuss their research with Jean Perrin and Georges Sagnac.

Sagnac was studying the secondary radiation produced by X-rays when they strike metals. Several researchers had attempted to detect the reflection of X-rays by metals and had failed. However, in some cases a dispersed radiation was observed coming from metals hit by X-rays. The initial interpretation was that the X-rays had been diffused or scattered by the metal; however, the diffuse radiation was less penetrating than the original one. Therefore, the metal had *transformed* the incident radiation. The phenomenon was similar to visible light fluorescence: the light emitted by a fluorescent substance has a smaller frequency than the incident radiation, according to Stokes' law. If the penetration of X-rays was related to their high frequency, then a secondary radiation of lower frequency was expected to be less penetrating.

In a paper where he described several properties of X-rays, including the production of secondary radiation, Sagnac marked the similarity between the Röntgen rays and Becquerel's rays:

> It is opportune to remind here the discovery due to H. Becquerel of new invisible radiations emitted during several months, without noticeable weakening, by uranium salts and especially by uranium, that have always been kept in darkness. Up to the present day it seems that there is no limit for the duration of those phenomena, for which S.-P. Thompson proposed the name *hyperphosphorescence*. We ignore if here there is really a transformation of radiations or simply a spontaneous radiation due to a new mechanism. Anyhow, those remarkable

time, studying the magnetism of several alloys. However, there might be another reason: the disagreement between Marie's results and Becquerel's ideas.

uranium rays are very close to the X-rays by their electrical properties. (Sagnac 1898, p. 314)

The production of secondary radiation (or S-rays, as Sagnac called them) was especially strong when X-rays stroke metals of high atomic weight, such as lead. In the case of low atomic weight metals, such as aluminum, the incident rays traversed the metal without producing noticeable secondary radiation.

The secondary radiation was less penetrating than the original X-rays. For that reason, it was strongly absorbed, and produced stronger effects (ionization and photographic effects). The most penetrating X-rays passed thorugh matter without noticeable energy loss, and therefore produced weak effects. The secondary radiation produced stronger effects, because its energy was easily absorbed by matter.

It is likely that Sagnac and the Curies discussed their mutual researches in the early months of 1898. Sagnac had been studying the secondary rays some months before, and several of his results had already been published, but he was continuing his researches during this period. The comparison between the two lines of research exhibited remarkable similarities. Marie Curie noticed that the rays emitted by uranium and thorium were similar to Sagnac's secondary rays:
1. Both the secondary rays and the uranium radiation were less penetrating than X-rays.
2. Only high atomic weight elements produced a large amount of easily absorbed secondary rays. The two elements that were known to emit Becquerel rays (uranium and thorium) were the elements with the highest atomic weight known at that time.

In her search for other substances that could emit penetrating rays, Marie Sklodowska Curie had noticed that some other elements (cerium, niobium, and tantalum) also seemed slightly active, but only uranium and thorium were very active. She commented:

> It is remarkable that the two more active elements, uranium and thorium, are those that have the highest atomic weights. (Sklodowska-Curie 1898a, p. 1102)

This striking similarity suggested either to Sagnac or to the Curies the hypothesis of a penetrating radiation that could account for the energy emitted by uranium and thorium. Inasmuch as Marie Sklodowska

Curie had already concluded that the emission of radiation by uranium was not similar to phosphorescence, and since the energy output seemed constant, the energy source could not be in the active material itself. It should come from outside, and the active substances just *transformed* some other form of energy existing in the environment into the Becquerel rays. The phenomenon could be analogous to the production of Sagnac's secondary rays by X-rays.

Marie Curie conjectured that a very penetrating unknown radiation existed everywhere. It produced no observable effects in ordinary matter but its transformation by heavy atomic weight elements could produce a detectable secondary radiation – the Becquerel rays.

This trend of ideas is not explicit in the early papers published by Marie Sklodowska Curie, but that seems a plausible reconstruction of the reasoning that led to the hypothesis of the penetrating radiation.

It seems that the hypothesis was not due to Sagnac. Indeed, in a paper on X-rays and secondary rays he published in 1898, Sagnac referred to the similarity between X-rays and the Becquerel rays, but did not compare them to the secondary rays. Also, as will be seen later, in 1901 this hypothesis was clearly ascribed to Marie Curie.

On the 1st of April, the laboratory notebook shows that the Curies had already begun to study the penetrating radiation conjecture. A series of experiments begun on this day, having the title "Effect of X-rays", attempted to detect changes in the amount of radiation emitted by uranium and other active materials when they were submitted to X-rays. The content of the notebook was described by Irène Joliot-Curie in the following way:

> The experimental conditions are not precisely described. It seems that the idea was the following: the active matter was irradiated through the support, that absorbed little; the active matter was covered by a plate that could absorb only part of its radiation, but almost completely the X rays (this plate could be made of lead). They searched whether the X-rays excited or not a radiation analogous to the normal activity of the active substances. The active materials used were uranium, uranium oxide, orangite and pitchblende. (Joliot-Curie 1955, p. 111)

It is quite obvious that, at this point, the relation between the secondary radiation produced by X-rays and the emission of Becquerel rays by uranium and other active substances was already at work, guiding the Curies' experiments.

On the same day, the Curies compared the penetrating powers of the rays emitted by thorium and uranium. They observed that the radiation emitted by uranium was less penetrating than that emitted by thorium. In the case of secondary rays, those emitted by elements with higher atomic weight were also less penetrating. Therefore, this experiment disclosed another important similarity between the radiation of uranium, thorium, and Sagnac's S-rays.

As described before, a few days later Marie Sklodowska Curie's first paper was read by Gabriel Lippman. It contained a clear presentation of the penetrating radiation hypothesis. No alternative hypothesis was discussed in that paper. This circumstance strongly suggests that the Curies were immediately convinced that this was a correct assumption.

The atomic property hypothesis and the penetrating radiation hypothesis were in mutual agreement, and reinforced each other. If the Becquerel rays were the outcome of the transformation of a penetrating radiation by elements of high atomic weight, this should be a property that depended on the properties of the *atoms* (not molecules), and the total amount of radiation produced in uranium compounds should only depend on the amount of the active element in the substance.

However, there were two empirical exceptions to the atomic property hypothesis: pitchblende and chalcolite, two uranium minerals, were more active than metallic uranium. If the atomic property hypothesis were a mere empirical generalization, it should have been rejected because of those exceptions. However, the Curies chose to retain this hypothesis, and added another supposition: that there was another, unknown active element, in pitchblende. This risky supposition was already presented in Marie Sklodowska Curie's first paper:

> Two uranium minerals, pitchblende (uranium oxide) and chalcolite (phosphate of copper and uranium) are much more active than uranium itself. This is a very remarkable fact and it leads to the belief that those minerals can contain an element that is much more active than uranium. (Sklodowska-Curie 1898a, p. 1102)

The strong confidence shown by the Curies in the atomic property hypothesis at this early stage of their researches is strong evidence that this hypothesis was not just an empirical generalization. It was part of a broader theoretical interpretation of the phenomenon, reinforced by Sagnac's work on the secondary radiation. Everything seemed to fit those hypotheses, and guided by those hypotheses the Curies set out into a strenuous search for the unknown active element in pitchblende. The hypothesis of the penetrating radiation, and the hypothesis that radioactivity was an atomic phenomenon (but without any assumption of atomic change) guided those investigations of the Curies, from April of 1898 onwards.

The hypotheses led them to the discovery, in 1898, of two new radioactive elements: polonium and radium. In their following papers describing the discovery of polonium and radium, the Curies did not mention the penetrating radiation hypothesis, but they did refer to the atomic property hypothesis.

It seems that the search for the new active elements absorbed most of their time, and they did not attempt to check the penetrating radiation hypothesis. Meanwhile, other researchers did it. In September 1898 Johann Elster and Hans Geitel submitted to the journal *Annalen der Physik und Chemie*, a paper in which they discussed several contrasting explanations of the Becquerel rays – including Marie Sklodowska Curie's penetrating radiation hypothesis.

After a theoretical discussion of the many suggestions, Elster and Geitel described an experimental test of Marie Sklodowska Curie's conjecture (Elster & Geitel, 1898). The hypothetical penetrating radiation should be able to penetrate the whole atmosphere (equivalent to about 10 meters of water), the walls of laboratory buildings and metallic apparatus used in radiation experiments, without noticeable absorption. However, it would be extravagant to suppose that it could penetrate any thickness of matter without suffering absorption. If radioactivity was produced by a penetrating radiation coming from space, it should be weaker in deep pits. Hence, they were led to test whether the emission of radiation by uranium suffered any change when it was observed in a very profound pit, about 850 meters deep. The experiment showed, however, that the activity of the radioactive sample was the same at the depth of 850 meters as at the ground level. The authors concluded:

> From those researches it seems to us that the hypothesis of production of Becquerel rays by other rays pre-existent in space is improbable to the highest degree. (Elster & Geitel 1898, p. 740)

Marie Sklodowska Curie became aware of this paper soon after its publication, in December 1898, and referred to its negative result in a long review article which she published in January of 1899 (Sklodowska-Curie, 1899a, p. 50). In that paper, Marie presented for the first time *several* explanations that had been suggested for radioactivity – including the penetrating radiation hypothesis.

The Curies acknowledged that the result of the experiment made by Elster and Geitel presented a difficulty for the penetrating radiation conjecture. However, they did not give up their hypothesis. They possibly thought that the radiation was not noticeably absorbed by the materials constituting the crust of the Earth, for depths of a few hundred meters, because the minerals that build up that crust do not contain a strong proportion of high atomic weight elements. They devised another test, which was shortly described in Marie Sklodowska Curie's thesis. The date of this experiment is unknown:

> We have measured the radioactivity of uranium at noon and at midnight, thinking that if the Sun were the source of the hypothetical primary radiation, this could be partially absorbed in passing across the Earth. Experience did not provide any difference between the two measurements. (Sklodowska-Curie 1903, p. 140)

Although 850 meters of rock did not produce any change, the whole Earth should produce a noticeable absorption. If the penetrating radiation came from the Sun, the activity of uranium should be greater at noon than at midnight. No difference was observed, however.

Notice that the Curies did not gave up the penetrating radiation hypothesis after Elster and Geitel's results. Notice also that their own experiment could only possibly *confirm* the penetrating radiation hypothesis, because the negative outcome could be interpreted in a very simple way: the penetrating radiation did not come from the Sun.

The penetrating radiation hypothesis had a strong influence on the interpretation of the Curies concerning "induced radioactivity".

They described their discovery of the phenomenon in the following manner:

> While studying the properties of strongly radioactive matter, prepared by us (polonium and radium), we have noticed that the rays emitted by those substances, acting upon inert substances, can communicate radioactivity to them, and that this radioactivity remains during a very long time. (Curie & Sklodowska-Curie 1899, p. 714)

Notice that in the very description of the discovery, the Curies assumed that *the rays* had induced radioactivity in other materials. A "neutral" description of the phenomenon would only specify that an inert body put close to a strongly radioactive source would become radioactive.

After describing the experiments that they made concerning the phenomenon, the Curies concluded:

> The phenomenon of induced radioactivity is a type of secondary radiation due to the Becquerel rays. However, this phenomenon is different from the one that is known for Röntgen rays. Indeed, the secondary rays of the Röntgen rays that have been studies up to now are born immediately when the bodies that emit them are hit by the Röntgen rays and cease immediately with the suppression of the later. (Curie & Sklodowska-Curie 1899, pp. 715-716)

Therefore, the hypothesis of the penetrating radiation and secondary rays was the basis of their initial interpretation of "induced radioactivity".

In 1899, new advances brought fresh difficulties for the interpretation of radioactivity. When the Curies began their studies on uranium and its radiation, nobody suspected that those rays could be classified into several different types. They seemed very similar to soft X-rays. The situation changed in 1899. Ernest Rutherford studied the absorption of radiation by thin metallic foils and distinguished the α and β rays. In the same year, F. Giesel, Stefan Meyer and Egon von Schweidler noticed that some of those rays could be deviated by a magnetic field. Now, the similarity between the Becquerel rays and X-rays began to dwindle, and this was a challenge to the viewpoints embraced by the Curies.

The possibility of deviating the rays was first confirmed by Becquerel, and Pierre Curie himself soon confirmed that some of the rays produced by radium and polonium could also be deviated by a magnetic field. Was this a clear proof that they were charged particles? Perhaps it was not. The Curies decided to check this point. They soon described an experiment where they separated and collected the magnetically deflected rays (Rutherford's β rays). They were able to detect that those rays carried a negative electric charge (Curie & Sklodowska-Curie 1900b). They seemed of the same nature as cathode rays. This finding threatened all their theoretical assumptions, because now the Becquerel rays could not be assumed to be similar to the secondary radiation of X-rays anymore.

The analogy could be maintained, however, if the X-rays also carried an electrical charge. The Curies tested this possibility, and did not find any clear evidence that X-rays conveyed electrical charges (Curie & Sklodowska-Curie 1900b, p. 650).

Of course, they must have discussed the uncomfortable situation with Sagnac, and their old friend came to their rescue. Indeed, in 1898 Sagnac had noticed that the secondary rays contained, besides neutral radiation, some electrically charged particles. The evidence he obtained in 1898 was not altogether clear, and so he had decided not to publish his discovery. However, in order to be able to claim priority afterwards, he placed a description of his research in a sealed envelope ("pli cacheté"), which was delivered to the French Academy of Sciences on July 18, 1898. In February of 1900, he asked the Academy to open the envelope. Its content was then read and published (Sagnac 1900).

That was a very important point. Pierre Curie and Georges Sagnac soon began a detailed joint investigation of this topic.[5] On April 9th, 1900, they presented to the Paris Academy of Sciences the result of their research (Curie & Sagnac 1900). They confirmed the previous result of the Curies that Röntgen rays do not carry a noticeable electric charge; however, "on the contrary, *the secondary rays* originating from the transformation of Röntgen rays *do convey electrical charges with them*, similar to cathode rays, as do the rays from radium" (Curie & Sagnac 1900, p. 1013; emphasis of the authors).

---

[5] Let us point out that this was the only joint research ever done by Curie and Sagnac.

The paper published by Curie and Sagnac did not mention the penetrating radiation hypothesis of radioactivity. However, the connection between the experiments and the hypothesis was made clear in another work on the same subject that they presented on the 3rd of May, 1901, to the French Physical Society.

> The weak penetration power of the secondary rays of heavy metals reminds us Lenard's cathode rays: they can only reach a few centimetres in the atmospheric air, where they are strongly diffused. This analogy led us to search whether the secondary rays, which are strongly absorbed by the air, carry with them negative electric charges, since this is the fundamental characteristic of the cathode rays. The deviation of the rays by a magnetic or electric field will be the probable consequence of their electrification. *There is no contradiction between this hypothesis and those that have been developed by one of us*, since the beam spontaneously emitted by the *radium* of Mr. and Mrs. Curie is a mixture of rays with negative electricity, analogous to the cathode rays, that can be deviated by the magnetic field and by the electric field, together with rays that cannot be deflected, analogous to X-rays, which seem devoid of electrical charges. (Curie & Sagnac 1902, p. 13; my emphasis)

The paper did not elucidate what the authors meant by the hypothesis that had been developed by one of them. Was that hypothesis proposed by Sagnac, or by Pierre Curie? An anonymous account of the meeting of the French Physical Society where they presented this paper leaves no doubt concerning this point: "The existence of electrified secondary rays producing a deflectable beam is in accordance with the analogy between the secondary rays and the spontaneous rays of radioactive bodies pointed out by Mrs. Curie" (Anonymous 1901, p. 499). Therefore, it is unlikely that Sagnac had suggested the penetrating radiation hypothesis. The two previous citations imply that it had been proposed by one of the Curies.

Pierre Curie and Georges Sagnac concluded from their experiments that the penetrating radiation hypothesis could be maintained in light of the new discovered properties of radiation. They had observed that the emission of negative charges together with the secondary rays was especially noticed in heavy metals – a circumstance that enhanced the similarity between this phenomenon, and radioactivity (Curie & Sagnac 1900, Curie & Sagnac 1902).

In 1900, the Curies presented a report on radioactivity to the International Congress of Physics which took place in Paris. At the end of that report, they discussed the nature of the Becquerel rays. They reported that those rays contain both charged rays, similar to the cathode rays, and others that were similar to X-rays. The occurrence of both kinds of rays seemed easy to explain:

> This mixture should not amaze us. In the vacuum tubes the X-rays are born at the walls hit by cathode rays. On the other side, when X-rays hit the bodies they produce the birth of the secondary rays studied by Mr. Sagnac, and those secondary rays seem also to be formed by a mixture of non-deflectable rays and rays charged with electricity, analogous to cathode rays. There is therefore a strong analogy between the spontaneous emission of the radioactive bodies and the secondary rays of the Röntgen rays. This analogy had hit us since the beginning of this study, and afterwards it always became stronger. [...]
>
> According to what has just been said, it is possible to regard the Becquerel rays as a secondary emission due to some rays analogous to X-rays that traverse all space and every body.
>
> If the emission in its totality is not a secondary emission, this could however be true for one of the two groups of rays; one could consider as primary rays either the non-deflectable rays, of the deflectable rays. (Curie & Sklodowska-Curie 1900a, pp. 113-114)

The Curies also mentioned, at the end of their paper, the idea of a changing atom, but ascribed this idea to William Crookes and J. J. Thomson – not to themselves. It is plain that at that time the Curies had a strong confidence in the penetrating radiation hypothesis, and thought that it would remain acceptable at least for one of the types of radiation emitted by radioactive bodies.

It is possible to find other evidences that from 1900 to 1903 in which the Curies still accepted this hypothesis, notwithstanding the new facts that were being discovered. In 1903, for instance, Pierre Curie and André Laborde published the first measurement of the energy released by a radium salt. They concluded that 1 g of radium liberates about 100 calories per hour. The authors discussed the hypothesis that the energy liberation was due to an atomic change, and then they emphasized: "The hypothesis of a continuous change of the atom is not the only one compatible with the release of heat by radium. This heat release can also be explained by supposing that the uranium makes use of an external energy of unknown nature." (Curie & Laborde 1903, p. 675)

This suggests that Pierre Curie had not yet given up the penetrating radiation hypothesis, at this time. It is also important to notice that when Becquerel and the Curies received the Nobel Prize for their researches, in 1903, the former researcher maintained that the penetrating radiation hypothesis was still acceptable – although he preferred the idea of atomic transformation:

> Among the hypotheses which are suggested to fill the gaps left by current experiments, one of the most likely lies in supposing that the emission of energy is the result of a slow transformation of the atoms of the radioactive substances. [...]
>
> In this scheme, there would still be scope to wonder whether the transformation of the atom comprises a slow, spontaneous evolution, or whether it is the result of the absorption of external radiation beyond the range of our senses. If such a radiation were to exist, one could still picture the radioactive substances transforming it without themselves being altered. So far no experiment has confirmed or invalidated these hypotheses. (Becquerel 1903, p. 15)

On the same occasion, Pierre Curie discussed the existing explanations of radioactivity. He presented a description of the earlier views of the Curies that is at variance with existing evidence:

> Since the beginning of our researchers we have noticed, Mrs. Curie and I, that to explain the phenomena it is possible to frame two distinct very general hypotheses that were presented by Mrs. Curie in 1899 and 1900. (Curie 1903, p. 5)

The two hypotheses are then presented by Curie: the penetrating radiation hypothesis and the hypothesis of atomic disintegration. As has been shown above, the only hypothesis described in Marie Curie's early research papers is the first one. The second hypothesis does appear, *among several others* (for instance, a violation of the second law of thermodynamics) in the papers published in 1899 and 1900, by Marie Curie; but this only occurred after the penetrating radiation hypothesis had been challenged by the experiment of Elster and Geitel.[6] Now, in 1903, Pierre Curie seemed convinced that the atomic

---

[6] In her 1899 paper, Marie Curie described *five* (not two) groups of hypotheses for explaining the emission of energy by radioactive bodies (Sklodowska-Curie 1899).

transformation hypothesis was the best explanation; and so he was careful enough to *conceal* that their initial assumption was the penetrating radiation hypothesis.

Conclusions

The penetrating radiation hypothesis had been very fruitful, in 1898, since it provided an explanation for the atomic property hypothesis that guided the discovery of polonium and radium. When the hypothesis encountered strong difficulties – such as Elster and Geitel's negative experiment in the late 1898 – the Curies maintained their hypothesis. When the conjecture was threatened by the discovery of the nature of the β radiation, in 1899, Pierre Curie and Georges Sagnac were able to sustain the hypothesis by showing that the secondary rays also contained particles with negative charge.

However, it is likely that this loyalty to the old hypothesis served as a barrier to understanding radioactivity, the following years. The Curies still kept their faith in this hypothesis at the time when Rutherford and Soddy began to develop the disintegration theory of radioactivity. They resisted the new theory, not because of their aversion to concrete, material hypotheses (as has been claimed), but because the new theory was incompatible with their own cherished explanation of radioactivity. In only a couple years, nonetheless, they had to give up their explanation because only Rutherford's theory of atomic disintegration and change could account for the wealth of evidence amassed by himself, by Frederick Soddy and by several other researchers.

Although the traditional accounts of the work of the Curies do not emphasize their use of conjectures (see Weill 1970, Wyart 1970), I claim that their radioactivity researches were guided by some definite hypotheses, in the same way as Becquerel's research. In both cases, their scientific papers convey the feeling that their research was purely empirical and that they avoided any specific hypothesis, but that was not the case. Rutherford's hypotheses were perhaps more detailed and they were explicitly presented by him, in his paper. But that is just a difference of degree, not a qualitative difference between the attitudes of Rutherford and the Curies.

References

[Anonymous] (1901), "Société Française de Physique. Séance du 3 Mai 1901. *Revue Générale des Sciences* 12: 498-499.

Badash, L. (1965), "Radioactivity before the Curies", *American Journal of Physics* 33: 128-135.

Becquerel, H. (1896a), "Sur les radiations émises par phosphorescence", *Comptes Rendus Hebdomadaires des Séances de l'Académie des Sciences de Paris* 122: 420-421.

Becquerel, H. (1896b), "Sur les radiations invisibles émises par les corps phosphorescents", *Comptes Rendus Hebdomadaires des Séances de l'Académie des Sciences de Paris* 122: 501-503.

Becquerel, H. (1896c), "Sur quelquer propriétés nouvelles des radiations invisibles émises par divers corps phosphorescents", *Comptes Rendus Hebdomadaires des Séances de l'Académie des Sciences de Paris* 122: 559-564.

Becquerel, H. (1903), "Sur une propriété nouvelle de la matière, la radio-activité", *Les Prix Nobel* 3: 1-15.

Crookes, W. (1887), *La genèse des éléments*. Trans. Gustave Richard. Paris: Gauthier-Villars.

Curie, E. (1939), *Madame Curie*, Paris: Gallimard.

Curie, I.J. (1954), *Oeuvres de Marie Sklodowska-Curie*, Warsaw: Panstwowe Wydawnictwo Naukowe.

Curie, P. (1900), "L'état actuel des recherches sur les substances radioactives", *Archive des Sciences Physiques et Natureles* 10 (4): 388-389.

Curie, P. (1903), "Conférence Nobel faite a Stockholm devant l'Académie des Sciences", *Les Prix Nobel* 3: 1-7.

Curie, P. & A. Laborde (1903), "Sur la chaleur dégagée spontanément par les sels de radium", *Comptes Rendus de l'Académie des Sciences de Paris* 136: 673-675.

Curie, P. & G. Sagnac (1900), "Électrisation négative des rayons secondaires produits au moyen des rayons Röntgen", *Comptes Rendus Hebdomadaires des Séances de l'Académie des Sciences de Paris* 130: 1013-1016.

Curie, P. & G. Sagnac (1902), "Électrisation négative des rayons secondaires issus de la transformation des rayons X", *Journal de Physique* (series 4) 1: 13-21.

Curie, P. & M. Sklodowska-Curie (1898), "Sur une substance nouvelle radioactive, contenue dans la pechblende", *Comptes Rendus de l'Académie des Sciences de Paris* 127: 175-178.

Curie, P. & M. Sklodowska-Curie (1899), "Sur la radioactivité provoquée par les rayons de Becquerel", *Comptes Rendus de l'Académie des Sciences de Paris* 129: 714-716.

Curie, P. & M. Sklodowska-Curie (1900a), "Sur la charge électrique des rayons déviables du radium", *Comptes Rendus Hebdomadaires des Séances de l'Académie des Sciences de Paris* 130: 647-650.

Curie, P. & M. Sklodowska-Curie (1900a), "Les nouvelles substances radioactives et les rayons qu'elles émettent", in Gillaume, C.-É. & L. Poincaré (eds.), *Rapports Présentés au Congrès International de Physique réuni a Paris en 1900*, Vol. 3, Paris: Gauthier-Villars, pp. 79-113.

Curie, P., Sklodowska-Curie, M. & G. Bémont (1898), "Sur une nouvelle substance fortement radioactive, contenue dans la pechblende", *Comptes Rendus de l'Académie des Sciences de Paris* 127: 1215-1217.

Davis, J.L. (1995), "The Research School of Marie Curie in the Paris Faculty, 1907-14", *Annals of Science* 52: 321-355.

Elster, Johann & Geitel, Hans. "Versuche an Becquerelstrahlen", *Annalen der Physik und Chemie* [2] 66: 735-740, 1898.

Jauncey, G. E. M. "The Early Years of Radioactivity", *American Journal of Physics* 14: 226-41, 1946.

Joliot-Curie, I. (ed.) (1954), *Oeuvres de Marie Sklodowska Curie/Prace Marii Skłodowskiej-Curie*, Varsovie/Warsawa: Panstwowe Wydawnictwo Naukowe.

Joliot-Curie, I. (1955), "Les carnets de laboratoire de la découverte du polonium et du radium", in Sklodowska-Curie, M., *Pierre Curie*, Paris: Denoël, pp. 103-124.

Malley, M. (1979), "The Discovery of Atomic Transmutation: Scientific Styles and Philosophies in France and Britain", *Isis* 70: 213-223.

Martins, R.A. (1997), "Becquerel and the Choice of Uranium Compounds", *Archive for History of Exact Sciences* 51 (1): 67-81.

Nye, M.J. (1993), "National Styles? French and English Chemistry in the Nineteenth and Early Twentieth Centuries", *Osiris* 8: 30-49.

Perrin, J. (1897), "Rayons cathodiques et rayons de Röntgen. Étude expérimentale", *Annales de Chimie et de Physique* (série 7) 11: 496-554.[7]

Rutherford, E. (1899), "Uranium Radiation and the Electrical Conduction Produced by It", *Philosophical Magazine* 47: 109-63.

Sagnac, G. (1896), "Les expériences de M. H. Becquerel sur les radiations invisibles émises par les corps phosphorescents et par les sels d'uranium", *Journal de Physique Théorique et Appliquée* 5 (3): 193-202.

Sagnac, G. (1898), "Luminescence et rayons X", *Révue Générale des Sciences* 9: 314-320.

Sagnac, G. (1900), "Rayons X et décharge: généralisation de la notion de rayons cathodiques", *Comptes Rendus Hebdomadaires des Séances de l'Académie des Sciences de Paris* 130: 320-323.

Sagnac, G. (1900a), "Propagation des rayons X de Röntgen", *Annales de Chimie et de Physique* (série 7) 22: 394-432.

Sagnac, G. (1900b), "Rayons secondaires dérivés des rayons de Röntgen", *Annales de Chimie et de Physique* (série 7) 22: 493-563.

Sagnac, G. (1900c), "Relation des rayons X et de leurs rayons secondaires avec la matière et l'électricité", *Annales de Chimie et de Physique* (série 7) 23: 145-198.

Sklodowska-Curie, M. (1898a), "Rayons émis par les composés de l'uranium et du thorium", *Comptes Rendus Hebdomadaires des Séances de l'Académie des Sciences de Paris* 126: 1101-1103.

Sklodowska-Curie, M. (1898b), "Poszukiwania nowego metalu w pechblendzie", *Swiatlo* 1: 54-62. (Reproduced in Joliot-Curie, I.

---

[7] This paper reproduces Perrin's PhD thesis.

(ed.) (1954), *Oeuvres de Marie Sklodowska Curie/ Prace Marii Sklodowskiej-Curie*, Varsovie/Warsawa: Panstwowe Wydawnictwo Naukowe, pp. 49-56.)

Sklodowska-Curie, M. (1899), "Les rayons de Becquerel et le polonium", *Révue Générale des Sciences* 10: 41-50.

Sklodowska-Curie, M. (1900), "Sur le poids atomique du baryum radifère", *Comptes Rendus de l'Académie des Sciences de Paris* 131: 382-384.

Sklodowska-Curie, M. (1902), "Sur le poids atomique du radium", *Comptes Rendus de l'Académie des Sciences de Paris* 135: 161-163.

Sklodowska-Curie, M. (1903), *Recherches sur les substances radioactives*, Paris: Gauthier-Villars, 1903.[8]

Sklodowska-Curie, M. (1923), *Pierre Curie*, Trad. Charlotte and Vernon Kellogg; with an introduction by Mrs. William Brown Meloney and autobiographical notes by Marie Curie, New York: MacMillan.

Soddy, F. (1905), "Radioactivity", *Annual Reports on the Progress of Chemistry for 1904 Issued by the Chemical Society* 1: 244-280.

Weill, A.R. (1970), "Curie, Marie (Maria Sklodowska)", in Gillispie, C.C. (ed.), *Dictionary of Scientific Biography*, Vol. 3, New York: Charles Scribner's Sons, pp. 497-503.

Wyart, J. (1970), "Curie, Pierre", in Gillispie, C.C. (ed.), *Dictionary of Scientific Biography*, Vol. 3, New York: Charles Scribner's Sons, pp. 503-508.

---

[8] This was Marie Curie's PhD thesis.

Galileo's Matter-Theory: *resolutio* and Infinite Indivisibles

Fernando Tula Molina

National University of Quilmes (UNQ)/
National Scientific and Technical Research Council (CONICET)

1. Introduction

In *Atomism and its Critics*, Andrew J. Pyle points out that:

> The cohesiveness of fluids also poses a mayor problem for the matter-theory of Galileo. Solid bodies, he claims in Day One of the *Discorsi*, are held together by the *fuga vacui* exerted by their interstitial microvacua; liquids such as water lack such point-vacua and are therefore without cohesion. (The melting of a solid body he explains in terms of fire-atoms or *ignicoli* into the interstitial vacua to neutralize their *fuga vacui*). Galileo continued to deny, in the face of some powerful evidence, that a fluid such as water possessed *surface tension* – such an admission would have proved fatal to his matter-theory. (Pyle 1997, pp. 494-495)

The main problem of any atomistic theory is the explanation of *body cohesion*. In the above citation Pyle correctly specifies that, in Galileo's case, the problem was in explaining the cohesion of *fluids* (or, more properly, its *lack* of cohesion). This point is, in my opinion, not only right but much deeper than general comments like, for example, that of A. Mark Smith who states that:

> It appears that the confluence of powerful physical, metaphysical and mathematical trends lead Galileo to his theory of indivisibles. (Smith 1976, pp. 571-588)

Here, the empirical and conceptual difficulties that Galileo had to face disappear under the mere enunciation of the convergent traditions behind him. Moreover, Pyle's citation has, to my ends, the advantage of briefly involving all of Galileo's atomism points that I want to comment in the following:
1. The relationship between cohesion of fluids and Galileo's matter theory.
2. The cause of cohesion and dissolution of solid bodies.
3. Galileo's conception of fluids.
4. The problem of surface tension and Galileo's atomism.
5. The relationship between theory and evidence.

2. Conflicting traditions at the back of Galileo's science

First of all I must refer, at least in a general way, to the main intellectual traditions converging on Galileo's science. In this way, I'll try to make clear what I consider the scope and the limits of Mark Smith's statement above.

I will refer mainly to the tension between the Archimedean tradition – very early adopted in Galileo's life to analyze the problem of the center of gravity of non-regular bodies – and the Veneto Aristotelism – the natural philosophy framework while he was student at the *Collegio Romano*. This tension relates directly to his early ideas about the constitution of matter, and its properties. In Archimedean terms, matter was atomized under the *specific weight* concept that establishes the relation of weight *per unit volume*, and which allows to be approached rigorously by the notion of *moment*. Nevertheless, the problem here is that this concept considers neither *force*, nor *velocity*, establishing a non-dynamical conception of matter. On the other hand, in Aristotelian physics, dynamics was intrinsically causal, but in the framework of hylomorphism the emphasis was put on the intellection of *form*, and not on the mathematical comprehension of the atomic configuration in the material continuum.

2.1. Sunspots and atomism

The day after Christmas in 1611 Galileo wrote the third and last letter to Marco Velsero expressing his opinions on the nature of sunspots scrutinized systematically with his new telescope. On the basis of detailed diagrams on the successive positions of the spots; and with the aid of projective geometry, Galileo was able to sustain that all of them *move jointly*, which could only be explained by means of the hypothesis of solar rotation, which was considered

> A very strong reason enough to demonstrate by itself the essence of our point. (Galilei 1890-1909, Vol. V, p. 121)[1]

This is the strongest of Galileo's arguments on sunspots location, and with it he gives up the controversy as can be seen in the letters to Marco Velsero, published later (in 1613). In spite of that, these letters do not include a different and relevant argument advanced by his disciple, Benedetto Castelli, privately communicated on the 8th of May 1612:

> [...] aimed by this great occasion to philosophize [...] and if I would philosophize on the nature of solar body with reference to our bright bodies, I will say not only that it is necessary that these spots were on the solar body, but that I can't think otherwise about them (Galilei 1890-1909, Vol. XI, letter 674).

This "great occasion to philosophize" allows Castelli to introduce his first defense of atomism in the physical sense relating to the nature of light:

> I add (according with my supposition on light) that every bright body is continuously vibrating and letting fly corpuscles with great velocity, [and] that the Sun is bright and, in consequence, that it lets loose continuously very swift corpuscles, when the body can't divide itself with that velocity and the corpuscles can't move with that velocity, they can't produce in me the appearance of what I call light: for that reason sunspots are necessarily on the Sun, that is what we see (Galilei 1890-1909, Vol. XI, letter 674).

Judging from the conceptual difficulties that Galileo faced later on trying to establish his atomistic position, there's no doubt that the reason why this argument did not get to print was that, during the time, he had not arrived to a definitive idea about the subject.

---

[1] My translation; the translation of Stillman Drake (1957) stops just at the line before. See also p. 126.

2.2. Hydrostatic and atomism

Almost accidentally Galileo began in August 1611 a polemic with Vicenzio di Grazia on the state of water, when it turns into ice. Di Grazia stated that the solidity of ice results from the fact that it is *condensed* water; Galileo replied that, in that case, it would be heavier than water in its natural state and, for that reason, would not float; this must lead us to conceive ice as *rarified* water. The answer given to that argument was the Aristotelic dictum that the cause of floating bodies was not *weight* but *shape*. This point became the focus of the whole the subsequent discussion (Galilei 1890-1909, Vol. IV, p. 66).

Several days later, a Jesuit friend of Di Gracia, Ludovico Delle Colombe showed experimentally that an ebony *sphere* sank in water, but a thin *tablet* also made of ebony did not sink, and thereby inferred, – against Galileo – the interdependence between *shape* and *flotation*. Delle Colombe considered his experiment to be conclusive and began a series of public demonstrations in front of Galileo, two of which had Francesco Nori as referee (Galileo 1890-1909, Vol. IV, p. 66).

In the following year (1612), the *Discorso intorno alle cose chestanno in sul'acqua e che in quella si muovono* was published because Cosimo II of Medici urged Galileo to put an end to his participation in public debates, considered improper for a representative of the court (Galileo 1890-1909, Vol. XI, pp. 213-214).

Galileo wrote his *Discorso* in the spirit of Archimedean tradition, acquired from the very beginning of his activity. His first work as a mathematician, promoted by Guidobaldo del Monte, was related to the calculation of the center of gravity of irregular bodies, completing the work of Federico Commandino regarding regular ones, using the Archimedean concept of *momento* (Galileo 1890-1909, Vol. I, pp. 178-207). Nevertheless, an important difference must be pointed out. The work done by Commandino and Guidobaldo was part of a program with the humanist purpose of recovering Greek texts; they were interested more in saving their *literary integrity* than their *use* for the *physical understanding* of the natural world (Rose 1975, caps. 9-12). Galileo instead, urged by the controversy, was more interested in showing Cósimo II that the *right* explanation of *natural motion* must refer to the Archimedean concept of weight, and not to the Aristotelian.

The first aim of Galileo was to refute the Aristotelian role of *shape* as cause of body floating or sinking. His strategy was to admit that shape is relevant to penetrate media, *only in the case that matter is apt*. In this sense, for example, the cutting edge of a knife will be of importance in bread cutting, but if the knife is made of wax, it will not matter how sharp we can make it. This way, *shape* was subordinated to "the aptitude of certain matters due to their own nature to surpass media resistance", and consequently he will say that the body's *form* must refer to the *gravità in specie* or, in ours terms, to specific weight.

Galilean historiography has referred many times to this debate between Delle Colombe and Galileo. However, no reference is usually made to Galileo's intellectual effort to understand the *cause* of the surface tension phenomenon (a concept unknown to him), which contradicts Archimedes' principles.[2] I want to show here the relationship between this problem and his later defense of an atomist matter theory.

Concerning Delle Colombe's experiment, what Galileo *sees* is that the body – a chip of ebony –, in fact sinks, i.e. the lower boundary goes under water level; but the sinking stops at certain point (Fig. 1).

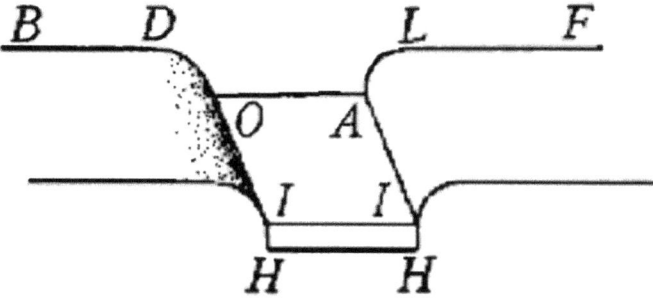

Fig. 1

He asks:

> But if the chip has already penetrated and vanquished the continuation of the water [level], and is by its nature heavier than water, what

---

[2] An exception is Biagioli (1993), but the interpretation given here is entirely different from Biagioli's. Full treatment of this point can be found in Tula Molina (2002).

is the reason that it does not go on down, but stops suspended within that little cavity that it has made by its weight in the water? I replay: Because in [gradually] submerging until its [upper] surface arrives that the water level, it loses part of its weight, and it goes on then losing the rest of it in going deeper down, and lowering itself beyond the surface of the water, while that makes a ridge and a bank around it. (Drake 1981, pp. 95-96)

His answer, completely mistaken to our eyes, is that:

It suffers this loss [of weight] by drawing down and making descend with it the air above itself by adherent contact, which air follows in to fill the cavity surrounded by the little ridges of water. Thus, what in this case sinks into and becomes situated in water is not just the gold [here the printer put *ferro* for *oro*] lamina or ebony chip, but a *composition* of ebony – [or gold] – and-air, from which results a volume [*solido*] no longer heavier than water as was the simple ebony or the simple gold (Drake 1981, p. 97; my emphasis).

It is interesting to note that this explanation confronts him with a new difficulty, that of explaining *how such a compound* of different matters *is possible*; how it is possible that air and ebony *combine* so that they can be considered a *single* body, thus justifying the statement that the compound's specific weight *is not superior* to that of water? He argues as follows:

Perhaps some of those gentlemen who dissent from me marvel that I affirm that the contiguous air above has the power to sustain the lamina of copper or silver that keeps itself on water, as if I would in a certain way give to the air some kind of magnetic virtue [virtù di calamita] of sustaining heavy bodies to which it is contiguous. To meet all the difficulties as well as I am able, I have been thinking of demonstrating with some other sensate experience how that little bit of air contiguous and above truly supports those solids that, though by nature fitted to sink to bottom, do no submerge when placed lightly on water if they have not first been wetted completely [...]. I have found that if such a body has sunk to the bottom, then without touching it but merely by sending to it a little air that joins with its top, this is sufficient not merely to sustain it, as before, but [even] to lift it and to bring it back up, where (in the same way as before) it stops and rests so long as the assistance of the air joined with it [...]. There exists, therefore, between air and other bodies, a certain affinity that holds them united, so that they are not separated without some little force (Drake 1981, pp. 102, 104).

On the other hand, in order to explain the features of that *affinity* Galileo refers to the well-known observation of the force needed to separate two well-polished marble tablets, where "there remains nothing between them". The reason of that coupling and adherence is a certain attractive force (*virtù calamitica*)

> [...] with firm coupling joins all bodies that touch without any interposition of yielding fluids.

He completes this immediately with the following philosophical comment,

> And who knows but that such contact, when it is most exact, is not a sufficient cause of the union and continuity of parts in physical body? (Drake 1981, p. 105)

At this point Galileo has to face the problem of material continuum that frames his answer in terms of *infinite indivisibles*, published 15 years later in the *Discorsi e dimostrazioni matematiche*, in 1638. As a reference in the remaining sections, the following points must be kept in mind:

1. As a *conceptual heritage* we can say that atomism was posited as a consequence of the Archimedean concept of *gravità in ispecie* (specific weight).
2. This was a key-concept in Galileo's understanding of floating bodies, but it fails to explain *physically* why the ebony *stopped* sinking.
3. Trying to explain this he introduced certain *attractive force* (virtù calamitica), which combines parts of the ebony with parts of air. Its action ceases if "a fluid medium" is interposed.
4. Galileo begins to speculate on the possibility that this *virtù* is the sufficient cause of the union and continuity of *all* natural bodies.

2.3 The evaluation of the Aristotle-Democritus controversy: specific weight as characteristic ratio of elementary units

The transition to a general matter-theory was neither swift nor easy. I want to highlight this fact in order to evaluate the scope and limits of some theses about this theory, such as those of Pyle or Smith. The road begins with Galileo's *evaluation* of the Aristotle-Democritus debate over the material continuum. Conceptually, the conclusion was that the concept of specific weight was put in Aristotelian clothes, as the *characteristic ratio of the four elements*, with their respective dynamic natural tendencies. Let us see this in greater detail.

In this controversy Aristotle denies Democritus' statement that some *fire atoms*, which continually ascend through water, may push up and sustains heavy bodies. His reason of his denial is that this should occur in greater measure in air, which is not the case. Democritus replies that in air these atoms do not act *together*. Galileo draws the following conclusion:

> Here I shall not say that the cause adopted by Democritus is true; I shall say only that he seems to me not entirely refuted by Aristotle, who says that if it were true that the hot atoms which ascend sustained heavy bodies that are broad, they ought to do that more in air than in water – perhaps because in Aristotle's opinion the same hot corpuscles ascend through air with greater force and speed than through water. If this is, as I believe, [the ground of] Aristotle's objections, it seems to me we have cause to ask whether he may not have been deceived on more than one count (Drake 1981, pp. 171-172).

The main Galilean reasons against Aristotle are:
1. To have considered as causes of a greater or lesser velocity only the difference in shapes and the greater or lesser *resistance of media to be penetrated by those shapes*, without any reference to the mobile's *gravity* and that of the media, "point of capital importance in this subject".
2. To have sustained the uncertain idea that bodies have an inherent and positive quality to ascend and descend.
3. Not to have recognized that bodies are heavier in air than in water.

For these reasons Galileo concludes that "in this particular Democritus philosophized better than Aristotle" (Drake 1981, p. 174).

Then Galileo tries to establish limits to his acceptance of Democritus' atomism and advances the following dichotomy:

> It is therefore necessary to say either that in water there are no such ascending atoms, or that if there are, they are not capable of lifting and pushing up any plate of material that without them would go to the bottom (Drake 1981, p. 176).

Up to this point my intention has been to present the context of problems and ideas in which Galileo immediately states: "I deem the second of these two positions true, supposing water in its natural state of coldness" (Drake 1981, p. 176).

After the letter to Castelli on sunspots, this is the first explicit statement of his atomistic conviction that, as has been explained, results from his efforts to explain the inexplicable phenomenon of surface tension, and the concept of *virtù calamitica*. To back up his admission of the existence of fire atoms he points us to the following experiment:

> If we take a vessel of glass or copper or any other hard material, filled with cold water, in which is placed a solid having a flat or concave shape, which exceeds water in specific gravity so little that it goes slowly to the bottom, I say that when under this vessel are placed burning coals, then as soon as new igneous corpuscles have penetrated the substance of the vessel, the ascend through that of the water; and doubtless in striking the aforesaid solid they will push it clear to the surface, and will hold it there as long as the incursion of the said corpuscles shall endure; but on the cessation of this with removal of the fire, the solid will return to the bottom, abandoned by its little points [of support] (Drake 1981, p. 177).

Nevertheless, Galileo knows that Democritean atomism is not a complete explanation for the sinking or floating of bodies because, as Democritus himself acknowledged,

> This cause exists only when we are dealing with the raising and sustaining of plates of material little heavier than water, or exceedingly thin, [...] whereas the adversaries' chips do not stop [sinking]except when their upper surfaces remain dry; nor is there any way, once they are within the water, of acting so that they do not fall to the bottom. So the cause of the swimming on water of the things Democritus speaks of is *different* from that of the things we speak of. (Drake 1981, p. 178; my emphasis).

Having established this point, Galileo takes up the controversy once again to consider Aristotle's objection against Democritus

> if what you suppose were true, then there will be a great bulk of water that will have more of fire than does some small bulk of air, and a great mass of air that will have more earth than some small mass of water, whence necessarily a great bulk of air must come down faster

> than some small quantity of water. But that is not seen in any case; therefore Democritus reasoned erroneously (Drake 1981, p. 178).

Galileo points out two reasons why Aristotle's argument is not conclusive. The first one refers to the Aristotelian relation between weight and velocity, which he counters with the Archimedean concept of specific weight:

> [...] if I am not mistaken, Aristotle's mode of deduction is either inconclusive, or if conclusive it can be turned against him [...] in the first place it would have to be true that a greater bulk of simple (*semplice*) earth is moved more swiftly than a lesser amount; but this is false, though Aristotle affirms in many places that it is true. It is not greater absolute heaviness, but greater specific heaviness, that is the cause of greater speed, nor does a ball of wood weighing ten pounds descend more swiftly than one of the same material that weights ten ounces. But it is true that a four-ounce lead ball descends more swiftly than a twenty-pound wooden ball, because lead is specifically heavier than wood. Hence it is not necessary that a great mass of air, by the much earth contained in it, should descend more swiftly than a small bulk of water; on the contrary, any bulk of water must move more swiftly than any other of air, there being a greater share of the terraneous part, specifically greater [in heaviness], in water than in air. For let Democritus grant to Aristotle that a great mass of air *can* (Drake 1981, pp. 178, 180, 182).

The second point is that

> [...] in multiplying the bulk of the air, there is multiplied not only what there is of earthy [substance], but also its fiery part as well, whereby the cause of going upward, by virtue of fire, is no less increased than that of going down on account of the multiplied earth (Drake 1981, p. 182).

Those are the main reasons why Galileo concludes that "the fallacy is greater in Aristotle's discourse". Nevertheless, he has no intention to close the controversy definitively here. He goes on adding, perhaps with some irony, a comment on the *evidence* and *authority* of Aristotle. He recalls that, trying to understand Aristotle's argument, he asked himself upon what experiment Aristotle relied to infer that a greater volume of air moves necessarily swifter than one of water:

> It is vain to think of seeing this [falling of air and water] in the element of water or in that of air, since water neither moves (or will ever move) in water, nor air in air, whatever shares of earth and fire are

> assigned to them. A still more inappropriate place for any such experience is earth, that being not a fluid body that yields to the mobility of other bodies. By Aristotle's own dictum, the void does not exist, and if it existed nothing would move in it. There remains only the region of fire, but since that is quite a distance away from us, what experience will be able to assure us, or can have assured Aristotle in the way he needs – as a thing well known to the senses – in affirming what he produces in refutation of Democritus; that a great bulk of air dos not move more swiftly than a small bulk of water? (Drake 1981, p. 182)

For my part, I wish to stress two points that I consider now sufficiently clear and that I shall want to recall later:
1. Although it is clear that he can state that it is not true that a greater volume of earth moves with greater velocity than a lesser one, thanks to the Archimedean definition of weight *per unit volume*, the reasoning is not mathematical but *physical*.
2. The second is to call attention on the particular way in which he combines the Archimedean notion of specific weight with the four elements via Democritean atomism. Here Galileo understands *specific weigh* as the *characteristic ratio* of the four elements units (water, air, earth, fire) in each natural material (wood, lead, gold). This link, not frequently recognized, is in my opinion of great importance in Galilean hydrostatics and, in my view, is a consequence of his efforts to understand why ebony stops sinking in Delle Colombe's experiment.

As we saw before, the evaluation of the Aristotle – Democritus debate did not result in accepting without judicious consideration the Democritean theses. On the contrary, he was critic of the possibility that fire atoms can resist body sinking and, for that reason, it was necessary once again to complete the explanation in terms of the difference of specific weights. This requires, in its turn, that water *offers no resistance to division* – contrary to the Aristotelian explanation in terms of medium resistance. In my view, it was as a result of trying to satisfy this requisite that Galileo arrived to his atomistic theory of *infinite indivisibles*.

3. Fluids cohesion and Galilean matter-theory

The theory of *infinite indivisibles* is the heart of Galileo's atomistic conception of matter. Its features are a result in part of the conceptual difficulties already mentioned, and in part of the peculiarities of Galileo's strategies to solve them. By this I mean to say that it is not just a legacy of early views on the material continuum, and that it contains aspects of its own that will not even be present in the works of his disciples (for example, in the method of infinite indivisibles developed and promoted by Bonaventura Cavalieri). In particular, matter *porosity* was a consequence of the necessity that air and ebony could combine themselves in a compound, in order to explain the *diminution* of specific weight. This led to a central problem: understanding the *nature* of water.

The steps to this comprehension were not easy and it took him 26 years to follow them, starting on the printing of the treatise on hydrostatics up to his last works, when he was already in house arrest. On the first day of the *Discorsi*, he states the basic problem: the material resistance to division and fracture. Galileo's worries were about the resistance offered by water to division, seeking in general the cause of cohesion *of any natural body*. This gives rise to a sub-problem: determining the sufficient force to overcome that which held its parts together.

There he says:

> But I do not wish now to digress on this subject, especially since you want to hear my thoughts about resistance to breakage on the part of other bodies, whose texture is not of filaments, as is that of ropes and most kinds of wood, but whose parts cohere by reason of other causes. These, in my opinion, may be reduced to two kinds, one of which is the celebrated repugnance that nature has against allowing a void to exist. The other, when this of the void is deemed insufficient, requires the introduction of some sticky, viscous, or gluey substance that shall tenaciously connect the particles of which the body is composed (Galileo 1974, p. 19).

Galileo begins mentioning the same archetypical example of the two well-polished marble tablets, and the resistance that they offer to a separation when there remains no air between them (Fig. 2). Then he adds:

But I will say that the void which tights and is vanquished between two plates is not in itself enough reason for the firm bonding [*collegamento*] of the parts of a solid marble or metal cylinder which, strained [*violentate*] by strong forces pulling them directly, are finally separated and divide. Now, if I can find a way to distinguish this known resistance, that depends on the void, from any other resistance, whatever it may be, that joins with this in strengthening the attachment, and if I make you see that the former one alone is far from sufficient for the whole effect, will you not then grant me that another [resistance] must be introduced? (Galileo 1974, p. 23)

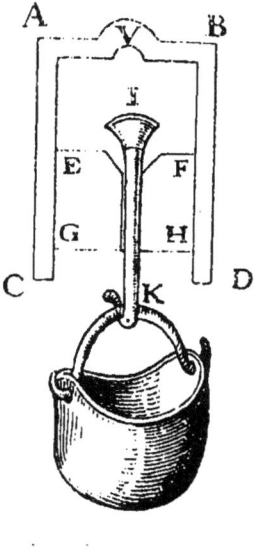

Fig. 2

Galileo needs to separate these forces, *horror vacui* and the one responsible for an *internal cohesion* of any continuous body. Ingeniously, he measured the weight that we have to hang from the cork of a *hollow cylinder* put upside down to take the cork down (this measures the *horror vacui force*), and compares it with the weight needed to break a *solid marble cylinder* of the same dimensions. He concludes that the force needed in the second case is five times greater than that of the first case.

Objections considered by Galileo, put in Simplicio's mouth, seem closer to the instrumental worries of Boyle than to the identification of a *new cause* to explain body cohesion. Simplicio objects: "Why should not air, or exhalations, or other more subtle substances, penetrate through porosities of the wood, or even of the glass itself?" (Galileo 1974, p. 24)

Since Galileo's purpose was not to demonstrate the existence of a vacuum, he replies:

> If in the upper part of the glass we make a small protruding indentation, s at V, the air or any more tenuous and spirituous material, penetrating through the substance or the porosity of glass or wood, will be seen to collect in the indentation V, the water giving way to it. But if those things are not observed, we may be assured that the experiment has been tried with all the proper precautions, and we shall know that water is not expansible, nor glass penetrable by any material however subtle (Galileo 1974, p. 24).

Still, the main problem will be to determine the possible cause of the *remaining* resistance, which Sagredo states in the following terms:

> What that gluey or viscous thing is that holds the parts of solids attached, in addition to the resistance which derives from the void. I cannot imagine any cement that cannot be burned and consumed in a very hot furnace over a period of two, three, or four months, let alone in ten, or a hundred. Yet silver, gold, or liquefied glass may remain in a furnace that long, and when united and attached together as before (Galileo 1974, p. 26).

It is precisely at this point, and with this question in mind, that Galileo states for the first time his hypothesis about the *infinite indivisibles* that constitute material continuum:

> I shall tell you what has sometimes passed through my mind on this; I do this not as the true solution, but rather as a kind of fantasy full of undigested things that I subject to your higher reflections. Take what you will from it, and judge the rest as suits you best. Sometimes, in considering how heat [*fuoco*, fire] goes snaking among the minimum particles of this or that metal, so firmly joined together, and finally separates and disunites them; and how then, the heat departing, they return to reunite with the same tenacity as before, without the quantity of gold being diminished at all, and that of other metals very little, even though these remain disunited for a long time, I have thought that this may come about because of very subtle fire-

> particles. Penetrating through the tiny pores of the metal, between which (on account of their tightness) the minimum [particles] of air and other fluids could not pass, these [fire-particles] might, by filling the minimum voids distributed between these minimum particles [of metal], free them from that force with which those voids attract one [particle] against another, forbidding their separation. And being thus able to move freely, their mass [*massa*] would become fluid, and remain so until the fire-particles between them depart. But when these go, leaving the pristine voids, the usual attraction returns, and consequently the attachment of the parts. (Galileo 1974, p. 27)

Replying to the immediate objection that, if the cause of cohesion were the result of minimal voids holding the parts together, then Galileo would not have succeeded in distinguishing two forces as he claimed, and so the *void* would be the only cause in both cases (hence turning unexplainable the alleged 5 to 1 ratio), he adds:

> And to Simplicio's objection it seems to me that one may replay that although such voids are very tiny, and as a result each one is easily overpowered, still the innumerable multitude of them multiplies the resistances innumerably, so to speak. The character and extent of the force resulting from an immense number of very weak momenta conjoined may be most evidently argued from our seeing a weight of millions of pounds, sustained by very thick ropes, ultimately yield and allow itself to be lifted by the assault of innumerable atoms of water, which, driven by the south wind or extended in a thin fog, go moving through the air to be driven between the fibers of the ropes; the immense force of the hanging weight being unable to prevent their entrance, they penetrate through narrow pores into the ropes, swelling and hence shortening them, by which means the enormous bulk is raised (Galileo 1974, pp. 28-29).

The connection is in my opinion clear when he finally concludes:

> From this, I think it is reasonable to argue that the minimum [particles] into which water seems to be resolved, since it has less consistency than the fines powder (or rather, has no consistency at all), are quite different from quantified and divisible minimum [particles], and I cannot find any other difference here besides that of their being indivisible. It also seems to me that their perfect transparency strengthens this conjecture. If we take the most transparent crystal that exists and begin to pound and break it, it loses its transparency when reduced to powder, and the more so the more degree, is yet diaphanous to the highest degree. Gold and silver, pulverized by aqua

> fortis more finely than by any file, still remain in powder[3] and do not become fluid; nor do they liquefy until the indivisibles of fire or of the sun's rays dissolve them (as I think) into their first and highest components, infinitely many, and indivisible (Galilei 1638, p. 86).

We can observe that this conclusion refers directly to the nature of water and its lack of cohesion, giving a belated answer to Delle Colombe's challenge. We can also see that *fire atoms* are considered as the only ones capable of filling the minimal interstitial voids in a metal. The *existence* of these atoms was admitted by Galileo from the first time following Castelli's suggestion, and then as a result of his analysis of Aristotle – Democritus debate. This is the reason why Galileo' first references to atoms were made by expressions such as *atomi ignei ascendenti, atomi ignei, atomi caldi, particole del fuoco* (I refer to them generally as *fire atoms*). Because of all that, we could say that the hypothesis of matter as constituted by *infinite indivisibles* is a more extended treatment of the problem to which he had to give a hasty answer in 1612, when he tackled the surface tension phenomenon (and, as explained above, tried to understand it in terms of the decrease of the specific weights due to the *combination* of ebony and air in the *water cavity*, which lead in turn to admit *porosity* in matter).

In this sense, I want to stress three points of continuity:
1. The action of fire atoms to fill the interstitial voids.
2. The denial of void as the cause of attraction of parts and as a consequence, of natural body cohesion.
3. The lack of cohesion as a central point in understanding fluids.

4. Mathematical or physical atomism?

In the previous sections, I've tried to introduce the problems and *physical* intuitions that frame the rise of Galileo's theory of matter. However, I've said nothing about the role of *mathematics* in this development. I will now introduce some comments on this subject, making also use of the opportunity to evaluate a recent thesis by Carla Rita

---

[3] Nitric or sulfuric acid. He does not consider the combination of nitric and hydrochloric acids, where the hydrochloric acid combines with the oxygen of the nitric acid, liberating chlorine which forms gold chlorides.

Palmerino, who suggests that Galileo's atomism evolves from a *physical* atomism to a *mathematical* one (Palmerino 2001, pp. 381-422).

Palmerino proposes an important connection between the theory of *infinite indivisibles* and Galileo's project to ground his theory of free fall by defining "rest" as the infinite degree of slowness. For that reason her paper (subtitled "a bridge between matter and motion theories") assigns great importance to Galileo's solution of the *rota aristotelis* paradox, which appears in the First Day of his 1638 treatise. She argues cogently that Galileo's strategy in solving the paradox may be seen as a way to *transform* a continuous theory of motion into an atomistic theory of space, time and matter – and also in the reverse order.

At the same time, the thesis intends to explain why Galileo abandoned the atomism introduced in *Il Saggiatore*, where atoms of different shapes and sizes produce primary qualities, by an atomism of infinity of homogeneous *indivisibles*. She describes this move as the transition from a *physical* to a *mathematical* atomism. In her opinion, although it is true that the subject was matter of great attention during 1970's, no clear reason was proposed to justify this change in Galileo's ideas on atomism (Palmerino 2001, p. 393, n. 31, with William Shea, Hugo Baldini and H.E. Le Grand in mind). The only exception she mentions during the 1980's is Pietro Redondi who defends the idea that Galileo's atomism is a consequence of his *prudence* in front of the Tridentine Council (having in mind that a physical atomism goes against the possibility of Eucharistic transubstantiation). Far from this *externalist* account, Palmerino believes that we must look for the reasons of Galileo's change of mind in relation to the problems he had to face concerning the behavior of natural bodies, and also to

> [...] provide an implicit justification to one of a kernel principle of his free fall theory (Palmerino 2001, p. 394).

I agree with Palmerino's suggestion that the answer that matters relates to the conceptual difficulties of Galileo in understanding natural phenomena. I will try nevertheless to defend all the same that Galileo's atomism was *physical* at all times.

As I've said before, Palmerino assigns a central importance to the *rota aristotelis* paradox – initially in Algazel's terms: how is it possible that in a revolving wheel, a point near the center and one near periphery describe *different circumferences at the same time?* (Palmerino 2001, p. 383). She also relies on the formulation of the pseudo-aristotelic *Quaestiones Mechanicae* where the problem was introduced by two circles of different diameter that move separately over its tangents, tracing in one revolution two tangent lines of the same length. We must notice that the supposition here – a supposition that Galileo will not make – is that *all the points* of each circle contact *all points* of its corresponding tangent.

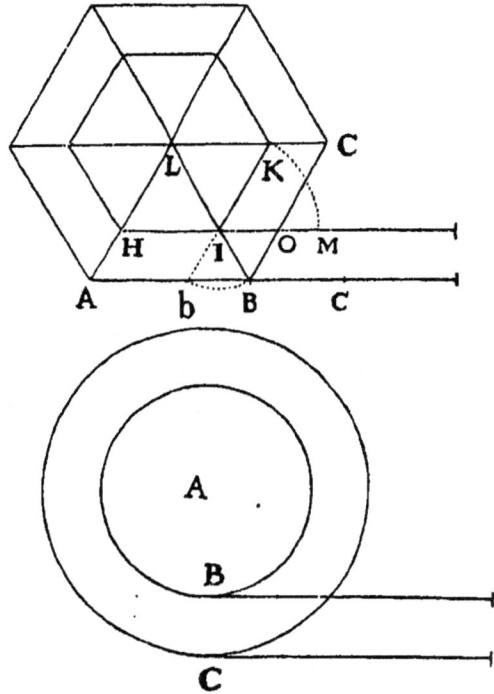

Fig. 3

What is really *new* in Galileo's account of this classic paradox is his *strategy* to solve it. Starting with the definition of "circle" as a polygon of *infinite* sides, then he can pass to the *finite domain* as a particular case, and analyze the problem of two homocentric *wheels* as two homocentric *hexagons*, reducing this way the comprehension difficulty of the problem to only six sides. This move allows him to demonstrate geometrically that the inner polygon, in rotating, traces a tangent line of the same length, but *interrupted* and not *continuous* (in the case of the figure, five times) (Palmerino 2001, p. 387).

He then translates this result again to the *infinite domain*, demonstrating that *infinity of non-extended voids* and *infinity of indivisibles* concur in a finite extension, solving this way the paradox. This thesis is the keystone of Galileo's theory of *infinite indivisibles*.

Galileo was not original, however, in linking this theory to the explanation of *condensation* and *rarefaction*. On the contrary, he accounted for the paradox *in order to* explain condensation and rarefaction in natural bodies. We must remember that this point was exactly the matter under question in the controversy with Di Grazia over the nature of ice. Mastering now the transition between infinite and finite domains in the way just explained, Galileo will explain *rarefaction* by means of the fact that it is the *outer* wheel which transmits motion. Side IK is moved *without* touching the tangent line leaving the segment IO empty. In this way the total extension of tangent line is *composed* of alternating full and empty segments.

On the other hand, when the *inner* wheel commands the motion, the voids of the outer circle tangent line are forced to compress, giving rise to condensation phenomenon (fig. 3).

Because of all this, and taking into account that the phenomena that were supposed to be explained are *physical* phenomena, there seems to be no reason to doubt that Galileo's atomism is of a *physical* kind. However, according to Palmerino, part of Galileo's analysis relies on the assumption of an "absolute isomorphism between physical and geometrical bodies" (Palmerino 2001, p. 390), turning *mathematical* the core of his atomistic proposal.

The point in discussion is, as we can see, in some degree terminological but, in my view, no less important in understanding Galileo's position. In a footnote, Palmerino rejects Stillman Drake's translation of the expression "no quanto" as non-quantifiable, and she explicitly blames this translation as a source of confusion in Galilean historiography. She proposes to translate "no quanto" as *without extension*,

> Given that the sense [...] is not that the minim could not be quantified, but that it has no quantity in the sense of spatial extension (Palmerino 2001, p. 338, n. 18).

Although it may not be of capital importance to get involved in this terminological discussion, Palmerino's translation has three problems for me:
1. It establishes a distinction that I don't see in Galileo's work.
2. It seems strange that what is *no quanto* should be considered the proper object of a *mathematical* atomism in Renaissance science.
3. Leaves open the problem, as Palmerino herself acknowledges, of how to understand that what has no extension be *operative* – produces changes – from a physical point of view.

In the following, I will try to justify an alternative translation for "no quanto" as *non-discrete* (not composed of different parts to be counted). In addition I will suggest that the expression refers to a physical *change of state* and not to a merely quantitative transformation. In my view, it is of central importance to bear in mind the fact that the basic intuition present throughout Galileo's account is – as we have seen – that of gold liquefaction in the crucible. If we consider this example too, we can appreciate that the *liquefaction point* implies a change of state to which we can confer no sense at all in terms of successive additions of caloric degrees. In considering the finite and divisible extension as *constituted* by infinite indivisibles as ultimate units, in my reading Galileo is not proposing a transition from a physical to a mathematical atomism but, on the contrary, showing how a *physical transformation* could not be completely accounted for neither in numeric nor geometrical terms.

As a first step in analyzing this point I wish to begin with *Il Saggiatore* (1623) where Galileo tries to distinguish between the *minimi quanti* and the *atomi realmente indivisibili*, which Palmerino explicitly takes as *extensive minims* and *non-extensive atoms* respectively. In referring to the minimal atoms, that of hotness or fire (*ignicoli*), Galileo states:

> And perhaps while rarefaction and friction are produced between minimal divisible parts (*i minimi quanti*), its motion is temporal and its action is only caloric; but, when it reaches its higher and last *resolution* in atoms truly indivisibles (*atomi realmente indivisibili*), light is produced with motion or – we can say – expansion and instant diffusion, capa-

ble of filling immense spaces by its – I don't know how to say – subtlety, rarity, immateriality, or another property different from all of them and without a name (Galilei 1890-1909, Vol. VI, p. 351; my emphasis).

Palmerino sees in this paragraph a point of transition point of Galileo's ideas on atomism, from the lack of extension as a property of the minimal particles of light in 1612 to the generalization of this attribute to *all* atoms (infinite and indivisibles), in 1638. In a reading different from Palmerino's, I can only conclude from this paragraph that Galileo is not sure how to describe the fact that the process outcome does not stop in ultimate *fire atoms*. I do not see here a clear statement that atoms of light, being *non quanti*, have no spatial extension. My suggestion is that we can find the key of Galileo's atomism in the citation above, although not in the *immateriality* idea, but rather in the concept of *resolution*.

5. Resolutio as key concept in Galileo's atomism

We have seen that the clue to solve hydrostatic problems – source of later conceptual difficulties – was to conceive water as offering *no resistance* to division *because* it is compounded by *indivisibles*. For that reason, in my opinion, at least part of the meaning of the term "indivisible" depends on that solution and, in this sense, refers to the fact that there is *nothing to divide*, and hence there is no resistance to overcome.

This interpretation avoids the problems that Palmerino must face, such as explaining how it is possible that a natural body can be *composed* of *non-extensional* parts. The difference of interpretations relies, in my opinion, on the identification of the main aim of Galileo's words: she identifies it with the understanding of the nature of *ultimate parts* (of natural bodies) considered *in isolation*, whereas in my view, Galileo's purpose is to understand the *relationship between* these parts. Consequently, if I am right, Galileo's atomism is not only more *physical* than *mathematical* in character, but it is also more physical than *metaphysical*. In this sense, Galileo's atomism would not state that having no extension the indivisibles offer no resistance to division, but that considered *altogether* there's no cohesion and adherence *between* them.

My interpretation assigns a central place to Galileo's worries about the "adhesive, glue or viscosity that strongly holds particles together" and which "does not burn nor consume in a red-hot oven; not in two, three, four, ten or even a hundred months", as mentioned above. This adhesive is a consequence of the interstitial micro-voids that produce a force five times stronger than that of the void considered *in toto*. As I noted before, particles of fire, in filling these interstices annul *horror vacui* as a cause of resistance to division, so the body separates in its parts; it *resolves* itself.

Briefly, this non mathematical, non-metaphysical, interpretation of Galileo's atomism, relates the lack of resistance to division with the fact that there's nothing to be divided *between* the disunited parts of a solid, in which the cause of cohesion has been annulled, whereupon the body has become a *fluid*. This interpretation obtains at least partial support from the following analogy offered by Galileo to clarify the point:

> The resistance we feel moving in water is similar to what we feel in moving through a crowd. The resistance experienced is not produced by the difficulty in dividing; we divide some of its waves moving people laterally and not altogether. In the same way, we experience resistance in trying to insert a stick in a dune, not because some of its parts must be divided, but only moved and elevated. Then, we have two ways to represent penetration: one for continuous bodies where division seems necessary, and the other related to bodies of which its parts are not continuous but contiguous. In this last case we need not to divide, but only to move (Galilei 1890-1909, Vol. IV, pp. 105-106).

Even though, as I believe, there is no metaphysical thesis here, we still need to explain how we can talk about *infinite* units in *finite* extension. To understand this we must remember that Galileo considers the material continuum as something *composed* by infinite material points *with* infinite interposed voids. On the other hand, as we have to set the doctrine of the *infinite indivisibles* in the frame of water resistance to division and to keep in mind the case of gold in the crucible, we must not forget the strategy followed in solving the *rota aristotelis* paradox: the mere addition of sides to a polygon *never* would result in a circle. This transition to a circle implies a *qualitative* step, a *mutation* of nature.

Galileo explicitly notes that those who want to find out the infinite points that compose a line by successive division "will be highly deceived, because eternity would be not enough for that" (Galilei 1890-1909, Vol. VIII, p. 82). In Galileo's mind "the only infinite number is unity" because it satisfies the "conditions and prerequisites of any infinite number, that is, to contain squares and cubes, and all numbers". In this way, the body *resolution*, involving at the same time all its unity, involves *at the same time* all its parts.

The idea of *resolution* appears immediately in what follows. Galileo clarifies:

> Here I want you to note how, if a line is resolved and divide into parts that are quantified and consequently numbered [*numerate*], we cannot then arrange these into a greater extension than that which they occupied when they were continuous and joined, without the interposition of as many void [finite] spaces. But imagining the line resolved into unquantifiable parts – that is, into its infinitely many indivisibles – we can conceive it immensely expanded without the interposition of any quantified void spaces, though not without infinitely many indivisible voids.
>
> What is thus said of simple lines is to be understood also of surfaces and of solid bodies, considering those as composed of infinitely many unquantifiable atoms (Galilei 1890-1909, Vol. VIII, p. 33).

Later Sagredo will protest that this theory, that merges considerations about the void, the infinite, the indivisibles, and instant motion, "is not proportionate to our mind". It seems quite possible to me that these words were said by Sagredo himself and are not merely the words of his character in Galileo's dialogue. If that were the case, I would not doubt Sagredo's sincerity. Perhaps this was the reason why Galileo adds another physical intuition:

> In this way there would be no contradiction in expanding, for instance, a little globe of gold into a very great space without introducing quantifiable void spaces – provided, however, that gold is assumed to be composed of infinitely many indivisibles (Galilei 1890-1909, Vol. VIII, pp. 33-34).

Anyway, the final conclusion will refer explicitly to the old problem of water resistance to division. He asks: "Must we therefore believe that fluids are what they are because they are resolved into indivisibles, infinitely many, [as] their prime components?" And he answers: "I cannot find any better expedient for solving some of the sensible appearances, among which is this" (Galilei 1890-1909, Vol. VIII, p. 47).

6. Concluding remarks

We can finally return to Pyle's first remarks on Galileo's atomism in order to clarify their meaning:

1. *The relationship between cohesion of fluids and Galileo's theory of matter*: if we take into account the ending of Pyle's citation, cohesion of fluids would be an *obstacle* that Galileo's theory of matter has to avoid in order to *apply* it to the *case* of fluids. On the contrary, in my opinion, Galileo's theory of matter *arises from* his reflections *on* fluids cohesion, as we have seen. In this sense, we obtain a better understanding if we approach Galileo's theory as trying *to solve* empirical and conceptual difficulties (its virtues and limitations depending on the degree of success of that solution), than if we approach it as a *theory with difficulties*.

    From a historical point of view the problem arises, in its turn, from a concrete debate with Ludovico Delle Colombe, in 1612, over the cause of the floating or sinking of bodies. From a conceptual point of view, the problem involves the integration of Archimedean hydrostatics with the search for the *physical cause* – in the sense of Aristotle, and the attempt to overcome Democritean atomism.

2. *Theory and cause of solid bodies' cohesion and dissolution*: the lack of cohesion in fluids responds, in Pyle's view, to a general theory of matter. In my view, for the reasons mentioned before, both theory of matter and its *degree of generality*, depend on the understanding of fluids, and in the case of Galileo, on the problem of water resistance to division.

3. *Fluids conception*: Pyle's reference to fluids as "lacking points-vacua" is not easy to understand and requires clarification. In my reading, fluids have to be understood as solids that have become disaggregated or dissolved as a consequence of losing the force that held its parts together.

4. *Surface tension and Galileo's theory of matter*: it seems to me that Galileo does not *deny* the surface tension phenomenon, but that he simply is not aware of it. Otherwise, he would have included (for the crucial experiment in front of Delle Colombe) the *complete immersion* requisite from the start; and he did not. Besides, this phenomenon

would in a sense be favorable to his position, in the sense that it involves a *secondary cause* of flotation, apart from the mere difference of specific weights of bodies, and the medium.

5. *Theory and evidence*: we have identified the *powerful evidence* which Pyle mentions only in a general way. It is the *perfect transparency of water*. In Pyle's account, it seems that Galileo is ready to admit anything in order to save his theory, even if it requires denying natural phenomena. In my opinion, this absolutely contradicts Galileo's entire intellectual biography. Besides, for the reasons exposed in this paper, the surface tension phenomenon, would not have been, and in fact was not, a *fatal* refutation of his theory. Moreover, if that had been the case, Galileo would not have developed his theory of *infinite indivisibles*, whatever its value for the later history of science.

References

Biagioli, M. (1993), *Galileo Courtier: The Practice of Science in the Culture of Absolutism*, Chicago: The University of Chicago Press.

Drake, S. (1957), *Discoveries and Opinions of Galileo*, New York: Doubleday Anchor Books.

Drake, S. (1960), "Galileo Gleanings VIII: The Origins of Galileo's Book on Floating Bodies and the Question of the Unknown Academician", *Isis* 51: 56-63.

Drake, S. (1981), *Cause, Experiment and Science: A Galilean Dialogue Incorporating a New English Translation of Galileo's «Bodies That Stay atop Water, or Move in It»*, Chicago: University of Chicago Press,

Galilei, G. (1890-1909), *Le Opere di Galileo Galilei* (edited by Antonio Favaro), 20 vols., Firenze: Edizione Nazionale.

Galilei, G. (1974), *Two New Sciences: including Centers of Gravity and Force of Percussion* (translated, with a New Introduction and Notes by Stillman Drake), Toronto: Wall & Thomson.

Palmerino, C.R. (2001), "Galileo's and Gassendi's Solutions to the *rota aristotelis* Paradox: A Bridge between Matter and Motion Theories", in Lüthy C., Murdoch, J.E. & W.R. Newman (eds.), *Late Medieval and Early Modern Corpuscular Matter Theories*, Leiden: Brill.

Pyle, A.J. (1997), *Atomism and Its Critics*, Bristol: Thoemmes Press.

Rose, P.L. (1975), *The Italian Renaissance of Mathematics: Studies on Humanists and Mathematicians from Petrarch to Galileo*, Genève: Librairie Droz.

Smith, A.M. (1976), "Galileo's Theory of Indivisibles", *Journal of the History of Ideas* 37: 571-588.

Tula Molina, F. (2002), "Microsociología y cambio teórico: en la corte de Mario Biagioli", *Llull: Revista de la Sociedad Española de Historia de las Ciencias y de las Técnicas* 25: 485-501.

T-Invariance, Irreversibility, Arrow of Time: Similar But Different

Olimpia Lombardi

National Scientific and Technical Research Council (CONICET)/
University of Buenos Aires (UBA)

1. Introduction

The problem of the arrow of time is undoubtedly one of the traditional problems of the philosophy of physics, and perhaps the kind of problem where physical concepts are more strongly linked with metaphysical questions. We perceive previous and posterior events in an immediate and intuitive way: the difference between past and future plays a central role in our lives to the extent that it organizes any perception. The problem arises when we try to find a physical correlate to this intuitive evidence.

Much ink has been spilled upon the problem of the direction of time. However, in the traditional discussions different concepts are usually identified or confused; although related to each other, these concepts possess their own specificity. In many cases, this lack of conceptual clarity is precisely what obscures the arguments, and prevents reaching a solution to the problem. In particular, the most frequently invoked concepts in the discussions about the direction of time are the concepts of time-reversal invariance (t-invariance, for short), reversibility, and arrow of time. In this paper, we will attempt to distinguish these three concepts with precision, showing that they not only refer to different properties, but they also apply to entities belonging to different categories. This conceptual clarification will allow us to stress the fact that different problems are frequently subsumed under the label "the problem of the direction of time"; each one of these problems, requires a precise formulation if we expect to find answers that result adequate, from a formal and a philosophical point of view.

2. T-invariance

T-invariance is a property of dynamical laws: it is usually said that a law is t-invariant if it is invariant under the transformation $t \rightarrow -t$, that is, if the law does not change when the sign of the variable t is changed. Mario Bunge adopts this characterization when he proposes the following definition:

> Let us call a lawlike sentence containing the temporal coordinate t $L(t)$. If $L(-t) = L(t)$, we say that the law is t-invariant, or invariant under time reversal (Bunge 1977, p. 319).

Thus, the concept of t-invariance seems to be the less controversial notion: t-invariance is conceived as a purely syntactic property of a dynamical law, which depends only on its formal structure. Since laws are linguistic entities to which we have direct access, it seems that we could decide whether a law is t-invariant or not by means of a mere inspection of its formal features.

The difficulty of this position relies on ignoring the fact that t-invariance requires the change of the sign not only of the variable t, but also of all the dynamical variables involved in the law. Therefore, the concept of t-invariance refers to a property that applies to a dynamical law L in the context of a theory T: we will say that a dynamical law L *is t-invariant in the context of a theory* T when it is invariant under the change of the sign of the variable t and of all the dynamical variables belonging to T. From this point of view, Newton's second law expressed as $F(x) = m\, d^2x/dt^2$ – where x represents the distance to certain point, m represents the mass of the physical body and $F(x)$ represents the force in the direction x – is t-invariant in the context of classical mechanics: since it is a second order differential equation, it is necessary to change the sign of the initial velocity v_0 which appears as an integration constant. On the contrary, Fourier's law of heat conduction, $\partial T/\partial t = K/C\rho_m \partial^2 T/\partial x^2$ – where x represents the distance to certain point, K represents thermal conductivity, C represents the specific heat, ρ_m represents the mass density, and T represents the temperature – is not t-invariant in the context of phenomenological thermodynamics.

Although t-invariance still seems to be mainly a formal concept, it possesses a clear physical meaning. Let us consider a system S in a state e_0 at a certain initial time, which evolves to a state e_1 after a time Δt. Let us now suppose that we have another system S', identical to S, which is in the time reversed state in relation to e_1 at the initial time; let us call this new state $\mathbf{T}(e_1)$. If the law governing the evolution is t-invariant, the system S' will evolve to the state $\mathbf{T}(e_0)$ after the time Δt, that is, to the time reversed version of the initial state of S. If we express the evolution law by means of an operator U_t such that $e_1 = U_{\Delta t} e_0$, the law is t-invariant if the following condition holds:

$$\mathbf{T}(e_0) = U_{\Delta t} \mathbf{T}(U_{\Delta t} e_0)$$

The concept of t-invariance can also be characterized in terms of the dynamically possible evolutions with respect to a dynamical law, that is, in terms of the solutions of the corresponding equation. An evolution – a sequence of states – $e_i \rightarrow e_j$ is dynamically possible relative to a law L if it is consistent with L, that is, if it is represented by a solution of L. Let us call again the time reversed state with respect to e, $\mathbf{T}(e)$. The law L is *t-invariant* when the following condition is satisfied: the evolution $e_i \rightarrow e_j$ is dynamically possible relative to L iff the time reversed evolution $\mathbf{T}(e_j) \rightarrow \mathbf{T}(e_i)$ is also dynamically possible relative to L (see Savitt 1995).[1]

But, what kind of states are the $\mathbf{T}(e)$? The time-reversal transformation $\mathbf{T}$ depends on which are the dynamical variables that define the state e, and this, in turn, depends on the particular theory to which the law L belongs to. For instance, in classical mechanics, if S is a system of point-like particles, its state at the time t is completely defined by the positions and the momenta of the particles at t; in turn, if the masses are constant, the momenta are functions only of the velocities of the corresponding particles. In this case, the time reversed state with respect to the state e is obtained when the particles are in

---

[1] Savitt (1995) also presents a stronger notion of t-invariance which will be not considered here because it is relevant only in the context of the foundations of quantum mechanics.

the same spatial position as in e, but each one of them possesses a velocity of the same absolute value and direction as the velocity that they possess in e, but inverted sense with respect to it.

3. Irreversibility

In contrast to t-invariance, the concept of *reversibility* does not apply to laws but to processes. A process P consisting of the temporal sequence of events $a_1, a_2,..., a_n$, is *reversible* if such a sequence can occur in this order or in the inverse order; P is *irreversible* if such a sequence always occurs in this temporal order, and never occurs spontaneously in the inverse order $a_n,..., a_2, a_1$.[2] When the concepts of reversibility and irreversibility are elucidated in this way, the events a_i are usually partial aspects of the states of a system. For instance, in classical mechanics, if the events are the positions of a particle, the time evolution of the particle's position is a reversible process; in thermodynamics, given a gas confined in the left half of a container considered when the division wall is taken out, if the events are the densities of the gas in the left half of the container, the time evolution of such a density is an irreversible process. It is worth insisting on the fact that the concepts of reversibility and irreversibility do not refer to the states of a system, but to the time evolution of a certain magnitude, which may be one of the variables defining the state of the system. This is particularly clear in mechanics: if the sequence of the positions of a particle in time is $x_1, x_2,..., x_n$, such a sequence can occur in the inverse time order $x_n,..., x_2, x_1$; but in this last case, it is necessary to time-reverse the mechanical states of the particle, in such a way that the time-reversed sequence does not consist of the original states, but rather that of the time-reversed states:

$$\mathbf{T}(e_n),..., \mathbf{T}(e_2), \mathbf{T}(e_1)$$

---

[2] The concept of irreversibility is usually illustrated by the idea of a movie where a certain process is filmed: if we obtain a possible process when the film is projected backwards, then the original process is reversible. However, this way of presenting the concept may lead to confusions: if 'possible' is interpreted as compatible with the laws governing the original process, the characterization refers to the concept of t-invariance and not to the concept of reversibility.

Nevertheless, the process to which the property "irreversibility" should be applied is the time evolution of the particle's position, and not the time evolution of the particle's mechanical states.

When expressed this way, the concept of irreversibility implies that certain processes, in particular those resulting from the time-reversal of irreversible processes, are excluded from physical reality. The origin of this exclusion distinguishes between two types of irreversibility. The irreversibility is *nomological* when certain processes are excluded by a physical law or a combination of physical laws. For instance, Fourier's law excludes the processes of heat conduction from lower to higher temperatures; the second law of thermodynamics excludes the processes that involve entropy decrease in isolated systems. On the contrary, the irreversibility is *de facto* in the case in which certain processes are excluded, not as a result of a law, but due to the fact that certain conditions never occur in nature as a matter of fact. When a dynamical law is expressed as an ordinary differential equation, its solution requires certain constants representing the value of the variables at the initial time, which must be obtained by empirical means – for instance, the position and the velocity of a particle at t_0 –; those values are the *initial conditions*. In the case of differential equations in partial derivatives, the previous procedure is not sufficient: it is necessary to empirically establish the constants representing the values of the variables in certain spatial regions – for instance, the value of the temperature in the extremities of a physical body –; these values are the *boundary conditions*. Therefore, the *de facto* irreversibility corresponds to those situations where certain initial or boundary conditions never effectively occur. For instance the equations describing wave propagation – mechanical or radiation waves – admit two kinds of solutions, those corresponding to retarded potentials, and those corresponding to advanced potentials: the first ones describe coherent waves propagating from a central point, and the second ones describe coherent waves propagating to a central point. The second kind of process never occurs, due to the fact that the boundary conditions necessary for their efectivization are never present in physical reality.[3]

---

[3] One of the first authors who considered the case of wave propagation in the discussion about the problem of irreversibility was Karl Popper, in a series of articles

4. Relationship between T-invariance and irreversibility

The characterizations of t-invariance and irreversibility presented in the previous sections allow us to establish the relationship between both concepts:

- *Nomologically irreversible* processes are described by non t-invariant laws; the excluded processes are precisely those corresponding to the dynamical equation, resulting from changing the sign of the time variable, and of all the dynamical variables in the original law.
- *De facto irreversible* processes are described by t-invariant laws; the excluded processes are those described by solutions corresponding to initial or boundary conditions which, as a matter of fact, never – or almost never – occur in nature.

Therefore, if a law is non t-invariant in the context of a theory, it describes nomological irreversible processes. If a law is t-invariant in the context of a theory, it either describes reversible processes, or it describes *de facto* irreversible processes when the non-occurrence of certain initial or boundary conditions excludes the reverse processes.

At this stage, it is worth repeating the relevance of identifying the theory in the context of which a law is or is not t-invariant. To disregard this point can lead to conclusions such as those of Henry Hollinger and Michael Zenzen (1982), who consider that the very concept of nomological irreversibility is internally inconsistent, and devoid of content. In order to decide whether a law is t-invariant or not, these authors require the *complete* analysis of each symbol of the corresponding equation. By applying this criterion to Fick's law of matter diffusion, $\partial c/\partial t = D\, \partial^2 c/\partial x^2$ – where x represents the distance to certain point, D represents the conduction coefficient and c represents the matter concentration –, they show that D changes its sign under the inversion of t when this coefficient is derived *from statistical-mechanical considerations*. By taking this example as a paradigmatic case, they conclude that, since all the fundamental laws of physics are t-invariant, the difference between nomological and *de facto* irreversibility collapses; as a consequence, it must be considered that legality implies no-

---

appeared in *Nature* between 1956 y 1967 (1956a, 1956b, 1957, 1958, 1965, 1967a, 1967b).

mological reversibility. However, in the argument of Hollinger and Zenzen, the derivation of the diffusion coefficient D does not correspond yet to the original theory, but it appeals to dynamical and statistical considerations that are completely alien to phenomenological thermodynamics, where the irreversible process of diffusion is described. Therefore, the authors' strategy amounts to suppose that the problem of the reduction of phenomenological thermodynamics to statistical mechanics is solved; but this is precisely one of the central points of the old problem of irreversibility. In other words, to consider that the only legitimate laws of physics are the fundamental t-invariant laws does not explain yet why the concentration c converges to uniformity, and why we never see the inverse evolution. For this reason, it is more fruitful to consider, for instance, Fourier's law or Fick's law as legitimate laws of physics: these laws are non t-invariant in the context of phenomenological thermodynamics, and such a t-invariance expresses a relevant aspect of our macroscopic physical experience.

5. The problem of irreversibility: Boltzmann versus Gibbs

In order to formulate with precision the problem of irreversibility, it is convenient to adopt the language of the phase space, that is, a d-dimensional euclidean space where each dimension represents a state variable of the system. In the cases studied by statistical mechanics, S is a system of N point-like particles: the corresponding phase space is a space of $6N$ dimensions, three representing the components of the position and three representing the components of the momentum of each particle.

Up to this point, it is necessary to remember the difference between the mechanical microstate and the thermodynamic macrostate of the system S:

- The *mechanical microstate* of S at time t is given by the value of the $3N$ components of position and the $3N$ components of momentum of each particle; therefore, it is represented by a *point* in the corresponding phase space. In turn, the mechanical evolution of S is represented by a trajectory in the phase space.[4]

- But the *thermodynamic macrostate* of S is compatible with – that is, can be realized through – a great number of mechanical microstates considered as equiprobable given the macrostate; therefore, the thermodynamic macrostate is represented by a region of dimension $d' \leq 6N$ in the phase space.

On the basis of these characterizations, the problem of irreversibility consists in explaining the thermodynamic evolution of the macrostates of a system in terms of the mechanical evolution of its microstates. The difficulties begin when the difference between the two kinds of evolutions is considered:

- From a thermodynamic point of view, the evolutions are *irreversible*: if the system starts from a non-equilibrium macrostate M_0 – for instance, a gas confined in the left side of a container when the division wall is taken out –, it evolves to the equilibrium macrostate M_{eq} – in the same example, the gas evenly distributed in all the container –; the inverse evolution is possible only with a fantastically low probability. In the phase space this means that, from a region Γ_0, the evolution leads to a region Γ_{eq} having a volume much greater than the volume of the original region, and which corresponds to the region of constant energy, since the system is isolated.

- In the mechanical description the Liouville theorem holds; according to this theorem, any region of the phase space evolves obeying the laws of classical mechanics in such a way that it preserves its constant volume through time. If we call the density of distribution of the points representative of the possible states of the sys-

---

[4] The instantaneous mechanical state $m(t)$ of the system is defined by the value of the $6N$ state variables: $m(t) = (q_i(t), p_i(t)) = (q_1(t), q_2(t),..., q_{3N}(t), p_1(t), p_2(t),..., p_{3N}(t))$. Its time evolution is governed by the *Hamilton equations*: $dq_i/dt = \partial H/\partial p_i$; $dp_i/dt = -\partial H/\partial q_i$ where the Hamiltonian $H(q_i, p_i)$ represents the total mechanical energy of the system. The solutions $q_i(t)$ and $p_i(t)$ represent the time evolution of the system, given the initial conditions q_{i0} y p_{i0}.

tem ρ, the theorem proves that, if the support[5] of ρ_0 is confined in a region Γ_0 of the phase space at the initial time, then the support of ρ_t will be confined in a region Γ_t of the same volume as the original region at any posterior time: this evolution is completely reversible, in agreement with the laws of classical mechanics.

Even if many interpretations about the problem of irreversibility have been proposed, the majority of them can be associated with one of the two main paths of research opened by Boltzmann and Gibbs. The way in which the problem was presented will allow us to understand in what sense both perspectives are different.

5.1. The approach of Boltzmann

Boltzmann's strategy consists in computing the number of different microstates compatible with the same macrostate. The more probable macrostate will be the macrostate having the maximum number of compatible microstates, and the macroevolution of the system will tend, with high probability, to that macrostate. This leads Boltzmann to identify the entropy of each macrostate with a measure of the number of its compatible microstates; in the language of phase space, the Bolzmann's entropy corresponding of a macrostate M_a is defined as:

$$S_B(M_a) = k \, log \, |\Gamma_a|$$

where k is Boltzmann constant and $|\Gamma_a|$ represents the volume of the region of the phase space associated with M_a. Since the region with maximum volume is the region corresponding to equilibrium – that is, it is the region with more compatible microstates –, in any evolution starting from a non-equilibrium macrostate M_0 and going to the equilibrium M_{eq}, the entropy will increase with high probability, in agreement with the second law of thermodynamics.

The question is how can one explain that we never actually see the inverse evolution? The answer rests upon the relationship be-

---

[5] The support of a function is the subset of its domain where the function has positive non-zero values.

tween probability and volume, in the phase space. The fact that macroevolutions tend to equilibrium with high probability – which justifies the non-observation of anti-thermodynamic evolutions – can be explained only if the probability of the equilibrium state M_{eq} is enormously higher than the probability of any initial macrostate M_0 of non-equilibrium. This requires a huge disparity between the volumes or the associated regions: $|\Gamma_{eq}| >> |\Gamma_0|$. But this relationship holds only in systems with *many degrees of freedom*. This is the case of gases: for a mol of a gas in a container of one liter, the relationship between $|\Gamma_{eq}|$ and $|\Gamma_0|$ is of the order of 2^N, where N, the number of particles, is of the order of 10^{20}. The order of magnitude of the probability involved in this kind of systems is what explains the macroscopic irreversibility of thermodynamic processes.

Another essential ingredient of Boltzmann's approach is the need of some additional assumption regarding the initial conditions of the system. The fact is that, even in the case of the equilibrium macrostate M_{eq}, there are compatible microstates whose further time evolution would lead the system to the initial non-equilibrium macrostate M_0, violating the second law. Boltzmann's answer, based on his probabilistic approach, relies on the extremely low probability of occurrence of those microstates in the efectivization of the equilibrium macrostate; in the language of the phase space, the microstates leading to anti-thermodynamic evolutions are "atypical" in the sense that they correspond to a volume that is lower in many orders of magnitude than the volume of the region corresponding to the equilibrium macrostate.

5.2. The approach of Gibbs

Gibbs' strategy consists in abandoning the attempt to describe the evolution of a particular system; on the contrary, he focuses his attention on the behavior of the *ensemble* representative of the system, that is, a set of systems with a structure similar to that of the system of interest, which are selected in such a way that each one of them is in a different microstate but always compatible with the macrostate of the system of interest. It is important to remember that the systems belonging to the ensemble must not be considered as interacting with each other: each one of them develops its own evolution, according to classical mechanics. Therefore, the ensemble is represented by a function ρ, *density of distribution* of the points representative of the systems of the ensemble in the phase space.

If the initial macrostate of the system determines a density ρ_0 whose support is confined in a region Γ_0, this region may change its shape and spread out reaching distant regions of the phase space; but since its volume is constant according to Liouville theorem, it cannot cover the entire region corresponding to the macrostate of equilibrium. In fact, Gibbs' entropy is defined as:

$$S_G(\rho) = -k \int_\Gamma \rho \, log\rho \, d\Gamma$$

where $\rho \, d\Gamma$ represents the probability of that the representative point of the system's microstate belongs to the elemental $d\Gamma$, and the integral is computed over the whole phase space Γ. Given the conservation of volume imposed by Liouville theorem, S_G is constant through all the evolution.

In Gibbs' approach, what really happens is that the initial region becomes distributed and smeared out up to cover the region corresponding to the equilibrium macrostate, in an apparently uniform way.[6] In order to account for the progressive deformation of the original region, a coarse-grained entropy S_{cg} can be defined: if the phase space is partitioned in cells and a probability P_i is assigned to each one of them – the probability of the fact that the point representative of the microstate of the system be included in the cell i –, S_{cg} is defined as:

$$S_{cg} = -k \, \Sigma \, P_i \, log \, P_i$$

---

[6] In order to illustrate this situation, Gibbs suggested an analogy known as 'Gibbs' drop': if we mix a drop of black ink in pure water, the water rapidly becomes grey; however, an observer with senses sufficiently sharp to perceive the individual molecules, would never see the grey color since he could follow the delocalized trajectories of the ink particles initially concentrated in a little region of the system. The idea that the homogeneous medium irreversibly becomes homogeneous would be, then, an illusion only due to the limited precision of our observational means.

It is reasonable to expect that it increases through the evolution as the original region covers more cells. Nevertheless, if a "perfect" observer described the evolution of the system initially in a non-equilibrium state by means of the behavior of its representative ensemble, he would see the progressive distortion and ramification in the phase space of the region corresponding to the initial macrostate, but he could also verify the validity of the Liouville theorem: the uniform distribution on the region corresponding to the equilibrium macrostate cannot be reached, because the volume of the initial region is constant during all the evolution. Therefore, from Gibbs' perspective the entropy increase stated by the second law for an isolated system refers to the coarse-grained entropy S_{cg}, and this implies an epistemological interpretation of irreversibility.

It is worth emphasizing that, in contrast to Boltzmann's approach; Gibbs' approach *does not require many degrees of freedom*. In principle, irreversible behavior may arise in simple mechanical systems, defined by few state variables. Another relevant aspect of this interpretation is the fact that, in order to increase the coarse-grained entropy S_{cg}, *the system must be mixing*, that is, the initial region must result *deformed* through the evolution. In turn, this implies that the system is ergodic, that is, its representative point travels over practically the whole region of the phase space corresponding to the equilibrium macrostate (see Lebowitz & Penrose 1973).

5.3. Boltzmann versus Gibbs

The contemporary followers of Boltzmann' approach attack Gibbs' position from different perspectives. For instance, Joel Lebowitz (1993) discredits Gibbs' entropy as a relevant physical magnitude to the extent that it is constant through the system's evolution; which in turn, he points out that the system must have many degrees of freedom to show an irreversible behavior (Lebowitz 1994). From a similar perspective, Jean Bricmont insists on the impossibility of endowing the micro/macro distinction with physical meaning in systems of few degrees of freedom (Bricmont 1995); as it physically does not make sense to speak of the temperature of a single particle, it is neither possible to define macroscopic variables in systems with few degrees of freedom.

In relation to the level of instability required, Bricmont claims that ergodicity is neither a necessary condition nor a sufficient condition for irreversibility. Ergodicity is not a necessary condition because there are ergodic systems with few degrees of freedom in which to speak of irreversible behavior makes no sense. In turn, ergodicity is not a sufficient condition to the point in which there exists non-ergodic evolutions which manifest an unequivocal irreversible character (Bricmont 1995); as an example, Bricmont appeals to a mathematical model as the Kac model which is non-ergodic but, in an adequate time scale, shows an evolution to the equilibrium value of its macroscopic variables. Other authors also adopt the same argumentative line: in explicit polemic with Lawrence Sklar (1993), who claims that mixing is an indispensable property for irreversibility, John Earman and Miklos Rédei (1996) argue that the typical irreversible systems studied in statistical mechanics are not even ergodic.

In addition to these criticisms, a new objection can be considered, which was posed by the Ehrenfests (1912) in a famous critical review about the state of the statistical mechanics and the kinetic theory of that moment, published in the *Encyclopedia of Mathematical Sciences*: Gibbs' interpretation of the second law cannot break the time symmetry between past and future. In fact, the entropy increases results from the progressive deformation and ramification of the region associated to the initial macrostate. The problem is that this entropy increase "toward the future" has a corresponding entropy increase "toward the past": if the time evolution of the system is described toward the past starting from an equilibrium situation, the initial region will suffer the same progressive deformation and ramification. In other words, although the entropy of the system increases in the future evolution, the system also comes from past macrostates of greater entropy than the entropy of the present non-equilibrium macrostate.

These difficulties have led many authors to completely discard Gibbs' perspective. However, Boltzmann's approach also faces difficulties which, although usually ignored, are not less importantly serious. The main challenge is the one posed by Liouville theorem. If the representative points of the microstates confined in a given region of the phase space evolve in such a way that the volume of that initial region does not change, how could it be explained, from a mechanical viewpoint, the increase of volume of the regions associated to successive macrostates, through the thermodynamic evolution of the system?

It seems quite curious that Lebowitz and Bricmont, followers of Boltzmann's approach, find the answer to Loschmidt's paradox in Liouville theorem. Let us remember that, according to Loschmidt's paradox, for any mechanically possible evolution leading to equilibrium, there is another equally possible evolution – which results from the inversion of the velocities of all the particles of the system – which describes the original evolution in the opposite sense, moving the system away from equilibrium and, therefore, decreasing its entropy. Let us see the authors' argument. Let:

- M_0 be the initial non-equilibrium macrostate, that is, the set of initial microstates.
- Δt be the time required by the system to approximately reach equilibrium.
- $U_{\Delta t}$ be the operator expressing the mechanical evolution of the microstates.
- M_{eq} the final macrostate of equilibrium, which is the final set of microstates.

The set M_0 mechanically evolves toward a set $M_t = U_{\Delta t} M_0$, preserving its volume constant ($|M_t| = |M_0|$). Loschmidt's paradox states that the time reversed states of M_t, $\mathbf{T}(M_t)$, must evolve according to $U_{\Delta t}$ toward the time reversed states of M_0, $\mathbf{T}(M_0)$:

$$\mathbf{T}(M_0) = U_{\Delta t} \mathbf{T}(M_t) = U_{\Delta t} \mathbf{T}(U_{\Delta t} M_0)$$

Lebowitz and Bricmont admit that, according to Liouville theorem, this equality holds. But they added that the microstates belonging to M_t and, therefore, to $\mathbf{T}(M_t)$, constitute a very tiny subset of M_{eq}; as a consequence, the subset of the states resulting from the inversion of velocities – which would lead to an anti-entropic evolution – is less probable, in many orders of magnitude, than the set of microstates that preserve equilibrium. The central point of the argument is that $M_t = U_{\Delta t} M_0$ is a very tiny subset of M_{eq} since, in the example of the gas confined in the left half of a container, most configurations of M_{eq} were not in the left half of the container at the initial time (Bricmont 1995, p. 173). When we face this claim, a question arises: where do the microstates of M_{eq} not resulting from the mechanical evolution of the microstates belonging to M_0 at the initial time come from? Given the validity of Liouville theorem, Boltzmann's approach does not provide a genuinely dynamical explanation of irreversibility.

Summing up, neither Boltzmann's approach nor Gibbs' approach supplies an adequate solution to the problem of irreversibility. Although Gibbs' interpretation proposes an exclusively dynamical account of the phenomenon of irreversibility, it cannot explain the fact that past states have lower entropy than the entropy of the present state, and it does not take into account the theoretical need of many degrees of freedom. On the other hand, Boltzmann's perspective adopts a purely probabilistic approach of the phenomenon of irreversibility, but it cannot account for the mechanical evolutions which give rise to the probabilities associated to the macrostates of the system.

6. The problem of the arrow of time

It is worth stressing that up to this point, the problem of the arrow of time has not been addressed, even if this problem is usually identified with the problem of irreversibility,. Those who adopt this position identify the privileged direction of time, past-to-future, with the direction in which irreversible processes proceed, in such a way that irreversibility supplies the foundation, defines time-asymmetry. In other words, this perspective attempts to reduce the relation "e_2 is posterior to e_1" in terms of an asymmetric non-temporal relationship between events, whether nomological or de facto. However, as Sklar (1974) points out, there are good reasons for rejecting this reductionist approach to the arrow of time. First, we understand the meaning of "posterior" and we can establish temporal relationships between events independently of our theoretical scientific knowledge. But, mainly, without this independent knowledge about the temporal order, the irreversibility introduced by t-invariant laws lose its empirical content and turns out to be an analytical truth; this *"overabundance of analyticity"* makes it

> impossible in principle for scientific change to ever lead us to conclude that, as a matter of fact, we were wrong in assuming a lawlike association of the two relations (Sklar 1974, p. 403).

The problem of the arrow of time owes its origin to the intuitive asymmetry between past and future: if two events are not simultaneous, then one of them is earlier than the other one. Moreover, we view our access to the past and future quite differently: we remember the past, and predict the future. The problem of the arrow of time arises when we seek a physical correlate of this intuitive asymmetry: does physics pick out a preferred direction of time?

The main difficulty to be encountered in answering this question lies in our anthropocentric perspective: the difference between past and future is so deeply rooted in our language and our thoughts that it is very difficult to shake off these asymmetric assumptions. In fact, philosophical discussions around the question are usually subsumed under the label "the problem of the direction of time", as if we could find an exclusively physical criterion for singling out the direction of time, identified with what we call "the future". But there is nothing in physics that distinguishes, in a non-arbitrary way, between past and future as we conceive them. It might be objected that physics implicitly assumes this distinction with the use of asymmetric temporal expressions, like "future light cone", "initial conditions", "increasing time", and so on. However, this is not the case, and the reason can be understood in simple conceptual terms.

Two entities are formally identical when there is a symmetry transformation between them that does not change the properties of the system to which they belong or in whose description they are involved. In physics it is common to work with formally identical entities: the two lobes of a light cone, the two spin directions, etc. When we call two formally identical entities by different names, we are establishing a *conventional* difference between them; this is the case, for instance, when we call the two lobes of a light cone "past lobe" and "future lobe", or the two spin directions "up" and "down". By contrast, the difference between two entities is substantial when they are not formally identical: we assign different names to them because of such a difference (see Penrose 1979, Sachs 1987). When asymmetric temporal expressions appear in the discourse of fundamental physics, they are used in a completely conventional way: if we exchanged each of them for its symmetric correlate, the resulting discourse would be indistinguishable from the original one, at least to the extent that the "directionality" of time is not introduced from the outside, that is, from our natural language.

Once this point is accepted, the problem cannot yet be posed in terms of singling out the future direction of time: the problem of the arrow of time becomes the problem of how to find a temporal asymmetry only grounded on physical arguments. But if this is our main problem, we cannot project our independent intuitions about past and future for solving it without begging the question. In spite of the fact that these observations are simple, they are usually ignored in the philosophical discussions. This is particularly evident in the widespread reductionist attitude regarding the arrow of time, whose ambition consists in identifying or reducing the relation of temporal priority to some lawlike or *the facto* feature of the physical world: it is supposed that there is a non-temporal asymmetric relation R between events such that $R(e_1, e_2)$ holds iff $E(e_1, e_2)$ holds, where E is the temporal relation "*is earlier than*". For some reductionists, the connection between R and E is a lawlike association. For others, the connection between R and E has a definitional nature. Nevertheless, both approaches rely on assuming our previous intuitions about what "earlier" means. The reductionist approach has been largely criticized in the literature on this subject (see Sklar 1974, Earman 1974), and this is not surprising. These attempts of solving the problem of the arrow of time are doomed to failure because they are misguided regarding what the problem is: how to find a temporal asymmetry only grounded on physical arguments.

If we want to address the problem of the arrow of time from a perspective purged of our temporal intuitions, we must avoid the conclusions derived from subtly presupposing time-asymmetric notions. As Huw Price (1996) claims, it is necessary to stand at a point outside of time, and thence to regard reality in atemporal terms.[7] This atemporal standpoint prevents us from using the asymmetric tem-

---

[7] Our agreement with Price's general proposal of adopting an atemporal viewpoint does not amount to a complete agreement: as the present paper will show, we do not accept the conclusions drawn by Price in the cosmological context.

poral expressions of our natural language in a non-conventional way. But then, what does "the arrow of time" mean when we accept this constraint? Of course, the traditional expression coined by Eddington has only a metaphorical sense: its meaning must be understood by analogy. We recognize the difference between the head and the tail of an arrow on the basis of its geometrical properties; therefore, we can distinguish between both of these directions, head-to-tail and tail-to-head, independent of our own perspective. Analogously, we will conceive the problem of the arrow of time in terms of *the possibility of distinguishing between the two directions of time on the basis of exclusively physical arguments*.

7. Arrow of time and thermodynamics

When, in the late nineteenth century, Boltzmann developed the probabilistic version of his theory in response to the objections raised by Loschmidt and Zermelo (for historical details, see Brush 1976), he had to face a new challenge: how to explain the highly improbable current state of our world. In order to answer to this question, Boltzmann offered the first cosmological approach to the problem. Since this seminal work, the traditional discussions about the arrow of time in cosmology have usually related the time direction past-to-future to the gradient of the entropy function of the universe: it has been usually assumed that the only way of distinguishing between the two temporal directions is by means of the second law of thermodynamics. In this sense, John Earman (1974, p. 15) points out:

> [W]hat has been taken as an unquestionable dogma: considerations about entropy are absolutely crucial to every aspect of the problem.

One of the most philosophically influential works on the problem of the arrow of time was *The Direction of Time* of Hans Reichenbach. In his classical book, Reichenbach *defines* the future direction of time as the direction of the increase of the entropy of the majority of *branch systems*, that is, systems which become isolated from the main system during certain periods. However, Reichenbach knew perfectly Loschmidt's irreversibility and Zermelo's recurrence objections: if a system in a state of less than maximum entropy is overwhelmingly likely to evolve into a state of higher entropy in the future, it is also overwhelmingly likely to have evolved from a state of higher entropy in the past; on the other hand, if in an isolated system any state will be revisited to arbitrary closeness, entropy cannot be a monotonically decreasing function of time. For these reasons, Reichenbach realized that his definition did not imply the existence of a global time direction for the universe:

> We cannot speak of a direction for time as a whole [...] whether there is only one time direction or whether time direction alternate, depends on the shape of the entropy curve plotted by the universe (Reichenbach 1956, pp. 127-128).[8]

Paul Davies also appeals to the notion of branch systems, but from his own interpretation of Reichenbach's theses. Instead of conceiving, like Reichenbach, branch systems as independent systems whose parallelism regarding entropy increase must be proved, Davies considers that branch systems emerge as the result of a chain or hierarchy of branchings which expand out into wider and wider regions of the universe; therefore,

> [t]he origin of the arrow of time always refers back to the cosmological initial conditions. There exists an arrow of time only because the universe originated in a less-than-maximum entropy state (Davies 1994, p. 127).[9]

Reichenbach and Davies are only two of the many authors, coming from philosophy and physics, which approach the problem of the arrow of time in cosmology in terms of entropy (see also Feynman *et al.* 1964, Layzer 1975). This approach rests upon two assumptions: that it is possible to define entropy for a complete instantaneous cross-section of the universe, and that there is only one time for the universe as a whole. However, both assumptions involve difficulties. Firstly, to confidently transfer the concept of entropy from the field of thermodynamics to cosmology is a controversial move. The definition of entropy in cosmology is still a very problematic issue, even

---

[8] On the basis of a detailed analysis of Reichenbach's argument for parallelism, Sklar (1993) concludes that it merely imposes parallelism on the systems without explaining it.
[9] In his *Physics of Time Asymmetry*, Davies (1974) also appeals to the notion of branch system, but from a perspective closer to Reichenbach's original view.

more than in thermodynamics: there is not a consensus among physicists regarding how to define a global entropy for the universe. In fact, it is common to work only with the entropy associated with matter and radiation because there is not yet a clear idea about how to define the entropy due to the gravitational field. But even leaving aside this problem, if the entropy of the universe is considered as entropy out of equilibrium, there are different definitions for it (see Mackey 1989). Secondly, when general relativity comes into play, time becomes a dimension of a four-dimensional structure: it is not yet acceptable to conceive time as a background parameter which, as in pre-relativistic physics, is used to mark the evolution of the system. Therefore, the problem of the arrow of time cannot be posed, from the beginning, in terms of the entropy gradient between the two ends of a linear and open time.

Nevertheless, these difficulties are not the main reason for denying the central role played by entropy in the problem of the arrow of time in cosmology: there is a conceptual argument for abandoning the traditional approach. Entropy, as defined by thermodynamics, is a phenomenological property: a given value of entropy is compatible with many different configurations of a system. The question is whether there is a more fundamental property of the universe which allows us to distinguish between both of the temporal directions. From our perspective, it is possible to address the problem of the arrow of time in cosmology in terms of the geometrical properties of the space-time, independent of the thermodynamic arguments. In this sense, we follow Earman's "Time Direction Heresy", according to which the arrow of time, if it exists, is an intrinsic feature of space-time "which does not need and cannot be reduced to nontemporal features" (Earman 1974, p. 20).

In other words, the geometrical approach has conceptual priority over the entropic approach, since the geometrical properties of the universe are more basic than its thermodynamic properties: the definition of entropy and the calculation of the entropy curve for the whole universe are possible only if the space-time has certain definite geometrical features. Therefore, to insist on entropic considerations for distinguishing between both temporal directions can only be the result of a reductionist attitude, and its attempt of reducing temporal relationships to non-temporal relationships between events.

8. Topological conditions for defining the arrow of time

Let us consider an object like, for example, the pyramid of Keops. Let us call the vertical axis "z-axis". If we divide the pyramid by a plane parallel to its base which intersects the middle point of its height, we cannot deny that the object is spatially asymmetric regarding this plane. Of course, this asymmetry does not distinguish between the two spatial directions along the z-axis, because the pyramid could change its orientation in space and because there are many other objects in the universe, in particular, other pyramids not pointing to the same direction. But, what would happen if the whole universe were reduced to the pyramid of Keops? In this case, the space would be confined to the pyramid-universe. It would be, then, possible to distinguish between both directions along the z-axis: the direction base-to-vertex, and the direction vertex-to-base. We could even fix the z-coordinate of a point by measuring its distance to, for instance, the base. In other words, the pyramid-universe is an object, and the geometrical structure of this object as a whole is what establishes the difference between the two directions in one of the dimensions of space.

The universe is a four-dimensional spatio-temporal object. As this kind of object, it may be symmetric or asymmetric along the temporal dimension. When the problem of the global arrow of time is considered, the question is to find out whether the universe is asymmetric along the temporal dimension: this temporal asymmetry is what would allow us to distinguish between the two temporal directions. What does it mean that the universe is a temporally asymmetric object? This means that the distribution of matter-energy in space-time is not symmetrically arranged along the temporal dimension. But we know that, according to Einstein's field equations, there is a close connection between the distribution of matter-energy and the geometrical properties of space-time. Therefore, the temporal asymmetry of the universe amounts to the asymmetry of the geometrical properties of the space-time along the temporal dimension.

Of course, things are never so simple. Many different space-times, of extraordinarily varied topologies, are consistent with the field equations, and some of them have features that do not permit the defining of the two directions of time in a global way, or even to speak of a unique time for the universe as a whole. In the following sections we will address each one of these matters.

8.1. T-orientability

In a Minkowski space-time there are two relevant sets of events relative to each event: the set of the events included in the future lobe of the light cone at the specified event, and the set of those included in its past lobe – where the labels "future" and "past" are conventional. In general relativity the metric can always be reduced, in small regions of space-time, to the Minkowski form. However, on the large scale we do not expect the manifold to be flat because gravity can no longer be neglected. Many different topologies are consistent with Einstein's field equations; in particular, the possibility arises of space-time being curved along the spatial dimension in such a way that the spacelike sections of the universe become the three-dimensional analogous of a Moebius band; in technical terms it is said that the space-time is non t-orientable. A space-time is *t-orientable* if there exists a continuous non-vanishing vector field on it which is timelike with respect to its metric. This definition implies that, in a non t-orientable space-time, it is possible to transform a future pointing timelike vector into a past pointing timelike vector by means of a continuous transformation that always keeps timelike vectors timelike (*e.g.* going around a spacelike "Moebius band"); therefore, the distinction between future and past lobes cannot be established on a global level

Earman was one of the first authors who emphasized the importance of t-orientability to the problem of the arrow of time. For him, a temporal orientation can be defined in a globally consistent manner only if space-time is t-orientable, and this is enough to justify a *Principle of Precedence* (PP) according to which "continuous timelike transport takes precedence over any method (based on entropy or the like) of fixing time direction" (Earman 1974, p. 22).

This means that, if time directions fixed by the certain method in two regions of space-time do not agree when compared by means of continuous timelike transport; then if one of the directions is right, the other is wrong: the method gives an erroneous result in some regions of the space-time. In this sense, Earman rejects Reichenbach's position, according to which the arrow of time may point to different directions in different spatio-temporal regions.

Although Earman's argument seems plausible, it is not accepted by all that t-orientability is relevant for the problem of the arrow of time. Geoffrey Matthews (1979) argues that the importance of the global structure of the universe for the solution of the problem has been overestimated. Matthews rejects the Principle of Precedence according to which, if an arrow of time does exist, it must be global. For Matthews, the space-time may be non t-orientable if it possesses regional arrows of time but not a global arrow of time. However, this position leads to a new difficulty. Let us suppose that the directions of the arrows defined by a law L in two regions of the space-time disagree when compared by means of continuous timelike transport: the trajectory of the transport will pass through a frontier point between both regions where the law will have a discontinuity. This fact contradicts a basic methodological principle of cosmology according to which the laws of physics are valid in all points of the space-time.[10] Therefore, it is not possible to reject the t-orientability of space-time as a condition for defining the arrow of time without ignoring certain basic principles of cosmology.

8.2. Cosmic time

As it is well known, general relativity replaces the older conception of space-through-time by the concept of space-time, where space and time are inextricably intertwined. On the one hand, time becomes a dimension of a four dimensional manifold. But when the time meas-

---

[10] Although we agree with Earman with respect of the need of t-orientability, we do not formulate the problem of the arrow of time in terms of *temporal orientation* because this seems to suggest that there is a privileged direction of time. In fact, following Earman's definition of orientation (1974, p. 18), the choice of an orientation is the choice of the set of the *future* pointing timelike vectors; but, what does 'future' mean in a non-conventional sense?

ured by a physical clock is considered, each particle of the universe has its own *proper time*, that is, the time registered by a clock carried by the particle. Since the curved space-time of general relativity can be considered locally flat, it is possible to synchronize the clocks fixed to particles whose parallel trajectories are confined in a small region of space-time. But, in general, the synchronization of the clocks fixed to all the particles of the universe is not possible. Only in certain particular cases all the clocks can be temporally coordinated by means of a cosmic time, which also has the features necessary to play the role of the temporal parameter in the evolution of the universe.

This problem can also be posed in geometrical terms. A space-time may be such that it is not possible to partition the set of all events into equivalence classes such that: (i) each one of the disjoint classes is a spacelike hypersurface, and (ii) the hypersurfaces can be ordered in time. This is the case when there are closed or almost closed timelike curves in space-time or, even without this kind of timelike curves, when it is impossible to find a smooth function which attaches to each event a real number, the time of the event, such that the number assigned to e_1 is less than that assigned to e_2 whenever there is a causal signal propagable from e_1 to e_2. In such cases, the space-time is not globally splittable into spaces-at-a-time, that is, into spacelike hypersurfaces each one of which contains all the events simultaneous with each other.

There is a hierarchy of conditions which, applied to a t-orientable space-time, avoid the "anomalous" features just described. In particular, a space-time (M, g), where M differential 4-dimensional manifold and g is its metric, possesses a *global time function* if there is a function t: $M \rightarrow \mathbb{R}$ whose gradient is everywhere timelike (see Hawking & Ellis 1973). This means that there exists a function whose value increases along every future directed timelike curve; the existence of such a function guarantees that the space-time is globally splittable into spaces-at-a-time, that is, into hypersurfaces of simultaneity ($t = const.$) which define a foliation (see Schutz 1980).

Some authors consider that the condition for obtaining the arrow of time is the possibility of defining a global time on the space-time (see Earman 1974). However, this position does not take into account that the fact that the space-time admits a global time function does not permit yet to define a notion of simultaneity in a univocal manner, and with physical meaning. So, it is necessary to choose a particular foliation among all the possible ones, in particular, the foliation according to which all the worldline curves are orthogonal to all the spacelike hypersurfaces defined by the foliation; moreover, the time between two hypersurfaces of simultaneity must be the same when measured on any worldline, and must be equal to the proper time of any particle (see Castagnino, Lombardi & Lara 2003). Only when these conditions are satisfied, it is possible to define a *cosmic time* which guarantees that all the processes of the universe can be coordinated by a single time.

Of course, the existence of a cosmic time imposes a significant topological and metric limitation on the space-time. In a completely general case it is not possible to define a cosmic time in terms of which the history of the universe as a whole can be conceived as the temporal sequence of the instantaneous states of the universe and, as a consequence, it makes no sense to speak of the two directions of time for the universe as a whole. This fact supplies a strong argument against the entropic approach to the problem of the arrow of time. By defining the time direction past-to-future in terms of the gradient of the entropy function of the universe, the entropic approach takes for granted the possibility of defining such a function. But this amounts to the assumption that: (i) the space-time can be partitioned in space-like hypersurfaces on which the entropy of the universe can be defined, and (ii) the space-time possesses a cosmic time or, at least, a global time on which the entropy gradient can be computed. When the possibility of space-times with no cosmic time is recognized, it is difficult to deny the conceptual priority of considerations about the geometrical structure of space-time over entropic considerations in the context of the problem of the arrow of time.

9. T-asymmetry

Traditionally it is supposed that if physics included a non t-invariant law, we would have a direct method for defining the arrow of time; the problem seems to arise because the fundamental laws of physics are t-invariant.[11] However, this traditional assumption deserves a deeper analysis.

In Section 2, we have pointed out that a law is t-invariant if, given the evolutions *dynamically possible* relative to it; the time-reversed evolutions are also dynamically possible. This characterization clearly shows that the definition of t-invariance says nothing about the properties that the possible evolutions must satisfy. In fact, a t-invariant law may be such that all or most of the possible evolutions relative to it are individually *t-asymmetric*. Price (1996) refers to this fact as a loophole which allows a t-invariant theory to have t-asymmetric consequences. As Steven Savitt (1996) says, the point may be more clearly posed in terms of the models of a theory: a theory T is t-invariant if the time-reverse $\mathbf{T}(m)$ of every dynamically possible model m of T is also a model of T; the loophole consists in the fact that a t-invariant theory may have t-asymmetric models.

Of course, this loophole is not helpful for solving the problem of the arrow of time when we are dealing with a multiplicity of systems. Even if all the dynamically possible evolutions – relative to the t-invariant law L – were t-asymmetric, for each system which evolves according to $S_i \rightarrow S_j$ there might be a system which evolves according to $T(S_j) \rightarrow T(S_i)$: this situation would restore the overall symmetry. But when we are studying the whole universe, such a situation is not yet possible. The universe is a single object: there is not another system which restores the symmetry when coupled with it. Therefore, the t-invariance of the global laws which govern the universe on the large scale is not an obstacle to the possibility of describing a t-asymmetric universe.

It is quite clear that these considerations are not applicable to the field equations of general relativity as originally stated; however, if there exists a cosmic time, such equations are t-invariant. But, as we have said, the t-invariance of the field equations does not prevent us from describing a t-asymmetric universe with them: each t-asymmetric solution of the equations represents a universe whose

---

[11] The only exception is given by the laws of certain elementary processes which involve the K meson; however, it is usually accepted that the effect of such processes is not relevant for macroscopic temporal asymmetry.

space-time is asymmetric in its geometrical properties, along the time dimension. This idea can also be formulated in terms of the concept of temporal isotropy. A t-orientable space-time (M, g) is *t-isotropic* if there is a diffeomorphism d of M onto itself which reverses the temporal orientations, but preserves the metric g. However, when we want to express the t-symmetry of a space-time having a cosmic time, it is necessary to strengthen this definition: a t-orientable space-time which admits a cosmic time t will be *t-symmetric* with respect to some space like hypersurface $t = \alpha$, where α is a constant, if it is t-isotropic, and the diffeomorphism d leaves fixed the hypersurface $t=\alpha$. Intuitively this means that, from the hypersurface $t = \alpha$, the space-time looks the same in both temporal directions. Therefore, if a t-orientable space time possessing a global time is t-asymmetric, it is possible to distinguish between the two directions of the global time exclusively on the basis of such a geometric asymmetry.[12]

However, we know that, if t is the cosmic time, then if m is a model of the Einstein's field equations, the time reversed model $\mathbf{T}(m)$ is also a model of those equations. In other words, we always obtain two solutions, each one of which is the temporal mirror image of the other, which are both possible relative to the laws of general relativity. At this point, the ghost of symmetry seems to threaten again: now we are committed to supplying a non-conventional criterion for picking out one of both nomologically admissible solutions (models). However, the threat may be surmounted when the implicit assumptions involved in the problem are explicitly stated.

When we accept the need of choosing only one of the solutions, we are assuming that each one of them describes a different possible universe: there are two possible objects, and we must decide which one of them corresponds to our actual universe. But why are the two possible universes different? The obvious answer is: they are different because they are arranged in time in opposed directions. This answer would be acceptable if we were trying to describe a system immersed in an environment: this background would allow us to distinguish

---

[12] These concepts can be applied to the standard models of contemporary cosmology; it is possible to prove that, in the set of these models, t-symmetric models have probability zero (see Castagnino, Lara & Lombardi 2003).

between both solutions and to decide which one of them adequately describes the system of interest. But when the system is the whole universe, there is no environment. The question is, then: what does it mean that both possible universes are temporally opposed?

The very idea of two temporally opposed possible universes presupposes that there is a single time, common to both possible universes, to which we can say that one is opposed to the other. But to suppose that we can meaningfully talk about a time common to two possible universes is completely contrary to the standard interpretation of general relativity. According to this interpretation, time – or better, space-time – coexists with the universe: each universe has its own space-time, and there is not a *temporal* viewpoint, external to both possible universes, from where we can compare them. In fact, two mathematical models for the universe, defined by (M, g) and (M', g') are taken to be equivalent if they are *isometric*, that is, if there is a diffeomorphism $\theta: M \rightarrow M'$ which carries the metric g into the metric g'. In particular, symmetry transformations are isometries: models related by a symmetry transformation are isometric. Therefore, two models m and $\mathbf{T}(m)$, related by time reversal, are equivalent descriptions of one and the same possible universe. Therefore, the new ghost of symmetry disappears: it is not necessary yet to find a non-conventional criterion for selecting one of two nomologically admissible solutions since both are different descriptions of a single possible universe.

It is interesting to notice that the thesis of the equivalence between m and $\mathbf{T}(m)$ does not depend on the t-invariance of the laws by means of which the models were constructed. Let us suppose that the theory T consists of a non t-invariant law L, according to which some magnitude α monotonically *increases* with time; this means that there is a model $m \in M_T$ of the universe such that $\mathbf{T}(m) \notin M_T$. Now we can construct a theory $T^* = \mathbf{T}(T)$ consisting of a non t-invariant law $L^* = \mathbf{T}(L)$ which states that the magnitude α monotonically *decreases* with time; of course, if $m \in M_T$, then $\mathbf{T}(m) \in M_T{}^*$. The question is: how could one decide whether T or $\mathbf{T}(T)$ is, in Earman's terms, "true"? We will consider that, say, T is true and $\mathbf{T}(T)$ is false because we know, by means of our observation of the processes in the world, that α increases toward the *future*. But this conclusion is based on *our perception* of the "direction" of time, which is independent of any theoretical consideration: only this previous intuition of the asymmetry between past and future allows us to decide between T and $\mathbf{T}(T)$. However, when the problem of the arrow of time is the question at issue, we cannot appeal to our inner perceptions: we must stand at a neutral point regarding time. As Price (1996) claims, from this atemporal standpoint we are not entitled to state that α increases or decreases with time; we can only say that there exists an unidirectional gradient of α between the two extremities of the universe, and such a gradient is adequately explained by both T and $\mathbf{T}(T)$. Therefore, when we do not independently presuppose the "correct" direction of time, there is no difference between the physical situations described by T and $\mathbf{T}(T)$ and, as a consequence, m and $\mathbf{T}(m)$ are equivalent descriptions of the same possible universe also in the case of non t-invariant laws. Summing up, the acceptance of the equivalence thesis does not depend on the t-invariance of the physical laws, but rather on the fact that we describe the universe as a whole without appealing to the privileged direction of time derived from our pre-theoretical perception.

10. T-invariance and the arrow of time

The arguments developed in the previous sections are useful for disentangling some questions frequently identified in the traditional discussions; in particular, they allow us to realize that, in addressing the issue of the arrow of time on the cosmological level, we must face two conceptually different problems. The "*symmetry problem*" consists in obtaining a t-asymmetric model of the universe where the two directions of time can be distinguished. Everybody agrees that there is no difficulty in constructing t-asymmetric models by means of non t-invariant laws; the problem seems to be in how it is possible to describe a t-asymmetric model by means of t-invariant laws. However, as we have seen, this is a pseudoproblem that arises from confusing an equation with its solutions: t-invariance is a property of equations – or laws –, t-symmetry is a property of solutions – or models –, and there is nothing which prevents the obtaining a t-asymmetric solution by means of a t-invariant equation. On the other hand, the "*choice problem*" consists in providing a non-conventional criterion for deciding between two solutions, each one of which is the temporal mirror image of the other. As we have argued, this problem vanishes when we realize that we are not committed to supplying such a criterion to the extent that both solutions are equivalent descriptions of the same possible universe.

On the other hand, these considerations show that the t-invariance of the physical laws is not as essential to the problem of the arrow of time as it has been traditionally assumed. In regards to the "symmetry problem", t-invariance does not prevent us from constructing t-asymmetric models. On the other hand, the "choice problem" arises whether or not the laws describing the two temporally "opposed" models are t-invariant. In fact, even a non t-invariant law or theory will have two models; one is of the temporal mirror image of the other: the need of deciding between them is independent of the features of the theory by means of which they were constructed. In other words, the "choice problem" is the result of the peculiar feature of a pair of models of a theory, and not of the property of t-invariance of the theory. In short, the problem of the global arrow of time requires that we focus our attention on the properties of the models of a physical theory: the properties of the theory itself – in particular, its t-invariance or non t-invariance – are rather less crucial to the problem than the traditional discussions suggest.

11. Concluding remarks

In the present paper, we have attempted to clarify the concepts that are most frequently used in the discussions usually subsumed under the label "the problem of the arrow of time". In particular, we have distinguished among the concepts of t-invariance – a property of laws –, reversibility – a property of processes – and t-symmetry – a property of models –. This distinction has allowed us to point out the difference between the problem of irreversibility and the problem of the arrow of time. Of course, we do not expect to have supplied a solution to these problems: the purpose has been to provide the conceptual elements necessary for addressing them with conceptual clarity, from a perspective that avoids confusions derived from identifying notions that are similar but different.

References

Bricmont, J. (1995), "Science of Chaos or Chaos in Science?", *Physicalia Magazine* 17: 159-208.

Brush, S. (1976), *The Kind of Motion We Call Heat*, Amsterdam: North Holland.

Bunge, M. (1977), *Treatise on Basic Philosophy, Vol. 3: Ontology I*, Dordrecht: Reidel.

Castagnino, M., Lombardi, O. & L. Lara (2003), "The Global Arrow of Time as a Geometrical property of the Universe", *Foundations of Physics* 33: 877-912.

Castagnino, M., Lara, L. & O. Lombardi (2003), "The Cosmological Origin of Time Asymmetry", *Classical and Quantum Gravity* 20: 369-391.

Davies, P.C.W. (1974), *The Physics of Time Asymmetry*, Berkeley: University of California Press.

Davies, P. C. W. (1994), "Stirring Up Trouble", in Halliwell, J.J., Pérez-Mercader, J. & W.H. Zurek (eds.), *Physical Origins of Time Asymmetry*, Cambridge: Cambridge University Press.

Earman, J. (1974), "An Attempt to Add a Little Direction to «The Problem of the Direction of Time»", *Philosophy of Science* 41: 15-47.

Earman, J. & M. Rédei (1996), "Why Ergodic Theory Does Not Explain the Success of Equilibrium Statistical Mechanics", *The British Journal for the Philosophy of Science* 47: 63-78.

Ehrenfest, P. & T. Ehrenfest (1912), *The Conceptual Foundations of the Statistical Approach in Mechanics*, Ithaca: Cornell University Press.

Feynman, R.P., Leighton, R.B. & M. Sands (1964), *The Feynman Lectures on Physics*, New York: Addison-Wesley.

Hawking, S.W. & G.F.R. Ellis (1973), *The Large Scale Structure of Space-Time*, Cambridge: Cambridge University Press.

Hollinger, H.B. & M.J. Zenzen (1982), "An Interpretation of Macroscopic Irreversibility within the Newtonian Framework", *Philosophy of Science* 49: 309-354.

Layzer, D. (1975), "The Arrow of Time", *Scientific American* 234: 56-69.

Lebowitz, J.L. (1993), "Boltzmann's Entropy and Time's Arrow", *Physics Today* (September): 32-38.

Lebowitz, J. L. (1994), "Lebowitz Replies", *Physics Today* (November): 115-116.

Lebowitz, J. L. y Penrose, O. (1973), "Modern Ergodic Theory", *Physics Today* 26: 23-29.

Mackey, M.C. (1989), "The Dynamic Origin of Increasing Entropy", *Reviews of Modern Physics* 61: 981-1015.

Matthews, G. (1979), "Time's Arrow and the Structure of Spacetime", *Philosophy of Science* 46: 82-97.

Popper, K. (1956a), "The Arrow of Time", *Nature* 177: 538.

Popper, K. (1956b), "Irreversibility and Mechanics", *Nature* 178: 382.

Popper, K. (1957), "Reply to Hill and Grünbaum", *Nature* 179: 1297.

Popper, K. (1958), "Reply to Bosworth", *Nature* 181: 402-403.

Popper, K. (1965), "Time's Arrow and Entropy", *Nature* 207: 233-234.

Popper, K. (1967a), "Time's Arrow and Feeding on Negentropy", *Nature* 213: 320.

Popper, K. (1967b), "Structural Information and the Arrow of Time", *Nature* 214: 322.

Penrose, R. (1979), "Singularities and Time Asymmetry", in Hawking, S. & W. Israel (eds.), *General Relativity, an Einstein Centenary Survey*, Cambridge: Cambridge University Press.

Price, H. (1996), *Time's Arrow and Archimedes' Point: New Directions for the Physics of Time*, Oxford: Oxford University Press.

Reichenbach, H. (1956), *The Direction of Time*, Berkeley: University of California Press.

Sachs, R.G. (1987), *The Physics of Time Reversal*, Chicago: University of Chicago Press.

Savitt, S.F. (1995), "Introduction", in Savitt, S.F. (ed.), *Time's Arrows Today*, Cambridge: Cambridge University Press.

Savitt, S.F. (1996), "The Direction of Time", *British Journal for the Philosophy of Science* 47: 347-370.

Schutz, B. F. (1980), *Geometrical Methods of Mathematical Physics*, Cambridge: Cambridge University Press.

Sklar, L. (1974), *Space, Time and Spacetime*, Berkeley: University of California Press.

Sklar, L. (1993), *Physics and Chance*, Cambridge: Cambridge University Press.

Principles in Cosmology

Antonio Augusto Passos Videira

Institute of Human Sciences and Philosophy, Philosophy Department
Rio de Janeiro State University (UERJ)

"As if the exact science of nature couldn't get to a point where meeting with metaphysics became inevitable!"
(Thomas Mann, *Experiências Ocultas* in *Mario and the Magician*)

It was thought for a long time that cosmology could never be a science such as physics, astronomy, or biology. We need only to call to mind the preclusions Auguste Comte used to make during the first half of the 19th century, against all attempts of investigation about astrophysical and cosmological matters which could never be resolved since it was not possible to dispose of observational data (i.e. empirical) to verify suggested answers.[1] Even if Comte aimed his critiques directly at the matter of the physical/chemical composition of the celestial stars, his opinion certainly embodied cosmology, since he worried about knowing the origin as well as the structure of the whole. Comte, a strict positivist convinced that cosmology kept dan-

---

[1] For more historical details see to Merleau-Ponty (1965), and Merleau-Ponty (1983).

gerous connections to religious and metaphysical thoughts – which he fiercely rejected, at least during the first phase of his philosophical career, – concluded that cosmology and astrophysics were nothing but childish chimeras. However, he was not successful in his prohibitions, not even having had the time to see them definitely fall in. Two years after his death in 1857, two German scientists – Robert Bunsen and Gustav R. Kirchhoff – discovered the spectral analysis method, which allowed the "decode" of the information about the physical/chemical composition of the stars hidden in the bright beams they discharged. This started the scientific study of the chemical composition and physical structure of the comets, stars and galaxies.[2]

In 1917, sixty years after Comte's death, Albert Einstein published an article through which he started the scientific research in cosmology. Even though Einstein's contribution had been fundamental, astronomy had already started, since the end of the 19th century, to worry about knowing if our galaxy, the Milky Way, would be the only one in the universe (see Hetherington 1993). There was already a concern about cosmology in the air. If the first defeat of positivism – the one that originated from the pioneering work of Bunsen, Kirchhoff, Huggins, Sechhi, and Jansen, among others – happened through the instauration of the possibility of the use of empirical data, the second, certainly more serious, was possible due to the fortunate conjunction of mathematics, philosophy, and intellectual audacity, all this based on a radically new physics (see Kragh 1996, A.L.L. Videira 2000).

As interesting as it is, my goal is not to analyze the philosophical or even scientific reasons that made Comte try to prohibit, without success, physical and chemical research concerning the celestial stars. Comte's unsuccessful try against astrophysics and cosmology – which held that the celestial mechanics of Newton and Laplace was the most perfect model of scientific theory – belongs today to the history of philosophy, as well as to the history of science. My reference to the French philosopher is due to the fact that his critiques touch a crucial point for science: the relationship that the latter keeps with the so called principles, since one of Comte's main philosophic objectives

---

[2] For more details, see Videira (1995).

consisted in building a conception of science through which the introduction of any topic related to metaphysics was not possible. In any case, Comte suspected of the use of principles.

It is not the latest thing to state that, apart from their nature and function, the position enjoyed by principles in science was never completely unperturbed or exempted of criticism. The least that can be said is that, sometimes, even among those who accept them, the importance of principles is disturbing. It cannot be denied that, even nowadays many scientists and philosophers believe that they can, in fact, make science turn its back to what is real, directing itself to metaphysics; that is, to a "wild and dangerous" speculation about reality. When this happens, many scientists, accompanied by philosophers, go back to lay hold of the flag of positivism, in an attempt to fight what seems to them to be a betrayal of science (see, for example, D'Espagnat s.d. and Popper's article a, s.d.).

The position just described can very well be exemplified by the critiques that the English astrophysicist Herbert Dingle directed to cosmologists such as Milne and Eddington, whom, between the 1930's and the 1940's developed cosmological models without worrying about verifying them observationally (see Gale & Urani 1993, Gale & Urani in Hetherington 1993 and Gale & Shanks 1996). To many of his contemporaries, Dingle adopted a conservative stance, exactly because he had worried about stating the dangers of an excessively speculative position, fed by an "irrational faith" in mathematics and in the heuristic potential of *a priori* principles. The origin of Dingle's critiques is precisely in his incomprehension of the role that mathematics performs in the process of elaboration of physical theories (see Chang 1993). To him, it was unacceptable that mathematics could be used as a guide for scientists in their activities of describing natural phenomena behavior. Even though his opinions have been strongly opposed to and criticized, he never changed his mind, keeping until the end of his life a deep suspicion before each and every physical theory that did not originate from empirical observations.

At least to what concerns cosmology, Dingle's position was not fruitful – neither could it be. Cosmology, deprived of principles, does not exist; neither could it exist as a science. This way, positivism's highest pretension – to base science upon observations and nothing else – cannot be respected by cosmology. And as in the relationship between science and philosophy, it is the first one that is "in charge", in the sense that it can determine the destiny of theories and philosophical principles – if a philosophical principle is not useful, fruitful to science, it can be simply abandoned and rejected.

I will make a last comment on positivism, and I will allow myself to do so without any proof. The associations between positivism and science have never been quiet and they never could be. Positivism demonstrates an excessive concern with metaphysics. This concern seems to be so strong that it is, in reality, the main reason for positivism's existence. The latter exists while it is still possible to keep up the battle against metaphysics. Positivism – and the examples from astrophysics and cosmology seem to be sufficiently strong to corroborate this opinion – is not fruitful, at least not to science. In other words, it does not have enough heuristic strength to promote the development – here understood as progress – of science, since its main concern is to avoid its contamination from the metaphysics. When it defends an anti-metaphysics position, positivism is throwing the baby out with the bath water. After all, metaphysics constitutes an important source of ideas to science, as Popper (see Popper b, s.d.) has very well emphasized since the first half of last century; or even Boltzmann, before him, between the end of the 19th century, and the beginning of the 20th century (see Boltzmann 1997).

Among physicists, particularly among cosmologists, the opinion that principles are necessary so that science is possible is disseminated. In the specific case of cosmology, this dependency is even stronger, since cosmology simply cannot exist without these principles. I present a few opinions to illustrate my statement:

1. "Given this situation [the universe is unique], *we are unable to obtain a model of the universe without some specifically cosmological assumptions which are completely unverifiable.*" (Ellis 1975, pp. 245-246; author's emphasis)
2. "But above all cosmology starts from a number of fundamental principles. [...] Cosmology is based on definite principles and can be compared to observations. [...] In any case it is important to be aware that scientific cosmology does rest on several metaphysical principles." (Lachièze-Rey 1993, p. 3)

3. "Cosmologists [...] do so by postulating a universal principle, which requires that our local sample of the universe be no different from more remote and inaccessible regions. There are strong philosophical reasons for advocating such a universal principle." (Silk 1980, pp. 3-4)
4. "Cosmology is exceptional amongst the sciences in the extent to which it makes use of 'Principles' in order to extract testable statements about the visible universe from the underlying laws of Nature. This is not entirely surprising; for astronomy in general, and cosmology in particular, suffer from limitations not shared by any of their sisters' sciences." (Barrow 1993, p. 117)

With the four statements above, all of them from approximately the last thirty years, I hope to make sufficiently clear that a significant number of scientists, at first, have nothing against the use of principles in science, particularly in cosmology. These quotes show equally that, in the case of cosmology, principles constitute one of the conditions of possibility. In this way, when facing the question "Cosmology: Science or Metaphysics?" I would have to answer: both (see Videira 2001). In reality, I do not believe that cosmology is a mix of science and metaphysics. I think that the latter is a condition of possibility that imposes itself due to the unique characteristics presented by cosmology's object of study: the universe. It is crystal clear that this is not only my opinion. Each and every cosmologist makes similar statements. The following are two examples:

Lachièze-Rey: "There is only one universe, and we are a part of it. This situation is different from the one usually encountered in science. Hence the methods and concerns of cosmology are distinct from the rest of physics."

Bondi: "A typical difficulty related to cosmology is the uniqueness of the object of its study, the universe. In physics, we are accustomed to distinguish between the accidental and the essential aspects of a phenomenon, by comparing it with other similar phenomena."

When I state that one of cosmology's conditions of possibility is the fusion of science and metaphysics, I am trying to express that cosmology is based upon an interaction between philosophy and observations, obviously accompanied by physical theory. In other words, one can characterize the mentioned interaction the following way: physics constitutes the arena or stage where philosophical principles and observations interact, originating the expected results, which is the knowledge in cosmology.

Because it has the universe as a whole as its object of study, cosmology cannot use the same criteria and methodological rules of other sciences, such as physics and astronomy. An elucidative distinction regarding this point is the following: there are experimental sciences (physics, chemistry and microbiology) and historical and geographical sciences (astronomy, geology and theory of evolution). In the experimental sciences, it is possible to do experiments with a class of identical or practically identical objects between themselves. The same thing does not happen in the so-called historical and geographical sciences, in which it is only possible to observe traits and characteristics of single events and objects. To the South African cosmologist George Ellis, cosmology is a mix of historical and geographical science, since "we necessarily observe distant sources in a far-away time, when its properties could have been different" [from the ones they have nowadays].

Yet in this point about the relations between object of study and method, there is an interesting consequence to the philosophy of science, when it is clear that it is not possible, at least in the case of cosmology, to sustain the thesis that method prevails over object. While this thesis was believed in, it was evident that cosmology had to be left out of the scope of science. It is impossible to adapt its object of study to the standard idea of a scientific method. In this way, in order for cosmology to be a scientific subject, it has to create its own method; a "mix" of common procedures in historical and geological sciences, but always trying to follow the most valuable principles of physics, as for example, the one that states that the laws of physics are universal. Even this last statement is not plain in cosmology. We are unappealingly limited to observe what is present in our cone of light. To believe that the laws of physics are universal corresponds to an act of faith, as it can be noticed in the words of the French cosmologist Lachièze-Rey:

> The laws of physics are the same everywhere. [...] Without this act of faith no scientific cosmology is possible. But once again it is a question of accepting an a priori principle. In fact, the very idea of a phys-

ical law implies its universality. But a law is only valid within a certain domain (Lachièze-Rey 1993, p. 3).

The idea that the laws of physics are universally valid is, in a strict sense, an audacious overstatement, and it cannot be proven. To a positivist, such an overstatement should be avoided. However, without it, cosmology is not possible. The British physicist D.J. Raine states that this idea is the most fundamental speculation of theoretical cosmology. The situation of the scientific laws gets worse in the case of cosmology, when it is reminded, as George Ellis does, that "an observational point is not capable of establishing the nature of a final cause relationship. Consequently, the concept of law becomes questionable when there is only one object to which it applies".

If cosmology intends to be coherent with its own definition – the study of the universe as a whole – it needs to overcome the limitation imposed by its limitation in observing the universe. As we have seen before, in order for this to happen, it avails itself of principles. These principles contribute to determine the method used in cosmology. In other words, method in cosmology is a consequence of the belief in certain principles. In Lachièze-Rey words:

> But above all cosmology starts from a number of fundamental principles. [...] Cosmology is based on definite principles and can be compared with observations. [...] In any case it is important to be aware that scientific cosmology does rest on several metaphysical principles. (Lachièze-Rey 1993, pp. 3-4)

One of the main obstacles that cosmologists went through for a long time was the difficulty to propose new ideas. Many times, other areas of science, especially in physics, came to my assistance. Two interesting examples of this situation are the **hot big bang**, proposed by Gamow and collaborators at the end of the 1940's, and the actual inflationary models, due to physicists such as Guth and Linde, among others. Gamow's ideas are due to the progresses made in nuclear physics, while the inflationary models became possible thanks to the success of the physics of elementary particles in his project to unite three basic forces (the strong nuclear force, the weak nuclear force, and electromagnetism) (see Kragh 1996, Guth 1997 and Videira 1998). The frequency through which cosmology makes use of other areas of physics should not be understood as a structural weakness.

On the contrary, when it is able to incorporate ideas originated in another field of action, cosmology shows the existence of a sophisticated, robust, and powerful conceptual network under the heuristic point of view (see A.L.L. Videira 2001).

After decades of suffering from terrible suspicion from the physicists, cosmology enjoys a unanimous situation to what regards its scientific character. I believe that there is almost no physicist who would, at least in public, state that cosmology is not a science. To the contrary, what can be read in specialized magazines, text books, and scientific articles is that cosmology is not only a science, but it already has a standard model, similarly to what happens in physics of elementary particles, as can easily be noticed in the statements below:

> Cosmology has progressed in the past 35 years [this article was published in August, 1999] from a mainly mathematical and philosophical exercise to an important branch of both astronomy and physics, and is now part of mainstream science, with a well-established Standard Model confirmed by various strands of evidence. (Ellis 1999, Box, p. 4.20)

> There is now a substantial body of observations that support directly and indirectly the relativistic hot big-bang model for the expanding Universe. Equally important, there are no data that are inconsistent. This is no mean feat: The observations are sufficiently constraining that there is no alternative to the hot big-bang consistent with all the data at hand. (Turner & Tyson 1999, p. 2)

Cosmology went from being a heterodox science to integrating orthodoxy. As always, this situation can bring problems to the community of cosmologists. After all, scientific ideas are born, live, and die. This seems to be the main characteristic of science. Even though it is positive to count on standard models, once they direct the research they cannot be used as a weapon – used to dismiss and exterminate different ideas that are not compatible with theirs. The danger represented by dogmatism is serious and should be avoided at all costs. Considering cosmology's distinctive peculiar nature, different from other branches of natural sciences, dogmatism can be especially pernicious because it negates the possibility of dialogue, preventing progress. In order for dogmatism not to become a reality in cosmology (the same being valid for other sciences) it is necessary, above all, to be conscious of the philosophical options made (see Ribeiro & Videira 1995 and Ribeiro & Videira 1998).

Another important element in the search to obtain transparency amongst the philosophical options made is directly related to the role that the definitions play in cosmology (see Videira 2000). In other terms, it is fundamental to analyze and understand the definitions proposed and effectively used. Cosmology's main definition, without a doubt, regards its object of study: the universe. What is the universe investigated by cosmology? Cosmology can be defined as the study of the whole or of everything else there is (even though it is important here to narrow down the definition in a way to exclude the living beings), or even of the structure of the universe on a large scale. It should be observed that, to many cosmologists, the expression 'structure of the universe in large scale' is more adequate than 'whole' or 'totality'. Whole, totality or existence are, to many of them, typical philosophical concepts, and therefore, "dangerous", since they are vague. A possibility to avoid the "dangers" of philosophy consists in defining adequately what is studied in cosmology and how its object is studied; in other words, what are its true and possible objectives.

According to George Ellis, there is no possibility of denying that philosophical options are really made in cosmology. This situation becomes clear when facing the following question: 'Why does the universe have one specific shape and not another when it is perfectly possible to think or to create other possibilities?' In other words, the initial conditions present and in action at the beginning of the universe, could be different from those that presided the formation of the universe as we know it and live in. To Ellis, it is inevitable, therefore, that metaphysical themes come up in cosmology. The philosophical choices become vital to the configuration of a theory. A key element in the process of choosing the philosophical options are to clearly know what the scope of the cosmological theory desired is. In Ellis's words:

> The specifically cosmological philosophical base becomes more or less dominant in shaping our theory according to the degree that we pursue with more or less ambitious explanatory aims. (Ellis 1999, p. 4.23)

The importance of clearly knowing the explanatory objectives is shown in an explicit and pressing way when we realize that the fundamental matters underlying cosmology are the following:
1) Why do the laws of physics have the shape they do?
2) Why are the conditions of configuration for the universe shaped the way they are?
3) Why are there laws of physics?
4) Why does something exist?
5) Why does the universe allow or require the existence of intelligent lives?

If these are the main points of scientific cosmology, there is no way to deny its resemblance with traditional cosmology, today banished to exist only in clearly philosophical inspirational manuals of neo-Thomism. Even if the answers to the above questions are not shown clearly in cosmological models, the latter have been conceived from the acceptance or refusal of the validity of science to answer or, at least, contribute to the "discovery" of some of the answers craved for. A very interesting historical example is directly related to the appearance and development of the stationary state theory. Not satisfied with some of the basic ideas of the **hot big bang model**, in particular the one that allowed the elaboration of pseudo-scientific speeches about the origin of the universe, Fred Hoyle decided to propose a model that avoided the possibility of cosmology becoming interested in the matter of the origin of the universe. In reality, Hoyle was worried about avoiding the fact that the matter of the origin was formulated. In this way, question number four from the list above could not be asked either, and much less, be answered. A considerable number of cosmologists agree with Hoyle's opinion, even though they do not accept his cosmological model. An example of this position can be noted through the words below:

> Today's physicists have nothing to say about how the expansion began. [...] the actual theory of physics cannot deal with a "beginning". [...] There is no evidence of the beginning of the universe and no theory can deal properly with that. (Zhi and Xian 1994, p. 187)[3]

---

[3] See Ribeiro & Videira (1999).

To notice the existence of similarities between scientific and neo-Thomist cosmology does not mean that I have the opinion that the latter can play any kind of positive role in the first. I want only to support and insist in the presence of philosophy, particularly of metaphysics, in cosmology. It is obvious that this thesis is not new. Many other physicists have already done the same, maybe even in a more radical way, as it is the case of Stephen Toulmin:

> Those who think of <u>metaphysics</u> as the most unconstrained or speculative of disciplines are misinformed: compared with cosmology, metaphysics is pedestrian and unimaginative. (Toulmin 1989, p. 409)

One of the interesting points of this short statement of Toulmin is that it seems to have happened an inversion in the relationship between science and metaphysics. As it has been known for a long time, once this movement started in the middle of the 19th century, the physicist kept a violent opposition against the philosophers because he thought they made inappropriate and non-veracious statements about reality (see Videira 1996). The opposition was so strong, that it originated some philosophical movements, developed by professional scientists or philosophers close to science – as it is the case of Comte's positivism and the logical positivism of the 1920's, 1930's and 1940's. In spite of the popularity and prestige which these two movements experienced among scientists and philosophers, they could not do what they wished for the most: to exterminate, once and for all, metaphysics. The latter has always shown to be more resistant than the attacks made against it.

Even the critiques and advice that Dingle addressed to his friends – especially the younger and most experienced ones, according to him – had no effect. The options and efforts of cosmologists from the 1940's, 1950's and 1960's, who were only a few then, were rewarded in 1965 with the discovery of the cosmic radiation background, since it was soon explained as a residue of processes occurred during the initial stages of the universe. The existence of the cosmic radiation background confirmed one of the main versions of the **hot big-bang model of** Gamow's and his collaborators. This discovery was so important that, to some scientists and science historians – as it is the case of Stephen G. Brush – that is what registers the beginning of scientific cosmology, since this discovery respected one of the main epistemological canons of science: the elaboration of a forecast about an unknown phenomenon that was later confirmed (see Brush 1992).

As we have seen before, metaphysics is present in cosmology. However, because it is present it does not mean that it has replaced cosmology. This seems to be the conclusion that Toulmin gets to. From the words of this north-American philosopher of science, we can suspect that, nowadays, the true, the authentic metaphysicists are scientists, since they are responsible for the elaboration and publishing of ideas that have no origin in the real, cannot be proved, and maybe never will be. In other words, the scientists seem to be, nowadays, the most responsible for the restoration of the value of metaphysics. Even if the great majority does not state this explicitly, their practice and results leave no room for discussion.

In his article, Toulmin analyzes the concern physicists of our time show with the beginning of the universe; a matter which, Toulmin himself remits to the Greek from the classical times and gets all the way to the present time – after going through characters like Kant. One of the main work fronts of cosmologists starting from the beginning of the 1980's is concentrated in the formulation of inflationary models, which could not only solve existing problems in the standard model, but also provide clues about how the first moments of the universe were. Yet, these models showed serious scientific difficulties, which made the original idea go through profound changes ever since the first time it was proposed – at least in the western scientific world – in 1981 by Alan Guth, and suffered serious epistemological difficulties, which is what made these ideas controversial. The main accusation directed to the inflationary models is that, because they were applied to areas where the values reached by energy are extremely high, they could never pass through the screen of experience (see Earman & Mosterín 1997, and Rothman & Ellis 1987).

If, as Torretti (1979) states that, scientific theories can change the significance of the philosophical principles, this must mean that the philosophical bases of the scientific theories can be changed; they would not be changed. This statement of Torretti seems to be natural, as there would be no reason to think that the philosophical component of theory would be the last one to remain intact, since this does not happen to mathematical, physical, and empirical (or observational) components. It has been acknowledged for some time that the mathematical structure, the physical component and the empirical content of a theory can be changed according to necessity. By using the word insight, Torretti seems to suggest that the statements of philosophical content would be important because they would constitute boundaries regarding the structure and behavior of nature during the elaboration process of scientific theories.

J. Merleau-Ponty thinks that there are two possible ways for philosophy to be interested in cosmology (Merleau-Ponty 2000). The first one concerns the intrinsic characteristics of this science and its methods. The second one concerns the task of placing scientific results of cosmology in a "more general picture" (these are the author's own words). However, what is this picture? How does this introduction take place? How is this picture composed (or built)? These questions are not answered by Merleau-Ponty in his article. Nevertheless, I believe that it is possible to interpret his statement as if it meant that, in cosmology it is not a simple thing to check a theoretical interpretation, or make sense out of observational results. For this to happen, it is necessary to dispose of a theoretical model, against which the observational results could be read and understood.

But, if this picture must exist before the observational results so that they can be understood, how can this picture be formed? A possible answer for this question can be given through the use of philosophical insights. However, within these pictures and especially due to the role that they perform, these insights receive a fundamental function, called principles. It is the philosophical insights that in the absence of empirical data tell us how nature behaves and what it is made of. While a science does not reach a level of maturity, the pictures would be basically formed by philosophical insights – some previous knowledge that can be used and employed by mathematical structures. However, the role and importance of these insights can undergo changes, as science grows more mature. This maturity can correspond to the progressive decrease of importance bestowed to the insights, according to what can be seen through the words of A. Albrecht:

> Of course, it is not uncommon to invoke philosophical arguments when one is trying to chart a way through unfamiliar territory. That is

> as true of the mainstream cosmology as it is of our detractors. The key to progress is that the philosophical arguments matter less and less as the data accumulate. (Albrecht 1999, p. 45)

It is important, however, to point out that these insights always play some kind of role in the theories. In other words, they are always present. If this interpretation of J. Merleau-Ponty's words is right, it seems to me that, strictly, it cannot be stated that there are two ways to philosophically approach cosmology. There is only one way, since the other one can imply changes of the first one. Or also, these two ways or paths, would be like the two sides of a coin, with the difference that the second way can have effects on the first one.

As we have seen, one of the main peculiarities of scientific cosmology is that it cannot refer to observations to justify its possibility of being, with all rights, a science. Due to the inescapable presence of the cosmological horizon "the Universe is divided for every observer into two parts: one part that is accessible and another that is not accessible to observations" (Rudnicki 1993, p. 169). To this same author, nobody has the right to demand everything in cosmology to be possible to observe. A resource extensively used by cosmologists to overcome this difficulty, is to resort to extrapolations of what they think to be valid for the possibility to observe regions, to the non-observable ones. To Rudnicki:

> The sole possibility of crossing the cosmological horizon is given by the power of human thinking. That cosmological principles form one possible pattern is just one example of such thinking. (Rudnicki 1993, p. 175)

If Rudnicki's words make sense, what makes it possible for them to be considered true by anyone is the fact that, cosmology is, above all, a rational science based on our rational capacity to overcome the limits imposed on us by the ordinary senses. Without the use of reasoning, there is no possibility of establishing cosmology as a branch of science. However, the history of science provides us with many examples of this problem, since every time reason excessively believed in its own capacity, mistakes were made. A philosophical analysis of the basis of scientific cosmology can, hence, help us to better understand the role that reason has in the process of elaboration of scientific theories. But it could also, and maybe this is its main lesson, alert us of the danger that an unlimited trust in the strength of reason represents. What a weird dilemma this is! Accepting it seems to be our destiny.

References

Albrecht, A. (1999), "Reply to 'A Different Approach to Cosmology'", *Physics Today*, April 1999, pp. 44-46.

Barrow, J.D. (1993), "Unprincipled Cosmology", *Quarterly Journal of the Royal Astronomical Society* 34: 117-134.

Boltzmann, L. (1997), "Uma Preleção Inaugural em Filosofia da Natureza", in *Escritos Populares-Ludwig Boltzmann*, Seleção, Introdução e Apresentação por Antonio Augusto Passos Videira, série Ciência & Memória (Observatório Nacional/MCT), n° 13/97, pp. 202-211.

Bondi, H. (1952), *Cosmology*, Cambridge: Cambridge University Press.

Chang, H. (1993), "A Misunderstood Rebellion – The Twin-Paradox Controversy and Herbert Dingle's Vision of Science", *Studies in History and Philosophy of Science* 24 (5): 741-790.

D'Espagnat, B. (s.d.), *Uma Incerta Realidade – O Mundo Quântico, o Conhecimento e a Duração*, Instituto Piaget, Lisboa, s.d.

Dingle, H. (1955), "Philosophical Aspects of Cosmology", in *Vistas in Astronomy* (edited by Arthur Beer), Vol. 1, London/New York: Pergamon Press, pp. 162-166.

Earman, J. & J. Mosterín (1999), "A Critical Look at Inflationary Cosmology", *Philosophy of Science* 66: 1-49.

Ellis, G.F.R. (1975), "Cosmology and Verifiability", *Quarterly Journal of the Royal Astronomical Society* 16: 245-264.

Ellis, G.F.R. (1990), "Innovation, Resistance and Change: The Transition to the Expanding Universe", in Bertotti, B., Balbinot, R., Bergia, S. & A. Messina (eds.), *Modern Cosmology in Retrospect*, Cambridge: Cambridge University Press, pp. 97-113.

Ellis, G.F.R. (1999), "The Different Nature of Cosmology", *Astronomy and Geophysics* 40: 4.20-4.23.

Fang Li Zhi & Li Shu Xian (1994), *A Criação do Universo*, Lisboa: Gradiva.

Gale, G. & J. Urani (1993), "Philosophical Midwifery and the Birth-Pangs of Modern Cosmology", *American Journal of Physics* 61 (1): 666-73.

Gale, G. & N. Shanks (1996), "Methodology and the Birth of Modern Cosmological Inquiry", *Studies in the History and Philosophy of Modern Physics* 27: 279-296.

Guth, A. (1997), *O Universo Inflacionário – Um Relato Irresistível de uma das maiores Idéias Cosmológicas do Século*, Rio de Janeiro: Campus.

Harrison, E. (1999), *Cosmology – The Science of the Universe*, 2nd ed., Cambridge: Cambridge University Press.

Hetherinton, N.S. (ed.) (1993), *Cosmology - Historical, Literary, Philosophical, Religious, and Scientific Perspectives*, New York/London: Garland Publishing.

Hoyle, F. (1962), *A Natureza do Universo*, Rio de Janeiro: Zahar Editores.

Kanitscheider, B. (1984), *Kosmologie – Geschichte und Systematik in philosophischer Perspective*, Sttugart: Reclam.

Kragh, H. (1996), *Cosmology and Controversy – The Historical Development of the two Theories of the Universe*, Princeton: Princeton University Press.

Lachièze-Rey, M. (1993), *Cosmology: A First Course*, Cambridge: Cambridge University Press.

McMullin, E. (1993), "Indifference Principle and Anthropic Principle in Cosmology", *Studies in the History and Philosophy of Science* 24 (3): 359-389.

Merleau-Ponty, J. (1965), *Cosmologie du Vingtième Siècle*, Paris: Gallimard.

Merleau-Ponty, J. (1983), *La Science de l'Univers à l'Âge du Postivisme: Études sur les Origines de la Cosmologie Contemporaine*, Paris: Vrin.

Merleau-Ponty, J. (2000), "Questions Philosophiques de la Cosmologie", *Épistémologiques (philosophie, science, historie)* 1 (1-2): 13-23.

North, J.D. (1965), *The Measuring of the Universe*, Oxford: Clarendon Press.

North, J.D. (1995), *The Fontana History of Astronomy and Cosmology*, New York/London: W.H. Norton & Co.

Popper, K.R. (a, s.d.), "Três pontos de vista sobre o conhecimento humano", in *Conjecturas e Refutações*, Brasília: Editora Universidade de Brasília, pp. 125-146.

Popper, K.R. (b, s.d.), "A Distinção entre ciência e metafísica", in *Conjecturas e Refutações*, Brasília: Editora Universidade de Brasília, pp. 281-321.

Raine, D.J. (1981), *The Isotropic Universe – An Introduction to Cosmology*, Bristol: Adam Hilger.

Ribeiro, M.B. & A.A.P. Videira (1995), "Cosmologia e Pluralismo Teórico", available in: <http://www.if.ufrj.br/~mbr/papers/sub-epcos.html>.

Ribeiro, M.B. & A.A.P. Videira (1998), "Dogmatism and Theoretical Pluralism in Modern Cosmology", *Apeiron* 15: 227-234.

Ribeiro, M.B. & A.A.P. Videira (1999), "O Problema da Criação na Cosmologia Moderna", in Susin, L.C. (ed.), *Mysterium Creationis – Um Olhar Interdisciplinar sobre o Universo*, São Paulo: Paulias, pp. 45-83.

Rothman, T. & G.F.R. Ellis (1987), "Has Cosmology Become Metaphysical?", *Astronomy* 15: 6-22.

Rudnicki, K. (1993), "Cosmological Principles", in Arp, H.C. *et al.* (eds.), *Progress in New Cosmologies: Beyond the Big Bang*, New York: Plenum Press, pp. 169-175.

Silk, J. (1980), *The Big Bang – The Creation and Evolution of the Universe*, San Francisco: W.H. Freeman and Co.

Torretti, R. (1979), "Mathematical Theories and Philosophical Insights in Cosmology", in Nelkowski, H. Hermann, A., Poser, H., Schrader, R. & R. Seiler (eds.), *Einstein Symposium Berlin*, Berlin/Heidelberg/New York: Springer, pp. 320-335.

Toulmin, S. (1988), "The Early Universe: Historical & Philosophical Perspectives", in Unruh, W.G. & G.W. Semenoff (eds.), *The Early Universe*, Dordrecht: Reidel, pp. 393-411.

Turner, M. & A.J. Tyson (1999), "Cosmology at the Millenium", *Review of Modern Physics* 71 (special Issue): S145.

Videira, A.A.P. (1995), "A Criação da Astrofísica na Segunda Metade do Século XX", *Boletim da Sociedade Astronômica Brasileira* 14 (3): 54-69.

Videira, A.A.P. (1997), "Notas Introdutórias ao Tema: As Relações entre Ciência e Filosofia na Passagem do Século XIX para o Século XX", in Dias, A.L.M., el-hani, C.N., de Santana, J.C.B. & O. Freire Jr. (eds.), *Perspectivas em Epistemologia e História das Ciências*, Feira de Santana: Universidade Estadual de Feira de Santana, pp. 11-24.

Videira, A.A.P. (1998), "A Gênese do Big Bang", *Ciência Hoje* 22 (145): 36-43.

Videira, A.A.P. (2000), "Para que servem as definições?", in *O que é Vida? Para entender a Biologia do Século XXI*, Rio de Janeiro: Relume Dumará/Faperj, pp. 16-29.

Videira, A.A.P. (2001), "Algumas Observações sobre a Questão da Cosmologia: Metafísica ou Ciência?", in Chagas Oliveira, E. (ed.), *Epistemologia, Lógica e Filosofia da Linguagem*, Feira de Santana: Universidade Estadual de Feira de Santana/Núcleo Interdisciplinar de Estudos e Pesquisa em Filosofia, pp. 43-60.

Videira, A.L.L. (2000), "De um Mundo sem História à História do Mundo: A Teoria da Relatividade Geral e o Nascimento da Cosmologia", *série Ciência & Memória (ON/MCT)*, nº 02/2000.

Videira, A.L.L. (2001), "O Estado da Cosmologia como Parte Integrante Legítima da Ciência Reforçado pela Emergência de Novas Questões e Desafios", Palestra proferida no I Simpósio Brasileiro de Filosofia da Natureza, Rio de Janeiro, 2001, 57 páginas.

Geometrical and Epistemological Aspects of the Schrödinger's Unified Field Theory

Víctor Rodríguez

Faculty of Philosophy and Humanities, National University of Cordoba (UNC)

Pedro W. Lamberti

Faculty of Mathematics, Astronomy and Physics, National University of Cordoba (UNC)/
National Scientific and Technical Research Council (CONICET)

1. Introduction

In this article, we analyzed certain aspects of the unified field theory developed by Erwin Schrödinger, from the perspective of his epistemological point of view and the evolution of his geometrical ideas. For this purpose, we make a schematic presentation, structured in such a way that the following aspects turn out to be apparent: a) philosophical and epistemological antecedents of his ideas, and the confluence of them in his late formulations on the unified field, and b) the evolution of his geometrical ideas and their incidence on his intellectual production in 1940. We finalized our paper with a brief conclusion.

2. The epistemology of Schrödinger

E. Schrödinger (1887-1961) is one of the most original and many-faced physicists of the XX Century. His scientific production presents very early important works, like his papers on General Relativity, and later on of the classical publication of Einstein of 1916 (see Lamberti and Rodríguez 2002), and a continuous activity of research on the nature of the physical universe until his last days. Late works like *Space-Time Structure, of 1950,* and *The Expanding Universe* (Schrödinger 1956), reflect in an elegant and clear way his old concern with the eventual geometrical background of a physical conception of the world. Naturally, his most known work is the one related to microphysics and in particular, to quantum mechanics.

Historians and philosophers of science have already extensively studied all of these facets. His reflections on physics have generated a voluminous literature. As an example of this, we have the two volumes of Mehra and Rechenberg (Mehra & Rechenberg 1987) dedicated to this author, on the historical development of the quantum theory.

His biographers, on the other hand, have elaborated profiles of his ideas associated to the diverse circumstances of his life, and some of them, such as Walter Moore (Moore 1989), have got an adequate equilibrium between his environment, his intellectual productions and his thought. Additionally, he has writings on different subjects that include topics so dissimilar like the Vedanta, Greek philosophy, or the nature of life from a physical-biological point of view. His philosophical interests, as erudite as diverse, make him a very special thinker of our epoch.

From all these contexts, and for the purpose of our work, we shall make a selection of epistemological topics oriented to give a framework sensitive to his scientific production of the decade of 1940 referred to theoretical physics, and especially to his unified field theory. A hypothesis that has guided this exploration is that in these works a considerable influence of his epistemological conception is perceived, and also it is possible to appreciate clearly the scope and limits, and a certain point of view about the nature of physics. The history of this discipline shows, in our view, strong thinkers that share this view in the XIX Century, just as did L. Boltzmann and H. Hertz (Baird, Hughes & Nordmann 1998, Lamberti & Rodríguez 2001). Schrödinger is not out of this tradition, because he received the early indirect philosophical influence from Boltzmann, through his old professor Exner, and the lecture of the *Populäre Schriften* of the Austrian physicist. Particularly, the influence of this scientist and philosopher seems decisive on his predilection for the adaptation of images to the mathematical notions that take part in the physical theories. Most of the classical questions about the nature of space-time were in the intellectual environment of the physicists of the countries of the center of Europe, at the beginning of XX Century. As it is known, the program of geometrization of physics had a strong support after the advent of the theory of general relativity.

We shall present a brief characterization of some aspects of Schrödinger's philosophical thought that have relevance to his philosophy of physics and, in particular, to his geometrical point of view. Naturally, given the goals of this work and the extension of it, we do not go into details related to the evolution of other ideas associated with the selected thematic core of analysis.

If we take into account just some of Schrödinger's monographs, like *Nature and the Greeks* (Schrödinger 1954), *Mind and Matter* (Schrödinger 1967), *Science and Humanism* (Schrödinger 1951), it is enough to realize about the difficulty for an adequate synthesis of his thought. Historians have found connections between his readings of Schopenhauer and the non-dualist philosophies of India, just to mention a very original part of his thought. It seems as though he found a certain parallelism between "the world as will and representation" as thought by this philosopher and his own way of thinking. It has been also studied his post-Kantian background in relation to his critical attitude towards "the thing in itself". He also openly recognizes the influence of other philosophers, like Spinoza, Mach, Semon and Avenarius on his thoughts. A subtle point about philosophical questions coming from scientists is the reach on the search of the influence they had with their specific scientific productions. In many cases, like with Schrödinger, in spite of his robust conviction about some philosophical arguments, the nexus with the papers of great scientific importance is not trivial. The limits accepted here are oriented toward the eventual epistemological background of his conception about the unification of the physical fields. The search for a unified field theory in physics has marked the research of several eminent physicists of the first half of the XX Century and, in our view, it exhibits in most of the cases under analysis an epistemological environment worthy of ulterior studies. In the case of Schrödinger, his interest is previous to his explicit proposals of a unified theory. Already in 1926, in his wave mechanics, his motivation to keep up a clear representation of space time emerged in an ostensible way. Scholars that have studied his thought, like de Regt (de Regt 1997), have focused their attention on the role of the concept of *Anschaulichkeit*, which we can translate as a subtle blend of the concepts of visualization and intelligibility. This concept plays an important role in explaining the realist or anti-realist background of the philosophy of our author. The doubts around this point are reinforced by the interpretation of the influence of Ernst Mach on his ideas. By "visualizability" we understand here the possibility of obtaining a space-temporal image of the world, trend that has a long tradition in classical physics. In the case of Schrödinger, his association of this concept with the possibilities of comprehension of a theory is direct: we can only understand a theory if we obtain an adequate space-temporal representation of it.

It is important to point out here that he does not consider the views of Mach and Boltzmann as mutually exclusive. He took from Boltzmann, and indirectly from Hertz, the concept of *Bild* that we can translate as image, painting, or representation. Among other things, Mach seduced him because of his view on the relation between perception and observational facts. In his own words,

> Boltzmann's idea consisted in forming absolutely clear, almost naïvely clear and detailed 'pictures' – mainly in order to be *quite* sure of avoiding contradictory assumptions. Mach's ideal was the cautious synthesis of observational facts that can, if desired, be traced back till to the plane, crude sensual perception (pointer reading). He was most anxious not to contaminate this absolutely reliable timber with any other one of a more doubtful origin.
> However, we decided for ourselves that these were just different methods of attack, and that one was quite permitted to follow one or the other provided one did not lose sight of the important principles

that were more strongly emphasized by the followers of the other one, respectively (Quoted in de Regt 1997, p. 466).

It is important to clarify that in Boltzmann the *Bild* did not represent yet an isomorphism between the theoretical image and the actual world. The relation was more subtle and similar to a methodological realism. Schrödinger chose this outlook, but added to it what has been called the "neutral monism" of Mach; basically, that body and mind do not differ in regard to its deep nature. To be more precise, as de Regt says (de Regt 1997), Schrödinger transformed the ontology of Mach, related to empirical elements, in a substantive monism, that is, that just exists a unique entity behind the empirical elements. In this sense, the *Anschaulichkeit* is more linked to our way of understanding reality than to the possible character of that reality. It would seem closer to a context of discovery than to a context of justification or, more specifically, to a general framework for a context of discovery. On this matter he comments

> Certainly the standpoint of *anschaulich* pictures, taken by de Broglie and me, is not yet far enough developed to account even for the most important facts. Moreover, it is quite probable that here and there we have taken a wrong turn, which must be left again (Quoted in de Regt 1997, p. 478).

It is our belief that, even though this philosophical position is not explicit in his works on the unified field in the decade of 1940, it shapes the epistemological environment that is implicit in the theoretical architecture of these essays. Moreover, in our view, this orientation allows him to have the freedom of choosing diverse conceptions about geometry; in particular, his approval of the strategy previously used by other authors of giving priority to the view that presupposes an affine geometry.

Even though his thought has suffered intellectual fluctuations, his epistemic valuation of continuity in relation to the conception of the physical world locates him as a relatively classical thinker in regards to a group of colleagues that visibly exhibited the growing influence of the quantum framework. But, in any case, it is not obvious the evolution of his idea around epistemological aspects of physics (see, for instance, Schrödinger 1995). There is a lot of work on Schrödinger's ideas around the years of 1925-1927, but the study of his posterior reflections on philosophy of physics is notably inferior. Already in the decade of 1920, he showed his doubts in relation to the epistemological status of the concept of causality (see Schrödinger 1929, Forman 1971), even coming to adopt a strongly acausal position at the atomic level. At that time he sustained the point of view that causality is just a convention. For him, as far as the physical laws are statistical, they do not require that certain individual successes be determined in a strictly causal way. Here it is clear the influence of Boltzmann's idea had on statistical thermodynamics. But he shows also the influence of Hertz, in particular, trough the notion of something adequate (*Zweckmässigkeit*) that was one of the criteria this author used for selecting representations. In this regard, Schrödinger says,

> In my opinion, this question (of causality) does not have to do with the real [*wirklich*] constitution of nature as it appears to us; it is instead a matter of adequacy [*Zweckmässigkeit*] and expediency [*Bequemheit*] of one or the other disposition of our thinking, with which we approach nature (Quoted in Bitbol & Darrigol 1992, p. 269).

The influence of this point of view on his conception of determinism is direct, even though when it is not an elementary view neither he adopts a naive realism, as we can appreciate in his comments on the works and perspectives of his colleagues in relation to the interpretations of quantum mechanics. In our opinion, it is highly feasible that his conception of the Ψ wave be the result of the tension between these two concepts. On this path, he seems to have accepted that the duality wave-corpuscle showed two ways of representation, the mathematical and the experimental. His discrepancy with the orthodox interpretation in regard to the concept of measurement in quantum mechanics seems to be a consequence of his viewpoint, but we will not go any further on this particular point given, since it is rather peripheral to our goal here. We brought up this point just to point out a style of thinking about some physical theories that, according to our view, goes on in his works on fields. In particular, with regard to these two modes of representation mentioned above, it is interesting to see the importance he gave to experimental results into the context of the highly formal developments of the unified field theory (Schrödinger 1943b).

An important aspect of his thought, partially inherited from Schopenhauer, and of his own interpretation of oriental philosophy, appears in his idea of the artificiality of the divisions between the world and the self. In our opinion, this interpretation crosses completely his unification program. However, as Bitbol comments (Bitbol 1991), it is convenient to attenuate the role of his philosophy on the domain of physics. If we consider his style of work in science, it seems attractive the idea that Schrödinger sustained two relatively incommensurable discourses with regard to quantum physics, and philosophy. In our interpretation, both versions are worthy of attention, seeming plausible that both views rise as referred to matters mainly methodological. Additionally, his conception of the world, been global, does not reflect direct simple connections with his scientific theories around the unification of fields. On this point, we want to clarify that another objective in this paper is to offer some details about the conceptions of this author on his ideal of unification, which is complementary to the excellent characterization that has been recently made on his late philosophy of quantum mechanics (Bitbol 1996).

Up to till now, we have described what we understand has been Schrödinger's epistemological position related to his proposal on the unification of physical laws. In the next section we will comment the main geometrical ideas that are underlying to his presentation of unified field theory.

3. The evolution of his geometrical ideas

Before describing Schrödinger's contributions to a unified field theory, we will comment the main milestones that marked the road toward a non-metrical formulation of the theory of electromagnetic and gravitational field. It seems very peculiar that, in spite of the fact that many important physicists had held in low esteem the affine geometrical framework as the adequate way to formulate a unified theory, in 1943 Schrödinger uses it to be the point of uprooting for his developments in this program of research.

3.1. Background

From a geometrical point of view, the basic variables of the general theory of relativity (GR) are the ten components of the metric of the 4-dimensional space-time, $g_{\mu\nu}$, $\mu,\nu=1,2,3,4$. The field equations of the theory, together with the specification of the distribution of matter in the space, give a "recipe" for the determination of the quantities $g_{\mu\nu}$. This way, a complete description of the gravitational field is obtained. As it is well known, immediately after the formulation of the theory of general relativity were attempts to obtain a mathematical generalization of the theory that would allow the inclusion of the other field known at that time: the electromagnetic field.

On the mathematical side, Levi-Civita had already noted at the beginning of XX Century that a fundamental entity to Riemannian geometry – and independent of the metric – is the affine connection, which prescribes the form in which a vector moves in a parallel way from one point to another in space-time. Formally, when carrying in parallel a vector of components A^μ along an infinitesimal path δx^ρ, the components of the vector change in

$$\delta A^\mu = -\sum_{\nu\rho} \Gamma_{\nu\rho}{}^\mu A^\nu \delta x^\rho$$

where the quantities $\Gamma_{\nu\rho}{}^\mu$ are the components of the affine connection. In Riemannian geometry one obtains a relation between the components of the metric and the components of the connection *via* the requirement that, when moving in a parallel way a vector, its module (length) is not altered. Another important point of Riemannian geometry is that the curvature tensor (Riemann tensor) is obtained from the quantities $\Gamma_{\nu\rho}{}^\mu$, independent of the existent connection between $\Gamma_{\nu\rho}{}^\mu$ and the metric $g_{\mu\nu}$. From a physical point of view, the curvature tensor is fundamental for writing the equations of general relativity.

These two facts led H. Weyl in 1918 to propose a theory in which the light rays were more fundamental objects than lengths and times (Weyl 1952). The way in which lengths and times are measured is given by the components of $g_{\mu\nu}$, while the propagation of light is determined by the rates of the components of $g_{\mu\nu}$. Geometrically, this means that Weyl gives an objective meaning to the relations of the lengths of two vectors (angles) instead of the module of each one of them. In particular, Weyl's affine connection requires that the parallel displacement keeps invariant the angle between two vectors, and not its lengths (as in Riemannian geometry). It is clear that to Weyl this is a purely formal supposition.[1] This determines the components $g_{\mu\nu}$ (with the exception of one factor) and four additional quantities ϕ_μ, that are physically interpreted as the electromagnetic potentials.

Arthur Eddington (1923) goes a little further with these ideas, and uses the affine connection as the only basic geometrical element of the theory, without considering the existence of a metric, which appears at the end as a deduced quantity. As was said above, the evaluation of the curvature tensor is carried out from the affine connection. Having got independence from the metric, Eddington allowed the Ricci tensor (derived from that of the curvature) to have a symmetrical part, and other anti-symmetrical (in "common" Riemannian geometry the Ricci tensor is symmetrical). In the Eddington theory the symmetrical part of the Ricci tensor is related to the gravitational field, whereas the anti-symmetrical part is related to the electromagnetic field. From a mathematical point of view, the affine connection (symmetrical) involves 40 quantities (the components $\Gamma_{\nu\rho}^{\mu}$). To its determination, Eddington proposes a functional $\aleph$ that depends upon these 40 quantities and a variational principle for this functional, which in turn lead to 40 equations for the $\Gamma_{\nu\rho}^{\mu}$. The structure of the quantities Γ to which he arrives corresponds to the Riemann theory with a modification that, in Einstein's words, "does not put aside from Riemannian geometry more than necessary". Finally, Eddington gives a particular form for the functional $\aleph$.

In the year 1923, Einstein criticizes Eddington's theory because in his view it is not a "simple and natural" recipe of how to determine the 40 quantities Γ, and intends to "cover this hole" proposing particular features for the functional $\aleph$ (Einstein 1923). With this, he gets to write field equations that involve just two constants that must

---

[1] Related to this point P. Bergmann remarks: "At the moment of the formulation of Weyl, the invariance of the line elements, $ds^2=\sum g_{\mu\nu} dx^\mu dx^\nu$, as well the invariance of the propagation of light, cannot be settled on solid physical (experimental) basis" (Bergmann 1976, p. 245).

be given through an experiment. In particular, he concludes that one of these constants must be "indefinitely small", because if that were not the case, every electromagnetic field would have an extremely large density of charge. Einstein worked several years with affine theories, until he expresses in 1927, after some vacillations,

> As a result of numerous failures, I have arrived to the conclusion that this road does not drive us to the truth.

In any case, this remark does not show the end of his motivation for affine theories. As a matter of fact, we find papers of Einstein in this line of work until the last years of his life (see, for instance, Pais 1982).

3.2. The contributions of Schrödinger

The first contact that Schrödinger has with Weyl's ideas of unification is in 1922 (Schrödinger 1922). In this work (more precisely, an unpublished note), he applies Weyl's concept of connection to an electron-proton system. He particularly explains the stability of the hydrogen atom by means of a *resonance* of the length of a vector that moves together with the electron. In this work he comments the following: "The equivalence of the generalization of Weyl to the general relativity and the rules of quantization of Bohr-Sommerfeld are a remarkable property".

Almost twenty years had to pass before Schrödinger was involved again with the problem of unification. In 1943, he begins to work on a unified theory of purely affine character (which means that the affine connection is the fundamental entity, and the metric is the derived concept) (Schrödinger 1943a). At the beginning of this work, Schrödinger ventures an explanation of why affine theories had failed up until that time: he speaks of an "esthetical displeasure" associated with the type of dependence of the Lagrangean of the theory (essentially, the quantity $\aleph$ mentioned above) with the components of the connection. After these considerations, he makes an exhaustive revision of affine geometry, studying then the features that should possess the Lagrangean on a physical basis. In his study of affine geometry, he carries out a totally general exposition. He liberates himself from the requirement that the components of the affine connection are symmetrical (that is, allows that $\Gamma_{\nu\rho}{}^\mu \neq \Gamma_{\rho\nu}{}^\mu$). Moreover, he considers the possibility that in the space time manifold there is more than one connection, which allows him to include other fields recently incorporated into physics: the meson field, and the Dirac field.

Schrödinger develops not only these "kinematical" aspects of the theory, but also proposes a functional $\aleph$ completely different to those considered up until that point in time. It is interesting to note also that the electromagnetism that emerges from Schrödinger's theory is different from Maxwell's theory. It is in this point where Schrödinger focuses on the eventual experimental verifications of his theory (Schrödinger 1943b, 1944). Basically, he looks for magnetic effects associated with the new theory in the Sun and planets. In one of his last works on the unified theory, Schrödinger expresses his satisfaction for the formal advances obtained in the theory. In this regard, he says:

> [...] I have at last completed a geometrical field theory on which I began work more than two years ago. Whether it is physically right or wrong [...] it must I think called the affine field theory since it rest almost entirely on the assumption that the fundamental connection of space-time is purely affine (Schrödinger 1946).

4. Conclusions

This exploration on the different facets of the intellectual production of Schrödinger has allowed us to establish certain connections between his scientific works related to the program of unification, and aspects of his epistemological and philosophical ideas. We have tried to show that the conception of this author on visual space-time representations of physics, together with the influence of epistemological points of view about the scientific method and its repercussion on the images of the world, played a very important role as a general framework for his strategy to tackle his unified theories, in the decade of 1940. This perspective of analysis does not exclude the incidence of other important factors, which may be alternative generators of strong motivations in the search for conceptual frameworks of theoretical physics. In this sense, it is perfectly feasible to intend another description, directly associated to the history of theoretical physics, of this scientific production of our author; for instance, more related to mathematics. We estimate that our small contribution has consisted in giving a complementary version which tries to integrate the motivations of this thinker around a unified theory with his continuous philosophical inquiry. In our view, this field of analysis is far from having been exhausted. The approach taken in this paper allows signaling a rich interaction between epistemology, and physics. Few scientists of the XX Century are as fructiferous as Schrödinger was to this purpose.

References

Baird, D., Hughes, R. & A. Nordmann (1998), *H. Hertz: Classical Physicist, Modern Philosopher*, Dordrecht: Kluwer.

Bergmann, P. (1976), *Introduction to the Theory of Relativity*, New York: Dover.

Bitbol, M. (1991), "Erwin Schrödinger: un filósofo entre los físicos", *Mundo Científico* 11 (111).

Bitbol, M. (1996), *Schrödinger's Philosophy of Quantum Mechanics*, Dordrecht: Kluwer.

Bitbol, M. & O. Darrigol (1992), *Erwin Schrödinger, Philosophy and the Birth of Quantum Mechanics*, Gif-sur-Yvette Cedex: Editions Frontieres.

de Regt, H. (1997), "Erwin Schrödinger, *Anschaulichkeit*, and Quantum Theory", *Studies in History and Philosophy of Modern Physics* 28 (4): 461-481.

Eddington, A. (1923), *The Mathematical Theory of Relativity*, Cambridge: Cambridge University Press.

Einstein, A. (1923), *Nature* 112 (2812): 448-449.

Forman, P. (1971), "Weimar Culture, Causality and Quantum Theory, 1918-1927. Adaptation by German Physicists and Mathematicians to a Hostile Intellectual Environment", *Historical Studies in the Physical Sciences* 3: 1-115.

Lamberti, P.W. & V. Rodríguez (2001), "¿Hay un programa de geometrización de la física en Hertz?", in Caracciolo, R. & D. Letzen (eds.), *Epistemología e Historia de la Ciencia*, Vol. 7, Córdoba: Universidad Nacional de Córdoba, pp. 250-254.

Mehra, J. & H. Rechenberg (1987a), *The Historical Development of Quantum Mechanics*, Vol. 5, part I, New York: Springer.

Mehra, J. & H. Rechenberg (1987b), *The Historical Development of Quantum Mechanics*, Vol. 5, part II, New York: Springer.

Moore W. (1989), *Schrödinger: Life and Thought*, Cambridge: Cambridge University Press.

Pais, A. (1982), *"Subtle is the Lord..." The Science and the Life of A. Einstein*, Oxford: Oxford University Press.

Rodríguez V. & P.W. Lamberti (2002), "Hertz, Schrödinger y la relatividad general", in Horenstein, N., Minhot, L. & H. Severgnini (eds.), *Epistemología e Historia de la Ciencia*, Vol. 8, Córdoba: Universidad Nacional de Córdoba, pp. 330-333.

Schrödinger, E. (1922), "Über eine bemerkenswerte Eigenschaft der Quantenbahnen eines einzelnen Elektrons", *Zeitschrift für Physik* 12: 13-23.

Schrödinger, E. (1929), "Was ist ein Naturgesetz?", *Naturwissenschaften* 17: 9-11.

Schrödinger, E. (1943a), "The General Unitary Theory of the Physical Fields, *Proceedings of the Royal Irish Academy* 49 A: 43-58.

Schrödinger, E. (1943b), "The Earth's and the Sun's Permanent Magnetic Fields in the Unitary Field Theory", *Proceedings of the Royal Irish Academy* 49 A: 135-148.

Schrödinger, E. (1944), "The Point Charge in the Unitary Field Theory", *Proceedings of the Royal Irish Academy* 49 A: 225-235.

Schrödinger, E. (1946), "The General Affine Field Laws", *Proceedings of the Royal Irish Academy* 51 A: 41-50.

Schrödinger, E. (1956), *Expanding Universe*, Cambridge: Cambridge University Press.

Schrödinger, E. (1954), *Nature and the Greeks*, Cambridge: Cambridge University Press.

Schrödinger, E. (1967), *Mind and Matter*, Cambridge: Cambridge University Press.

Schrödinger, E. (1951), *Science and Humanism*, Cambridge: Cambridge University Press.

Schrödinger, E. (1950), *Space-Time Structure*, Cambridge: Cambridge University Press.

Schrödinger, E. (1995), *The Interpretation of Quantum Mechanics*, Woodbridge: Ox Bow Press.

Weyl, H. (1952), *Space, Time and Matter*, New York: Dover.

Map of Interpretations of Quantum Theory

Osvaldo Pessoa Jr.

Department of Philosophy, Faculty of Philosophy, Literature and Human Sciences
University of São Paulo (USP)

1. General considerations

Quantum theory, i.e., the physics of the microscopic world, has a remarkable aspect associated to it, which is the existence of dozens of different "interpretations". Those who have some familiarity with this theory know that there is an "orthodox" interpretation, and that it is opposed to an interpretation with "hidden variables". The popularization literature makes frequent reference to a "many-worlds" interpretation, and in discussions about non-locality one sometimes writes that the interpretation Einstein gave to the world would be wrong.

How is it possible that there are so many different interpretations for a theory that is considered so fundamental? A bit of reflection shows that this situation, far from being pathological, should be considered common. An *interpretation* is usually understood as a set of theses or images that are added to the minimal formalism of a theory, without affecting in any way the observational predictions of the theory.[1] These theses make statements about the reality existing behind the observed phenomena, or furnish norms about the inadequacy of making such statements. Clearly, an interpretation is equivalent to a philosophical or metaphysical stance, which the scientist is free to choose.

The fact that the quantum theory refers to a domain of reality which is very distant from us (and did not play a selective role in the biological evolution of our cognitive apparatus) makes us consider it counterintuitive; since it is located at the limits of our knowledge, it is difficult to test any conjecture concerning the reality that lies behind our tenuous experimental measurements. Thus, it is natural that there are a great number of hypothetical constructions concerning the nature of this reality which hides behind the observations. In other words, there is a strong subdetermination of interpretation by the minimal formalism of the theory.

Once we have a general theory which is successful in making predictions and in explaining all kinds of measurements, the first guide for postulating what should be the nature of the underlying reality is the structure of the theory itself. If the theory makes use of a mathematical entity which is analogous to a wave, like the wave function $\psi(r,t)$ of Schrödinger's wave mechanics, then the "natural" interpretation of this theory is that there be a referent (in reality) for this wave function. There are other approaches to non-relativistic quantum mechanics that furnish the very same experimental predictions as wave mechanics, like matrix mechanics or Feynman's sum over histories. There are proofs that these approaches are mathematically equivalent, but still each approach "suggests", by means of the mathematical entities that are emphasized (waves, trajectories, possible trajectories), what are the real entities that have priority. Each mathematical formalism *suggests* a different ontology, each one has a different natural interpretation.

---

[1] It may happen that an interpretation makes predictions that are in disagreement with a theory, so that in this case one should speak of a "different theory"; however, if the disagreement is so small that one cannot make a crucial experiment to choose between the theories, then it is customary to consider that the different theory is also an "interpretation".

Still, there is nothing that forces a physicist that works with wave functions to believe or defend that such waves exist in reality. The "official" interpretation adopted by a scientist does not have to reflect the natural interpretation suggested by the theory[2]. In effect, there is nothing to force a physicist to defend any thesis whatsoever (concerning non-observable reality). If, in fact, he adopts this position of suspending his judgment about reality, that does not mean, however, that he lacks an interpretation concerning the theory, but that he adopts an interpretation which rejects associating a picture of the world to any non-observable part of reality. This attitude is known as *positivism* or, more precisely, as "descriptivism" (according to this view, science should only attempt to describe the observed reality, being "meaningless" to talk about that which is not observable). The orthodox interpretations of quantum theory are to a large extent positivist, while most of the alternative interpretations assert something about non-observable reality, an attitude that is known as *realism*. Any interpretation may be analyzed from the perspective of its degree of positivism/realism. In this paper, a classification of the interpretations of quantum theory is proposed, based on this distinction.

A second criterion for classifying interpretations concerns the proposed *ontology*. In the case of quantum theory, a fundamental ontological distinction is between particle and wave interpretations. This distinction reflects the more general dichotomy between "well-defined properties" and "smeared or fuzzy properties". What we call "wave" or "undulatory" interpretations (following Reichenbach, 1944) should be understood as views that do not attribute well-defined properties to certain quantum-mechanical magnitudes, such as position. What we call "particle" or "corpuscular" interpretations include views that attribute simultaneously well-defined values to any observable, including energy or spin component.

Most of the interpretations of quantum theory answer in a clear way to the following questions: "are there particles?", "are there waves?" Thus, there are three broad interpretative groups: *particle*, *wave*

---

[2] On the other hand, one may argue that there are "private interpretations" that the scientist uses, even without noticing, during his or her work, and which may differ from the "official interpretation" which he or she adopts publically (see Montenegro & Pessoa 2002).

and *dualism* (views that accept the existence of both), besides some approaches which avoid any ontological commitment. In this paper, a classification of all the interpretations of quantum theory is proposed, based on how each of them is located along the epistemological (positivism or realism) and the ontological axes (particle, wave, dualism or without ontology).

There is, however, a third axis that would be significant for classifying the interpretations, but whose elusive nature makes it difficult to apply. It consists of the "intentional" or even "emotional" aspect, which people attach to their interpretative positions. There are individuals who defend emphatically or even aggressively an interpretation, and the emotionally laden debate involving two or more parties may result in a "scientific controversy", which may even affect the professional or social levels. We will not use the *intentional-emotional* aspect in our classification of interpretations, although its relevance should be noted.

Consider the following interesting example of how the intentional-emotional aspect affects the cognitive area. Some authors propose new formalisms for quantum theory, introducing new concepts that might suggest an original "natural interpretation". However, if such authors are not interested in proposing a new interpretation, the theory is usually seen as part of the orthodox interpretation. A typical example is the approach of the Wigner distribution (see, for example, Freyberger & Schleich 1997), which introduces the concept of "negative probability". The positivist attitude of Wigner was to consider that such a concept is only a mathematical instrument, but if he had had a more realist attitude (concerning the natural interpretation of his approach), maybe he could have defended a "realism of potentialities" in which such a concept would refer to the "degree of impossibility" of a situation (Feynman 1987). In other words, a more thorough study of interpretations should consider not only situations in which scientists *declare* that they are presenting an interpretation, but also cases in which they *don't declare* even though they *could declared*.

2. Four broad interpretative groups

Following the comments made in the last section, concerning the classification of the interpretations based on the epistemological (positivism or realism) and ontological (particle, wave, or dualist) axes, one can form four broad groups of interpretations of quantum theory. In each of them, we will mention a "naïve" version, which has been used in Pessoa (2003) for an initial contact of physics students with this theory.

(1) *Wave interpretation (realist)*. This point of view considers that the quantum mechanical wave function corresponds to a reality, an undulatory or smeared out (fuzzy) reality, or maybe a potentiality. An undulatory view was explicitly defended by Erwin Schrödinger, but it was extremely hard for him to account for phenomena without the notion of "collapse". In a naïve version of the wave interpretation, the reality to which the wave function refers to would suffer collapses every time it interacted with a measurement apparatus. A conceptual problem is that such collapses are "non-local", that is, involving effects that propagate in an instantaneous way (see Einstein, in Solvay, 1928, p. 254). This view is similar to John von Neumann's, with the difference that the latter did not associate the wave function with reality (he had a positivist attitude: the wave function only represents our knowledge), so that non-locality was not problematic. The relative states interpretation of Everett (1957), the decoherence approach of Zeh (1993), and the spontaneous localization view (Ghirardi *et al.* 1986) are other examples of realist wave interpretations.

(2) *Particle interpretation (realist)*. This is the view according to which the microscopic entities (or at least those with nonzero rest mass) are particles, without an associated wave. This position was explicitly defended by Alfred Landé (1965-75), within the statistical ensemble interpretation. The great difficulty for the particle interpretation is in explaining the interference patterns obtained in experiments with electrons. In spite of this problem not being satisfactorily overcome, it is very common to find particle interpretations in literature and also, in a more naïve way, between students. Interpretations that attribute simultaneously well-defined values to incompatible observables (like position and momentum), and that don't introduce smeared magnitudes, are also classified as "corpuscular". An example is the interpretation implicit when using quantum logic.

(3) *Realist dualist interpretation*. This interpretation was originally formulated by Louis de Broglie, in his "pilot wave" theory, and ex-

tended by David Bohm (1952) to include also the measurement apparatus. The quantum object divides into two parts: a particle with a well-defined trajectory (but generally unknown), and as an associated wave (or a "quantum potential"). The probability for the particle to propagate in a certain direction depends on the amplitude of the associated wave, so that in regions where the waves cancel out there is no particle. In the naive level of an introductory course, this approach is free of the problem of non-locality, and the only conceptual problem is the existence of "empty waves", that don't carry energy. The problem of non-locality only appears when two correlated particles are considered, as shown by John S. Bell.

(4) *Positivist dualist interpretation*. This expression especially denotes the complementarity interpretation of Niels Bohr (1928), which identifies a limitation in our capacity for representing macroscopic reality. According to the experiment being made, one may use either a corpuscular description, or a wave picture, but never both at the same time (these excluding aspects, however, "exhaust" the description of the object). This does not mean, however, that the quantum object *is* a corpuscle or *is* a wave. According to any positivist interpretation (in the context of physics), one can only assert the existence of observed entities. To assert, for example, that "an unobserved electron suffers a collapse" would be meaningless. A wave phenomenon is characterized by the measurement of an interference pattern, and a corpuscular one by the possibility of inferring (or "retrodicting") a well-defined trajectory. The point-like aspect of every detection (considered by interpretation 2 as the best evidence for the corpuscular nature of quantum objects), which occurs even in wave phenomena, is considered the fundamental principle of quantum theory, and which Bohr called the "quantum postulate". There are many variations of this approach, constituting the so-called "orthodox" interpretations. More recently, one may mention the consistent histories of interpretations of R.B. Griffiths (1984), and Omnès (1992).

3. Key questions for distinguishing the interpretations

A criterion for distinguishing interpretations is to take note of the answers given by each one for different questions. We have developed this exercise in Pessoa (2003), and in the following we present some of the questions that were examined (in Pessoa 1998 we have already examined these same questions, explained through some detail experiments using electrons).

3.1. Two slit experiment

How to explain the behavior of a quantum, like a photon or an electron, in the two slit experiment? On the one hand, the photon or electron behaves like a particle, as it is detected in a point-like manner; on the other, it behaves like a wave, since the probability of it falling on each point follows an interference pattern. But how is it possible that an entity can be, at the same time, wave and particle, if such attributes are contradictory?

Question I: How to explain the two slit experiment for a single quantum?

(1) *Wave interpretation.* The photon or electron that passes through the two slits is, in reality, a wave, not a particle. In this way, it is easy to explain the formation of the interference pattern on the detecting screen. The appearance of a point on the detection screen occurs because of a "collapse" of the wave, which during the measurement is forced into a very narrow "wave packet", which has the appearance of a point particle.

(2) *Particle interpretation.* The photon or electron is in reality a particle, which is manifested in the point-like outcome of the detection. There is no associated wave: the interference pattern must be explained as the result of the momentum exchange between electron and diffraction grating (or of any other property involving the device used to separate and recombine the beam).

(3) *Realist dualist interpretation.* In reality there exists a particle (with well-defined trajectory) *and* an associated wave (which doesn't carry any energy), as postulated by L. de Broglie (1926) in his "pilot wave" theory. The probability of a particle propagating in a certain direction depends on the amplitude of the associated wave, so that in regions where the waves cancel out, there can't be a particle. This explains in a natural way the occurrence of interference fringes.

(4) *Positivist dualist interpretation.* According to Niels Bohr's complementarity interpretation, the "phenomenon" in question is undulatory (that is, the conceptual framework we use is in accordance with the physics of waves), and not corpuscular (we cannot infer the past

trajectory of a detected quantum). The point-like aspect that we observe as a result of detection is due to the "quantum postulate" mentioned above, which claims the existence of an *essential discontinuity* (an indivisibility) in any atomic process, as for example in the ionization of atoms in the detection screen.

3.2. Mach-Zehnder interferometer

Instead of using a double slit, it is possible to observe an interference pattern with a Mach-Zehnder interferometer. In this apparatus, developed for the use of light (there is a version for electrons, see Pessoa 1998), one splits the beam in two by means of a half-silvered mirror S_1, leading to paths A and B. These are then recombined in another half-silvered mirror, S_2. The result, in the case of perfect alignment, is that the whole beam unites again in a certain direction D_1, while in the other available direction, D_2, it disappears completely (destructive interference) (see Pessoa 2003, ch. 2).

What happens when only *one* photon or electron enters the interferometer? Quantum theory furnishes a simple answer: it will be detected with probability 1 (assuming perfectly efficient detectors and neglecting losses) in D_1 and with probability 0 in D_2. But what happens when the photon or electron is located *inside* the interferometer, before being detected? In this case, each interpretation will give a different answer.

Question II: What happens when the electron is inside the interferometer?

(1) *Wave interpretation*. The electron, which can be identified with a wave packet propagating in space, splits in two after the first half-silvered mirror S_1, in accordance with what classical physics of waves would predict. These "half electrons" would then recombine in S_2, and due to the destructive interference that occurs in the direction of D_2, the whole packet arrives in D_1. What remains to be explained is why half electrons are never detected (see the following section).

(2) *Particle interpretation*. Since the electron can never be split, it *either* follows path A (and nothing goes along path B), *or* path B (and nothing goes along A). However, if the electron moves with certainty along path A (which can be guaranteed by removing S_1), the probability of it being detected in D_2 is different from zero; and if it moves along B (introducing a reflector of electrons in S_1), the probability is

also different from zero. However, the probability of detection in D_2 is 0! Therefore, one cannot simply say that the electron went *either* by A or by B. A way out of this dilemma is to argue that the logic at the quantum level is of a non-classical type, thus invalidating the preceding argument (see Pessoa 2005).

(3) *Realist dualist interpretation*. This point of view also asserts that the electron is not split, but it escapes the aforementioned dilemma by postulating that the wave associated to the corpuscle splits in two in S_1 and recombines in S_2, leading to interference. The particle behaves like a "surfer" that can only move where there are waves; since the waves cancel out in the direction of D_2, the electron is forced to surf towards D_1.

(4) *Positivist dualist interpretation*. According to the view of Bohr, a phenomenon may be either undulatory or corpuscular, but never both at the same time. The examined experiment is a wave phenomenon; therefore it is *meaningless* to ask where the electron is.

3.3. Anti-correlation experiment

The two experiments previously examined are considered "wave phenomena" by the complementarity interpretation. Let us now see how the different interpretations explain a "corpuscular phenomenon".

Consider a beam of light which falls on a *single* half-silvered mirror S_1. Naturally, the beam will split in equal portions among paths A or B. It so happens that if there is only one photon, it will be detected *either* in D_A *or* in D_B (assuming perfectly efficient detectors), but never in both at the same time. This phenomenon is known as "anti-correlation". In other words, when detected, the photon maintains its individuality and does not have its energy divided. How do the different interpretations explain this phenomenon?

Question III: How to explain the anti-correlation experiment?

(1) *Wave interpretation*. After reaching S_1, the wave packet associated to the photon splits in two, which is expressed by the wave function $\psi_A + \psi_B$. However, once the photon is detected, say in D_A, then the probability of detection in D_B becomes zero instantaneously! The initial state is reduced, in this case, to ψ_A. Since, in this interpretation, the state corresponds to a "real" probability wave, one concludes that a process of *collapse* of the wave packet took place.

(2) *Particle interpretation.* In this case the explanation is straightforward: the particle simply followed one of the possible trajectories (*A* or *B*), ending up in one of the detectors, D_A ou D_B. One does not need to speak of "collapse".

(3) *Realist dualist interpretation.* This view also considers that, after S_1, the particle follows one of the trajectories *A* or *B*, falling on the corresponding detector. There might be an associated wave, which splits in two. The part that is not detected would be an "empty wave" that does not carry energy, and cannot be detected. This leads to a proliferation of entities, but without any undesirable observational consequence.

(4) *Positivist dualist interpretation.* Once the measurement is completed, the complementarity interpretation would consider this phenomenon as being corpuscular. Therefore, the photon can be considered a particle that followed a well-defined trajectory. Such an inference concerning the past history of the detected quantum is called *retrodiction*. When examining the uncertainty principle, both Bohr ([1928] 1934, p. 66) and Heisenberg (1930, pp. 20, 25) emphasized that retrodiction is a metaphysical hypothesis which does not need to be accepted (in spite of its acceptance not leading to any contradictions); however, when he defined "phenomenon", Bohr ended up making implicit use of this hypothesis.

3.4. The quantum-mechanical state

A main concept to be interpreted is that of a "state" $|\psi\rangle$. To what does this theoretical term refer? Let us see how each point of view approaches this issue.

Question IV: To what does the quantum state refer?

(1) *Wave interpretation.* Interprets $|\psi\rangle$ in a "literal" way, attributing reality to the state or to the wave function, and claiming that nothing else exists, besides what is described by the quantum-mechanical formalism. But what kind of reality is this? It is not an "actualized" reality, which we can observe directly. It is an intermediate reality, a *potentiality*, that establishes only probabilities, but that notwithstanding evolves in time as a wave. The biggest problem of this interpretation of state is that, for *N* quantum objects, the wave function is defined in a 3*N*-

dimensional configuration space: would that mean a 3*N*-dimensional reality?

(2) *Particle interpretation.* The state $|\psi\rangle$ is an essentially statistical description, which represents an average of all the possible positions of the particle. In technical language, the state represents a statistical "ensemble", associated to an experimental preparation procedure. Thus, this view considers that the quantum state represents an *incomplete* description of an individual object.

(3) *Realist dualist interpretation.* Considers that there exist "hidden variables" behind the description in terms of states; such variables are the positions and velocities of the particles. The state $|\psi\rangle$ expresses a real field in 3 dimensions that "guides" the particles. Such a "pilot wave", however, does not carry energy, because the energy is concentrated in the particle. The description given by the quantum state would be incomplete, and would only be completed with the introduction of the hidden parameters.

(4) *Positivist dualist interpretation.* Considers that the state $|\psi\rangle$ is only a mathematical instrument for making calculations and obtaining predictions (this view is called "instrumentalism"). Heisenberg (1958, p. 55) expressed this in a radical way by writing that the discontinuous change in the wave function is a "discontinuous change in our knowledge", which amounts to an *epistemic* view of the quantum state. The statistical ensemble interpretation (item 2 above) also shares this view; the difference, however, is that the complementarity interpretation considers that the quantum state is the most "complete" description of an individual quantum object. Emphasis is also given to *relationism*: the reality of a quantum phenomenon only exists in the relationship between a microscopic object, and a measurement apparatus.

3.5. Measurements in quantum physics

The historian of science Max Jammer defends the thesis that Bohr, before adopting the relationist stance, had an "interactionalist" conception: in general, a particle only acquires a well-defined value p_x of momentum (for example) after interacting with the measurement apparatus and the outcome p_x being obtained. Pascual Jordan (1934) expressed this in a more radical way: "we ourselves produce the results of the experiment" (see Jammer 1974, p. 161).

There is a certain consensus that the magnitude that is directly measured, either in measurements in classical or quantum physics, is *position* (velocity, momentum, etc. would be indirectly measured, from direct measurements of position and from the counting of events). Let us see, in this section, how the different interpretations consider the measurement of a magnitude such as the position x.

Question V: What can be said about the prior existence of a measured value of position x?

(1) *Wave interpretation*. In the case in which the quantum object is in a superposition of the position eigenstates (that is, the wave function $\psi(x)$ is not sharply peaked around a value of x), then one cannot attribute a well-defined value for position. After the measurement, assuming that the value x_0 was obtained, a collapse of the spread out wave to one sharply peaked around x_0 occurs (according to the projection postulate). After the measurement, therefore, one may attribute a well-defined value for position, but not before.

(2) *Particle interpretation*. In this interpretation, it is common to accept that the position measurements are *faithful*: they reveal the value of the position possessed by the particle before the measurement process. Furthermore, immediately after the measurement the position of the particle remains the same. However, in order to adequately explain experiments in which incompatible observables are measured in succession, one must admit that the measurement of position *disturbs* in an uncontrollable and unpredictable way the momentum of the particle. This, in fact, was the interpretation adopted by Heisenberg in his semi-classical derivation of the uncertainty principle (see following section).

(3) *Realist dualist interpretation*. According to this view, position measurements are faithful, revealing the value possessed before the measurement. Such a measurement introduces an instantaneous change in the associated wave, which affects the momentum in an unpredictable way (the change in the wave would depend on the microscopic state of the measurement apparatus, which is never known by the scientist).

(4) *Positivist dualist interpretation*. For an interpretation that tends to attribute reality only to what is observed, it is meaningless to ask what the position of the particle was before measurement. This is ex-

pressed by the "interactionalism" mentioned above with the quotation from Jordan. However, in its "relationist" version, the complementarity interpretation ends up adopting retrodiction. In this case, therefore, it is plausible to say, *after* the detection of a quantum in a certain position x_0 (for either particle or wave phenomena), that the position of the quantum object right before the measurement was x_0 (but *before* the measurement it is incorrect to say that "it has a well-defined but unknown position", since the detector may be quickly removed and an interference between the different paths may be introduced).

3.6. Interpretations of the uncertainty principle

To conclude this chapter, let us examine how the different interpretative groups account for the *uncertainty relations* for pairs of "incompatible" magnitudes, originally derived in 1927 by Heisenberg. To simplify the discussion, we will consider the relation involving position x and the momentum component p_x: $\Delta x \cdot \Delta p_x \geq \hbar/2$.

Question VI: What is the meaning of the uncertainty relation?

(1) *Wave interpretation*. Attributing reality only to the wave packet (without postulating the existence of point particles), Δx measures the extension of the packet, indicating that the position x of the quantum object is undetermined or not well-defined by a quantity Δx. Thus, the relation expresses a principle of *indetermination*: if x is well-defined, p_x is not well-defined, and vice-versa.

(2) *Particle interpretation*. The proponents of statistical ensemble interpretation tend to assert that it is possible to have simultaneous knowledge of x and p_x with good resolution. One way of doing this, for a free particle, would be first to measure p_x, assuming that this variable is conserved (since it is a "non-demolition" variable), and then measure x. Using the hypothesis that the position measurement is faithful (see previous section, item 2), one would have simultaneously well-defined values for x and p_x, right before the second measurement! In this way, according to this interpretation, the uncertainty principle would not prohibit the existence of simultaneous well-defined values for the same particle. What happens (following the argument of Margenau 1937, p. 361) is that if one prepares the same quantum state

$|\psi\rangle$ many times, and measures p_x and x for each preparation, then one would obtain values that vary from one measurement to the other. If these values are put in a histogram for x and p_x, one obtains the standard deviations Δx and Δp_x. Therefore, the uncertainty principle would be an exclusively statistical thesis, contrary to the claim of the other interpretations (see also Ballentine 1970).

(3) *Realist dualist interpretation*. According to this view, the particle always has simultaneously well-defined x and p_x but these values are unknown. If we measure x with good *resolution*, we necessarily have a large *uncertainty* or ignorance of p_x, because the measurement of x by a macroscopic apparatus disturbs in an uncontrollable way the value of p_x. In regards to the uncertainty principle, this interpretation is quite close to the corpuscular view seen above.

(4) *Positivist dualist interpretation*. We have seen that a phenomenon cannot be corpuscular and undulatory at the same time. In an analogous way, it would be impossible to measure simultaneously x and p_x with resolutions smaller than Δx and Δp_x given by the uncertainty relation. Curiously, the original argument given by Heisenberg to justify the uncertainty relations, by means of a gamma ray microscope, may be classified in interpretations 2 or 3 (being for this reason sometimes called a "semi-classical" argument). But since he shared a *positivist* thesis, according to only that which is observable has reality, he could conclude in this case (after the determination of position) that "it is meaningless" to speak of a particle with well-defined momentum.

4. The main interpretations of quantum theory

We have divided the interpretations of quantum theory into four broad groups, according to two criteria: (i) *Ontology*: what is the ultimate nature of physical reality? Is it particles, waves, or some kind of dualism? (ii) *Epistemology*: to what extent does the theory describe this reality? Does it only describe the reality that can be observed and measured (positivism) or does its theoretical concepts also correctly represent (or attempt to represent) a reality which stands beyond observation (realism)?

The four groups of interpretations obtained were: (1) Wave (undulatory), (2) Particle (corpuscular), (3) Realist dualist, and (4) Positivist dualist. The wave and the particle interpretations tend to be realist, but they also come in more positivist versions, and the transition between the different groups is quite smooth, as we will see. Let us start by comparing the division presented here with the usual classifications of interpretations.

In the chapters of his celebrated book on the philosophy of quantum mechanics, Max Jammer (1974) presents five groups of interpretations: (*i*) the semi-classical pioneering views, (*ii*) the complementarity conception, (*iii*) hidden variables theories, (*iv*) stochastic views, and (*v*) the statistical ones. One may also add a further group, suggested by Redhead (1987, ch. 2) and others: (*vi*) potentiality interpretations.

4.1. The first semi-classical theories

The pioneering *semi-classical* theories considered by Jammer are realist interpretations that appeared between the years 1926 and 1927. They consist basically of what we have called wave and dualist interpretations. The undulatory ones include the initial electromagnetic view of E. Schrödinger (1926) and the hydrodynamical interpretation of E. Madelung (1926), the latter being later developed by other physicists, including the Brazilian Mário Schönberg (1954). One of the dualist views was the pilot-wave theory of L. de Broglie (1926), abandoned the following year and rehabilitated in 1952.

Among the semi-classical theories, Jammer also includes the initial probabilistic interpretation of Max Born (1926), according to which $|\psi(r)|^2$ expresses the *probability* of finding *one classical particle* in a certain region. In order to explain interference phenomena, such a particle would be accompanied by a "ghost field" (term used by Einstein), a "probability wave" which would propagate in space. This renders the dualist view, although Jammer preferred to consider it corpuscular.

Subsequently, this interpretation of Born was weakened, and $|\psi(r)|^2$ became the probability of *measuring* a quantum by means of a detector located in a certain region. Since this thesis was incorporated into the minimum formalism of quantum theory, we shall call it "Born's rule" (and not "Born's probabilistic interpretation"). Strictly speaking, Born's rule shouldn't even refer to "probability", but rather to "relative frequency", which is the directly observable datum in the empirical basis. To consider that the relative frequency is a "probability" is, strictly speaking, an *interpretation* of the formalism. Accepting this interpretation of quantum theory (as is usual), one arrives at different views of the quantum world, according to the interpretation adopted for the notion of probability (within the theory of probabilities).

4.2. The complementarity interpretation

The interpretation taken to be the most widespread among physicists is the *complementarity interpretation* developed by Niels Bohr in the years 1927-35, whose theses were presented above as representation of the positivist dualism. It is also known as the Copenhagen interpretation, referring to Bohr's hometown and where Heisenberg worked at the time, and also where Pauli met them in June, 1927, to reconcile their divergent opinions. Heisenberg had written his famous paper on the uncertainty principle, emphasizing a corpuscular perspective. Bohr, who had developed his idea of complementarity during a skiing trip to Norway, in March, found several mistakes in the paper, and emphasized that both a wave and a particle picture were necessary to derive the uncertainty principle. Pauli and Bohr succeeded in convincing Heisenberg that complementarity was consistent with the uncertainty principle, and thus was born the new interpretation that soon would become consensual in the community of physicists, leaving behind the semi-classical views mentioned in the previous section.

The *principle of complementarty* claims that an experiment can be represented either in a corpuscular picture, or in an undulatory picture, according to the situation. To say that such representations are complementary means that they are mutually exclusive, but together they exhaust the description of the atomic object. An experiment is in accordance with a corpuscular representation if it is possible to infer the past trajectories of the detected quanta. It is in accordance with a wave representation if it presents an interference pattern. It is an empirical thesis (that is, a thesis for which acceptance does not depend on the adopted interpretation) that a same experimental setup cannot exhibit both clear interference patterns and unambiguous trajectories (see Pessoa 1998).

Why wouldn't it be possible to encompass a quantum object in a more general single picture? Because, according to Bohr, we are limited by the language of classical physics, the language we use to communicate to others how an experimental arrangement is set up and what are the results of measurements taken, the language that describes the macroscopic world. We can only have access to the quantum world by means of apparatus describable in classical language. Would this imply *macrorealism*, that is, the thesis that macroscopic objects (like Schrödinger's cat) cannot exhibit quantum properties? Not necessarily: what Bohr defends is that it is always necessary to use a classical apparatus to measure quantum properties, but parts of this apparatus may be treated as a quantum system.

As mentioned in section 3.1., Bohr's starting point was the "quantum postulate", which attributes to any atomic process an "essential discontinuity" or "individuality". According to Bohr, one consequence of this is the impossibility of controlling or predicting the disturbances arising in the quantum object due to the interaction with the measurement apparatus.

In 1935, Einstein, Podolsky & Rosen (EPR) published their famous article in which they argued that quantum mechanics is an incomplete theory (a thesis shared by the statistical ensemble interpretation). The argument involved a pair of correlated particles located at a distance from each other. Assuming that the measurement operations in one of the particles could not instantaneously affect the other particle (the thesis of *locality*), they concluded that there would be elements of reality which quantum theory could not describe (and in this sense it would be incomplete).

To answer EPR, Bohr had to refine his interpretation, giving emphasis to the *wholeness* which encompasses the experimental setup and the quantum object, and coining the term "phenomenon" to refer to an instance of this wholeness. Thus, even if an apparatus has parts which are separated at a great distance, a change in one of these parts would modify the wholeness of the phenomenon, modifying the elements of reality. Therefore, there would not be any elements of reality that are not describable by quantum mechanics: the theory would be complete. The essence of Bohr's argument seems to have been the (not very explicit) rejection of the notion of locality of Einstein, with his conception of wholeness (see Bohr 1949). The change of a distant part of the apparatus followed by a measurement would result in an instantaneous modification of the overall wave function. However, since the wave function does not refer to reality (according to this interpretation), this would not violate in an explicit way the assumption of locality (only in 1952, with Bohm, would such an assumption be explicitly questioned).

Thus, in his answer to EPR, Bohr gave priority to the wholeness involving apparatus and object, resulting in a "relationist" conception, according to which the quantum state is defined by the relation between the quantum object and the whole measurement apparatus.

In section 4.7., we will survey these and other opinions of the founders of quantum mechanics, which form the group of views which constitute the *orthodox interpretations*.

4.3 Hidden variable theories

Hidden variable theories are proposals that introduce additional parameters to quantum theory. Such parameters are not directly observable, but their values are taken to determine in a unique way the result of a measurement and, on the average, they furnish the expected values of quantum mechanics. According to Jammer, the Russian J.I. Frenkel, Born's assistant, sketched an interpretation of this kind in 1926. In 1932, von Neumann presented his famous proof of the impossibility of hidden variables, but such a proof did not encompass all the possible types of hidden variables theories, as J.S. Bell would show clearly only in 1966. Von Neumann's proof did not consider, besides other things, the possibility that the hidden variables belong to the measuring apparatus.

This was the property (called *contextualism*) that rendered possible the realist dualist interpretation of David Bohm (1952). Writing the wave function as $\psi(x) = R(x)\exp[iS(x)/\hbar]$, where S and R are real functions, Bohm assumed that $\psi(x)$ described an ensemble of particles with position x and momentum given by $p = \nabla S(x)$. Position and momentum would thus be the hidden variables of his interpretation. He then obtained the Newtonian equation of motion, $ma = \square \nabla V(x)$, where the $V(x)$ is the sum of the classical potential function and the *quantum potential* $U(x)$, which has the following form: $U(x) = \square\, (\hbar^2/2m)\, \boldsymbol{\nabla}^2 R(\boldsymbol{x})/R(\boldsymbol{x})$. Note that even if the absolute value R of the wave function has a small value (corresponding to a distant tail of ψ), the potential might have a significant value (since R appears both in the numerator and in the denominator). The potential $U(x)$, which expresses the undulatory aspect of the model, has the property of "non-locality" (that is, it acts in an instantaneous way even at long distance), besides not having a definite source. More recently, there has been an interest in "Bohmian mechanics", but the quantum potential has been treated in a non-realist manner, as an unnecessary hypothesis (see Cushing *et al.* 1996).

The *pilot wave interpretation* proposed by L. de Broglie in 1926-27 is formally similar to Bohm's for a single particle, but differs for more particles. For de Broglie, the particle is considered a "singularity" of its own field ψ (behaving like a soliton), and the waves of this field propagate in the physical 3-dimensional space, and not in configuration space, as for Bohm. One experimental consequence of this interpretation has been proposed by Croca *et al.* in 1990, but its prediction has been refuted by Wang, Zou & Mandel (1991), which falsified the pilot wave interpretation in 3-dimensional space.

Interpretations which introduce hidden variables may be corpuscular, undulatory or dualist, or they lack a physical interpretation. The Bohm & Bub (1966) theory, for example, introduces an additional Hilbert space (without a physical interpretation), in such a way that the vector in this space (distributed in a random manner) is the hidden variable (see Belinfante 1973).

4.4. Stochastic interpretations

Stochastic interpretations are hidden variable theories that are inspired by the theory of Brownian motion, and by the fact that the Schrödinger equation is formally identical to a diffusion equation with an imaginary coefficient. Such theories are essentially classicist, and are usually corpuscular and attempt to be local. For F. Bopp (1954), the matter waves of quantum physics are the result of the collective motion of submicroscopic particles (as in the case of sound). More recently, the so-called "stochastic electrodynamics" has retained the corpuscular ontology for particles with mass, but considers light as a classical wave with boundary conditions which include fluctuations in the electromagnetic vacuum (Boyer 1975). Usually such interpretations are able to derive the Schrödinger equation, but have difficulty in explaining the measurement process (see survey in Ghirardi *et al.* 1978).

4.5. Statistical ensemble interpretation

The *statistical ensemble* interpretations (or simply "statistical interpretations") assert that the wave function does not refer to an individual system, but to an ensemble of systems prepared in a similar way. The American physicists J. Slater (1929) and E. Kemble (1937) defended such views, which became quite popular in the Soviet Union (Blokhintsev), as a reaction against the subjectivism of the orthodox interpretations. K. Popper, H. Margenau and A. Landé are other thinkers associated with this view, and the latter declared explicitly: "Particles, yes! Waves, no!" The notions of "wave-particle duality", and also that of "collapse of the wave packet", are rejected by this corpuscularist view.

L. Ballentine, in an influential paper published in1970, defended that the statistical ensemble interpretation does not have to commit itself to an ontology, which led to the distinction between: (*i*) a *"minimal" ensemble interpretation*, which adds to the minimal formalism of the theory only the thesis that the state represents an ensemble, leaving open the question of the nature of the elements of this ensemble; (*ii*) and an interpretation involving hidden variables, usually corpuscular, which is sometimes called *ensemble interpretation with intrinsic values*. The latter is clearly realist, while the former is more positivistic (for an example of a positivist ensemble interpretation, see Park 1973).

Maybe the most attractive aspect of the ensemble interpretation is its analysis of the uncertainty principle, presented in section 3.6.

The greatest difficulty of any corpuscular view is explaining interference experiments. Landé (1965-1975) argued that this explanation can be based on an old proposal of W. Duane (1923), according to which there is a discrete transfer of momentum from the crystalline lattice (which causes diffraction) to the particle (which is diffracted). Such an explanation, however, does not work for interference experiments which do not involve rigid lattices, such as the electron biprism (as pointed out by Rosa 1979; see also Home & Whitaker 1992).

4.6. Potentiality interpretations

Michael Redhead (1987) has classified the interpretations of quantum mechanics into three main groups, according to the answer given to the following question (compare with section 3.5): what can be said about the value of an observable Q, when the system is not in an eigenstate of the corresponding operator? (View A:) Hidden variable theories claim that Q has a well-defined but unknown value. (View C:) Complementarity asserts that the value of Q is not defined or is "meaningless". (View B:) The last group suggests that Q has a not well-defined value, a diffused, smeared out or fuzzy value.

This latter view B proposes, according to Redhead, that, in reality, the system does not possess well-defined values, but propensities or *potentialities* for producing different measurement results. This Aristotelian notion, of potentialities that are actualized during measurement, appear in the writings of Heisenberg in the 1950's, which may be classified as an orthodox interpretation. The idea is also formulated by Margenau (1954), with his "latent" magnitudes (ensemble interpretation). Redhead concludes that this is a realist view.

Such notion of potentiality or intermediary reality can also be attributed to the interpretations that we have called "undulatory". It will be argued, in section 4.8, that this is an important class of interpretations, although books like Jammer (1974) tend to omit this group (Jammer describes some of these interpretations in different chapters of his book). The notion of potentiality is also close to the "implicate order" recently proposed by David Bohm.

It is curious that different classes of interpretations (which we have called corpuscular, wave and positivist dualist) make use of this notion of potentiality, or potential reality.

4.7. The orthodox interpretations

We will now survey the slight differences that exist between different interpretations usually classified as "orthodox". Generally, they have a commitment with *dualism*, but the boundaries with corpuscular interpretations, on the one hand, and wave interpretations, on the other, are rather diffuse. Most of them also present a positivistic attitude, but once again the boundary with realist dualism is smooth.

(a) *Complementarity interpretation*. This is the "Copenhagen interpretation" which is defended by Bohr since 1927, and with a greater emphasis on relationism since 1935 (see section 4.2.). Pauli and Rosenfeld kept very close to this view, while Heisenberg and Born stood a little farther away. The positivist stance is expressed by the impossibility of attributing a type of phenomenon (wave or particle) to an experiment before the measurement is completed. However, after the measurement is completed, Bohr accepted the use of retrodiction.

(b) *Positivist wave interpretation*. This term refers to the position assumed by von Neumann (1932), by Wigner (1963), and by many theoretical physicists. Emphasis is given to the state vector $|\psi\rangle$, which is reduced (collapses) after measurements; even the measurement apparatus is described by a state vector. This position is sometimes called the "Princeton interpretation". It does not explicitly attribute reality to $|\psi\rangle$ (in this sense, it is positivist), but the calculations are as if $|\psi\rangle$ corresponded to a reality.

(c) *Subjectivist interpretation*. This is the approach adopted by London & Bauer (1939), occasionally defended by Wigner (1962) and some others (like Jeans, Eddington, and Heitler), and which reappeared in the 1990's (for example, with H. Stapp). Adopting an undulatory view, it argues that human consciousness is responsible for the collapse. In the words of London & Bauer: "the irreversible transformation in the state of the measured object" would be due to the "faculty of introspection" or to the "immanent knowledge" that the conscious observer has of his own state. This position is a development of view (b), while $|\psi\rangle$ may be treated as a real entity. In this case, it is not a positivist (descriptivist) view, but an idealist one, in the sense that the reality described by quantum mechanics depends upon the presence of a human observer.

(d) *Macrorealist complementarity interpretation*. The Russian school that defended complementarity (Fock 1957, and Landau, according to Bell 1990, section 6) did not accept the position of Bohr and von Neumann, according to which the boundary between the classical and quantum worlds could be drawn at any point in the chain connecting the object to the *observer* ("psychophysical parallelism"). In a more objective way, this Russian school attributed attributed classical properties to macroscopic objects in general. A similar position was proposed by Ludwig (1961), who postulated that non-linear corrections to the Schrödinger equation would impose classical behavior for macroscopic bodies.

(e) *"Eclectic" interpretation.* Jammer (1974, p. 68) attributes to Heisenberg the following position, in the beginning of 1927: both an exclusively corpuscular and an exclusively undulatory interpretation could be associated to the quantum mechanical formalism. In 1930, Heisenberg still thought along these lines, but stressed that each representation had its limitations. This eclecticism is sometimes adopted in quantum field theory to explain both the success of Feynman's corpuscular view and of Schwinger's undulatory approach.

(f) *Realist readings of complementarity.* This is a path to be explored in the future. In 1927-1928, Bohr presented the principle of complementarity by opposing "definition" (a pure state of a closed system) e "observation" (a measurement renders the system open and introduces indeterminism). However, he dropped this characterization since it did not make sense for positivism to refer to a non-observed system. Realist readings, however, make pick up this type of complementarity again. David Bohm, in his text book of 1951, also made a more realist reading of complementarity (failing in a few points), stressing that unpredictability is connected to the coupling of the quantum object to the Universe as a whole (during measurement). In another direction, realist readings of complementarity lead to paradoxical situations, such as the assertion that "the photon knows what will be the future experimental setup", which helps to increase the mystery of quantum theory for the larger public. John Wheeler makes this kind of realist reading, concluding (in the delayed-choice experiment, due to retrodiction) that "the past does not have existence while it is not registered in the present" (Wheeler 1983, p. 194).

(g) *Radical instrumentalism.* In a review of possible interpretations of the measurement problem, Wigner (1983) mentioned the view according to which the aim of quantum mechanics would not be to describe reality, but to furnish statistical correlations between successive observations. This "instrumentalist" point of view is quite common among physicists, radicalizing the positivism of the orthodox interpretation and the epistemic view of the quantum state. J. Park (1973), a former student of Margenau, arrived at this position from the statistical ensemble interpretation: "Quantum Mechanics is a theory about the statistics of measurement results".

(h) *Stroboscopic interpretation.* Within the latter radical view, one may place a *stroboscopic* corpuscular interpretation, according to which the particles in nature give discontinuous leaps from one position to the other, according to macroscopic track left by the particles, for example, in a Wilson cloud chamber. Heisenberg (1927, p. 63) discusses this possibility, stressing that in this case an instantaneous velocity is not well defined (see also Bohm 1951, p. 144-148).

(i) *S-matrix interpretation.* Another instrumentalist version is the interpretation given by the S-matrix theory. This approach describes scattering processes by considering only the asymptotic initial and final states, and S-matrix which relates one to the other. Under certain conditions, one can show that this approach is identical to the use of the Schrödinger equation, having however the advantage of being easily extended to the relativistic domain (Stapp 1971).

(j) *Sum over histories interpretation.* In 1948, Feynman presented his "sum over histories" approach, developed in relativistic quantum field theory, as a new interpretation for quantum theory. A particle would follow all possible paths, and the wave function would be a sum of these amplitudes (histories). This approach stresses a corpuscular representation, but it is worth investigating up to what point it is not an undulatory view.

4.8. Wave interpretations

The wave (or undulatory) interpretations consider that the quantum state corresponds to some kind of reality (in opposition to the orthodox views), and deny the existence of point particles that follow continuous trajectories. Thus, in agreement with the complementarity interpretation, and contrary to the ensemble, stochastic and realist dualist interpretations, they accept that the description by means of the quantum state is complete, and that systems prepared in the same state are in fact identical.

Max Born, on a certain occasion, defended the reality of $|\psi\rangle$ when he wrote: "I personally like to consider a probability wave, even in $3N$-dimensional space, as a real thing, certainly more than an instrument for mathematical calculations. For it has the character of an invariant of observation" (Born 1949, pp. 105-106). In opposition to this, but for the same reason, Heisenberg (1958, p. 129) prefers to consider the ψ wave as something "objective", but not "real".

In the last decades, there has been an increase in the number of interpretative proposals that are akin to the undulatory view, assuming that the wave function corresponds to a reality. A positivist argument used against this view is that one cannot attribute reality ψ because it would be impossible to determine the quantum state from a single measurement. Attempting to refute this argument, Aharonov et al. (1993) proposed a new kind of measurements, called "protective", that would allow the determination of the quantum state. Such a proposal, however, has been much criticized.

Let us now give an overview of the tradition of wave interpretations, the unity of which has received little attention (one member has already been examined in section 4.9.c).

(a) *Electromagnetic interpretation*. In Schrödinger's original proposal (mentioned in section 4.1.), $e|\langle\psi_i|\psi\rangle|^2$ represented a classical charge density (where e is the system's total charge), so that one would have "matter waves" and not "probability waves". Such waves would propagate in a deterministic way, recovering classical visualization. Particles would be, in reality, wave packets.

The arguments presented at the time, which undermined this proposal were: (*i*) *High dimensionality of ψ*. For N particles, $|\psi\rangle$ is defined in $3N$-dimensonal configuration space. How could this be interpreted? (*ii*) *Particles as wave packets*. Wave packets disperse as time goes by, contrary to what happens in the special case examined by Schrödinger, in the quantum-mechanical harmonic oscillator. (*iii*) *Discreteness of atomic processes*. How to explain quantum leaps, charge quantization, and how to associate discrete atomic frequencies to discrete energies ($E=h\nu$)? (*iv*) *State reduction during measurement*. How to explain the apparent state collapse that occurs during measurements, expressed by the projection postulate, and the non-locality that is involved?

More recently, some authors have reexamined Schrödinger's original proposal, offering solutions to the problems mentioned above (Dorling 1987, Barut 1988). Some of these solutions will be mentioned below.

(b) *Hydrodynamical interpretation.* Starting from Schrödinger's equation and writing $\langle \psi_i | \psi \rangle = \alpha\, e^{i\beta}$, Madelung (1926) obtained a hydrodynamical equation for α, thus suggesting that a fluid with distributed charge and mass composes the basic structure of the world. Such an approach would be reconsidered by Bohm (1952), who added a new particle. Bohm & Vigier (1954) presented a hydrodynamical model in which the fluid is coupled to stochastic fluctuations at a subquantal level (see Jammer, 1974, pp. 33-38, 49-54).

(c) *Naïve wave interpretation with collapses.* A realist undulatory view may be obtained by adapting von Neumann's positivist interpretation (section 4.7.b). In this case, collapses would be real processes, the causes of which could be associated to resonances due to the interaction of the apparatus with the environment, or simply accepted in an *ad hoc* way. Non-locality would be present both in the process of collapse and in measurements of correlated particles associated to Bell's theorem.

(d) *Relative states interpretation.* In 1957, H. Everett postulated that the universe as a whole could be described by a single wave function that evolves deterministically, according to Schrödinger's equation. The apparent collapse associated to measurements would, in reality, be an illusion, linked to the fact that our brain is also coupled to quantum objects. The brain would participate in a superposition of states associated to different readings of the measurement results, and each one of these "memory configurations" would not have access to the others. The world would branch out in this way in many parallel worlds, during each measurement. In spite of the apparent absurdity of this interpretation, it raised a lot of interest around 1970 (DeWitt 1970), and today it has generated once again much discussion, with David Albert and others, in different variations: many worlds, many minds, and bare theory (see Barrett 1999).

(e) *Wave interpretation with decoherence.* The "decoherence" approach attempts to explain the emergence of classical behavior in a quantum system (for example, after measurements) from the interaction between object, apparatus, and environment. Authors like Zurek have initially placed themselves closer to the complementarity interpretation, while others like Zeh & Joos adopted an undulatory view. Zeh (1993) has asserted that "There are no quantum leaps, and there are no particles!" The approach of these authors offers a solution to problem (*ii*) mentioned in entry (*a*) above: as a free wave packet disperses, collisions with other particles induce a "localization" of the system (which, however, ceases to be in a pure state).

(f) *Spontaneous localization interpretation*. Ghirardi *et al.* (1987) and also Gisin & Percival (1992) have attributed reality to the wave function, but assume that the process of collapse (for a wave packet narrowly centered on a certain position) is spontaneous or stochastic (which places this approach also within the stochastic interpretations). In order to eliminate subjectivism, they suppose that all the particles have a very small probability of suffering a localization, which would not affect the validity of Schrödinger's equation for few particles. In the case, however, in which a macroscopic object couples to a measurement apparatus with octillions of particles, the probability of localization becomes very large, thus explaining the state reduction that accompanies direct measurements of position.

(g) *Transactional interpretation*. This approach is based on the "transaction" between an emitter and an absorber, which takes place by means of retarded waves (the usual ones) and advanced waves (which propagate with negative energy towards the past), according to the proposal of Wheeler & Feynman (1945). This interpretation of quantum mechanics developed by Cramer (1986) is temporally symmetric, non-local, and considers that the wave function is a wave in a 3-dimensional space.

4.9. Interpretations that question classical logic

In this section, we grouped some of the views that propose modifications of classical logic in order to explain the interpretative problems of quantum mechanics. What they have in common, besides questioning different aspects of classical logic, is certain sympathy for the attribution of well-defined values for all observables, which brings them close to corpuscular views or to hidden variables theories.

(a) *Quantum logic*. Since the pioneering work of G. Birkhoff & von Neumann (1936), it is common to assert that the logic of the microscopic world is of a special type, called "non-distributive logic" (see for instance Hughes 1981). Such a conclusion is defensible, but it presupposes a corpuscular interpretation (dispersion-free values) for quantum theory.

(b) *Operational approach*. A certain approach to quantum logic (that does not assume a corpuscular ontology) considers the theory not as a description of physical nature, but as a description of the behavior of a scientist while he prepares and measures microscopic objects in the (Foulis & Randall 1974).

(c) *Modal interpretation*. In a broad sense, this name applies to any interpretation that is inspired by modal logic, which makes use of the categories of "possibility", and "necessity". More specifically, it refers to the interpretation proposed by Kochen (1985), which considers the problem of what are the *properties* (that is, what are the observables with well-defined values) of a subsystem that is quantically correlated with another (making use of Schmidt's decomposition theorem). Such a relational realism (the properties exist in relation to the chosen environment) furnishes an explanation to the EPR paradox without assuming non-locality.

(d) *Consistent histories*. A "history" is a series of well-defined properties occurring in an temporally ordered sequence (for exemple, $p_x(t_1)$, $x(t_2)$, $p_x(t_3)$). In 1984, R. Griffiths introduced the notion of "family of consistent histories", to which one may attribute a probability to each history. Given an initial event D and a final event F, this approach furnishes a probability for the occurrence of a history of intermediary events E_1, E_2, etc. If the initial event D is $S_x=+½$ (after the measurement of spin in the x direction) and the final F is $S_z=+½$ (after a measurement of spin in the z direction), the probability of an intermediary event E being $S_x=+½$ is 1, and the probability of being $S_z=+½$ is also 1! However, since these two histories are not consistent, one cannot deduce that $S_x=+½$ *and* $S_z=+½$ with probability 1, for the same event E. This violates classical probability calculus (see criticisms of d'Espagnat 1989).

Other authors, like Omnès, Gell-Mann and Hartle, worked on this interpretation proposing that it is a development of the orthodox interpretation, since the latter only attributes probabilities to the moment of measurement, while the consistent histories interpretation would allow attributing probabilities to past events. Omnès (1992) even defended the use of what he called "quantum logic", but it is simply an approximation rule that eliminates very small quantities. Implicit in Griffiths' approach is the acceptance of retrodiction, of the epistemic view of states, and of faithful measurements. His view is clearly dualist, since retrodiction may also lead to states involving superposition of trajectories.

5. Map of the interpretations

Now that we have become familiar with many of the interpretations of quantum theory, let us make a sketch of the position of each of them in relation to the *ontological* (particle, wave, dualism or without ontology) and *epistemological* (realism or positivism) criteria. In the map of Fig. 1, the horizontal axis presents the ontological criteria, while the vertical axis is divided into realism (on the bottom), and positivism. Certain regions are highlighted, corresponding to the following interpretations: orthodox (ORTH.), statistical ensemble (ENS.), hidden variables theories (HVT.), wave (WAVE), stochastic (STOCH.), and quantum logics (LOG.). In general, the hidden variables theories may be considered a particular case of the ensemble interpretation.

Interpretations that are related appear with a dashed line in-between them.

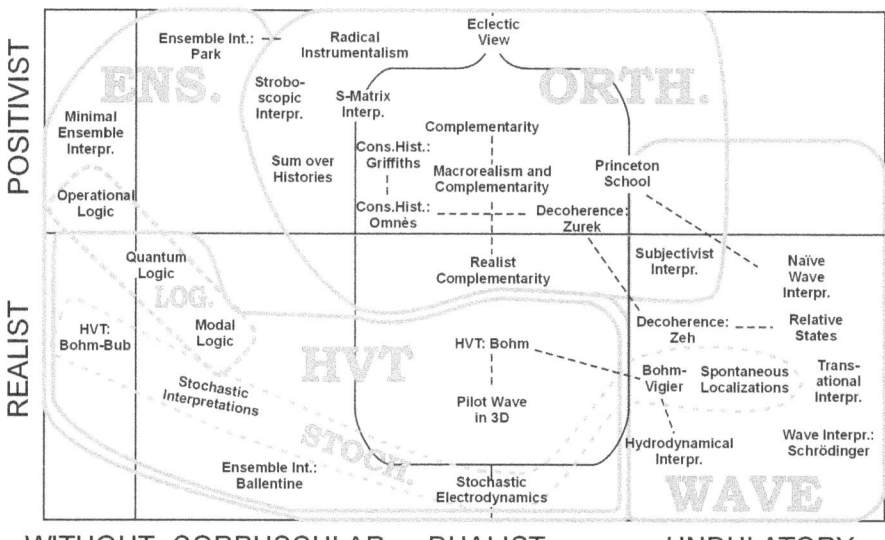

Fig. 1: Map of interpretations of quantum theory

6. Conclusion

The *systematic* study of the interpretations of quantum theory is still a vast and not much explored field. It is the task of "philosophy of physics" to try to systematize the comparative study of interpretations, pointing out which theses each view answers in a clear way, which assertions in fact correspond to a specific ontology and which are only the attribution of a label, which problems are swept under the rug, and how to group the interpretations in a satisfactory way. Furthermore, it would be interesting to take into account the intentional-emotional aspects mentioned in section 1, and extend the study not only to the "declared" interpretation, but also to the "natural" interpretations of alternative formalisms (like the Wigner distribution).

References

Aharonov, Y., Anandan, J. & L. Vaidman (1993), "Meaning of the Wave Function", *Physical Review A* 47: 4616-4626.

Ballentine, L E. (1970), "The Statistical Interpretation of Quantum Mechanics", *Reviews of Modern Physics* 42: 358-381.

Barrett, J.A. (1999), *The Quantum Mechanics of Minds and Worlds*, Oxford: Oxford University Press.

Barut, A.O. (1988), "The Revival of Schrödinger's Interpretation of Quantum Mechanics", *Foundations of Physics Letters* 1: 47-56.

Belinfante, F.J. (1973), *A Survey of Hidden-variables Theories*, Oxford: Pergamon.

Bell, J.S. (1990), "Against 'Measurement'", in Miller, A.I. (ed.), *Sixty-two Years of Uncertainty*, New York: Plenum, 1990, pp. 17-31. Reprinted in: *Physics World* 3: 33-40.

Bohm, D. (1952), "A Suggested Interpretation of the Quantum Theory in Terms of 'Hidden' Variables, I and II", *Physical Review* 85: 166-193. Reprinted in: Wheeler & Zurek (1983), pp. 369-396.

Bohr, N. (1928), "The Quantum Postulate and the Recent Development of Atomic Theory", *Nature* 121: 580-590. Reprinted in: Bohr, N., *Atomic Theory and the Description of Nature*, Cambridge: Cambridge

University Press, 1934, pp. 52-91; in: Wheeler & Zurek (1983), pp. 87-126.

Bohr, N. (1949), "Discussion with Einstein on Epistemological Problems in Physics", in Schilpp, P.A. (ed.), *Albert Einstein: Philosopher-Scientist*, Evanston: The Library of Living Philosophers, 1949, pp. 200-241. Reprinted in: Wheeler & Zurek (1983), pp. 9-49.

Born, M. (1949), *Natural Philosophy of Cause and Chance*, Oxford: Oxford University Press.

Boyer, T.H. (1975), "Random Electrodynamics: The Theory of Classical Electrodynamics with Classical Electromagnetic Zero-point Radiation", *Physical Review D* 11: 790-808.

Cramer, J.G. (1986), "The Transactional Interpretation of Quantum Mechanics", *Reviews of Modern Physics* 58: 647-87.

Cushing, J.T., Fine, A. & S. Goldstein (eds.) (1996), *Bohmian Mechanics and Quantum Theory: An Appraisal*, Dordrecht: Kluwer.

Dewitt, B.S. (1970), "Quantum Mechanics and Reality", *Physics Today* 23: 30-35.

D'Espagnat, B. (1989), "Are there Realistically Interpretable Local Theories?", *Journal of Statistical Physics* 56: 747-766.

Dorling, J. (1987), "Schrödinger's Original Interpretation of the Schrödinger Equation: A Rescue Attempt", in Kilmister, C.W. (ed.), *Schrödinger: Centenary Celebration of a Polymath*, Cambridge: Cambridge University Press, 1987, pp. 16-40.

Everett III, H. (1957), "Relative State Formulation of Quantum Mechanics", *Reviews of Modern Physics* 29: 454-62. Reprinted in: Wheeler & Zurek (1983), pp. 315-323.

Feynman, R.P. (1948), "Space-time Approach to Non-relativistic Quantum Mechanics", *Reviews of Modern Physics* 20: 367-387.

Feynman, R.P. (1987), "Negative Probability", in Hiley, B. J. & F.D. Peat (eds.), *Quantum Implications*, London: Routledge, pp. 235-248.

Fock, V.A. (1957), "On the Interpretation of Quantum Mechanics", *Czechoslovakian Journal of Physics* 7: 643-656.

Foulis, D.J. & C.H. Randall (1974), "The Empirical Logic Approach to the Physical Sciences", in Hartkämper, A. & H. Neumann (eds.), *Foundations of Quantum Mechanics and Ordered Linear Spaces*, New York: Springer, pp. 230-249.

Freyberger, M. & W.P. Schleich (1997), "True Vision of a Quantum State", *Nature* 386: 235-248.

Ghirardi, G.C., Omero, C., Rimini, A. & T. Weber (1978), "The Stochastic Interpretation of Quantum Mechanics: a Critical Review", *Rivista Nuovo Cimento* 1: 1-34.

Ghirardi, G.C., Rimini, A. & T. Weber (1986), "Unified Dynamics for Microscopic and Macroscopic Systems", *Physical Review D* 34: 470-491.

Gisin, N. & C. Percival (1992), "The Quantum-State Diffusion Model Applied to Open Systems", *Journal of Physics A* 25: 5677-5691.

Griffiths, R.B. (1984), "Consistent Histories and the Interpretation of Quantum Mechanics", *Journal of Statistical Physics* 36: 219-272.

Heisenberg, W. (1927), "Über den anschaulichen Inhalt der quantentheoretischen Kinematik und Mechanik", *Zeitschrift für Physik* 43: 172-198. English translation: "The Physical Content of Quantum Kinematics and Mechanics", in Wheeler & Zurek (1983), pp. 62-84.

Heisenberg, W. (1930), *The Physical Principles of Quantum Theory*, Chicago: University of Chicago Press.

Heisenberg, W. (1958), *Physics and Philosophy*, London: Allen & Unwin.

Home, D. & M.A.B. Whitaker (1992), "Ensemble Interpretations of Quantum Mechanics: A Modern Perspective", *Physics Reports* 210: 224-317.

Hughes, R.I.G. (1981), "Quantum Logic", *Scientific American* 245: 146-157.

Jammer, M. (1974), *The Conceptual Development of Quantum Mechanics*, New York: Wiley.

Kochen, S. (1985), "A New Interpretation of Quantum Mechanics", in Lahti, P. & P. Mittelstaedt (eds.), *Symposium on the Foundations of Modern Physics*, Singapore: World Scientific, 1985, pp. 151-169.

Landé, A. (1965, 1966, 1969, 1975), "Quantum Fact and Fiction. I. II. III. IV", *American Journal of Physics* 33: 123-127, 34: 1160-1166, 37: 541-548, 43: 701-704.

London, F. & E. Bauer (1939), *La théorie de l'observation en mécanique quantique*, Paris: Hermann. English translation in: Wheeler & Zurek (1983), pp. 217-259.

Ludwig, G. (1961), "Gelöste und ungelöste Probleme des Me☐ prozesses in der Quanten-mechanik", in Bopp, F. (ed.), *Werner Heisenberg und die Physik unserer Zeit*, Braunschweig: Vieweg, 1961, pp. 150-181.

Margenau, H. (1937), "Critical Points in Modern Physical Theory", *Philosophy of Science* 4: 337-370.

Margenau, H. (1954), "Advantages and Disadvantages of Various Interpretations of the Quantum Theory", *Physics Today* 7: 6-13.

Montenegro, R. & O. Pessoa Jr. (2002), "Interpretações da teoria quântica e as concepções dos alunos do curso de física", *Investigações sobre Ensino de Ciências* 7 (2). On-line: <http://www.if.ufrgs.br/public/ensino/vol7/n2/v7_n2_a1.html>

Omnès, R. (1992), "Consistent Interpretations of Quantum Mechanics", *Reviews of Modern Physics* 64: 339-382.

Park, J.L. (1973), "The Self-Contradictory Foundations of Formalistic Quantum Measurement Theories", *International Journal of Theoretical Physics* 8: 211-218.

Pessoa Jr., O. (1998), "As interpretações da física quântica", in Aguilera-Navarro, M.C.K., Aguilera-Navarro, V.C. & M. Goto (eds.), *Anais da III semana da física*, Londrina: Editora da Universidade Estadual de Londrina, 1998, pp. 137-187.

Pessoa Jr., O. (2000), "Complementing the Principle of Complementarity", *Physics Essays* 13: 50-67.

Pessoa Jr., O. (2003), *Conceitos da física quântica*, Vol. 1, São Paulo: Editora Livraria da Física.

Pessoa Jr., O. (2005), "Towards a Modal Logical Treatment of Quantum Physics", *Logic Journal of the IGPL* 13: 139-147.

Redhead, M. (1987), *Incompleteness, Non-locality, and Realism*, Oxford: Clarendon.

Reichenbach, H. (1944), *Philosophic Foundations of Quantum Mechanics*, Berkeley: University of California Press. Reprinted: New York: Dover, 1998.

Rosa, R. (1979), "Electron Interference: Landé's Approach Upset by a Recent Elegant Experiment", *Lettere al Nuovo Cimento* 24: 549-550.

Solvay, Institut International de Physique (1928), "Discussion générale des idées nouvelles émises", in *Électrons et photons – rapports et discussions de cinquième conseil de physique*, Paris: Gauthier-Villars, 1928, pp. 248-289.

Stapp, H.P. (1971), "S-Matrix Interpretation of Quantum Theory", *Physical Review D* 3: 1303-1320.

Von Neumann, J. (1932), *Mathematische Grundlagen der Quantenmechanik*, Berlin: Springer. English translation by Princeton University Press, 1955.

Wang, L.J., Zou, X.Y. & L. Mandel (1991), "Experimental Test of the de Broglie Guided-Wave Theory for Photons", *Physical Review Letters* 66: 1111-1114.

Wheeler, J.A. (1983), "Law without Law", in Wheeler & Zurek (1983), pp. 182-213.

Wheeler, J.A. & W.H. Zurek (eds.) (1983), *Quantum Theory and Measurement*, Princeton: Princeton University Press.

Wigner, E.P. (1961), "Remarks on the Mind-Body Question", in Good, I. J. (ed.). *The Scientist Speculates*, London: Heinemann, 1961, pp. 284-302. Reprinted in: Wheeler & Zurek (1983), pp. 168-181.

Wigner, E.P. (1963), "The Problem of Measurement", *American Journal of Physics* 31: 6-15. Reprinted in: Wheeler & Zurek (1983), pp. 324-341.

Zeh, H.D. (1993), "There are no Quantum Jumps, nor are there Particles!", *Physics Letters A* 172: 189-192.

Randomness vs. Arbitrariness in Classical Statistical Mechanics or Statistical Mechanics?[*]

Eduardo H. Flichman

National University of General Sarmiento (UNGS)/
University of Buenos Aires (UBA)

1. Purposes

The theoretical views related with isolated systems of particles ruled by classical statistical mechanics present many problems. Two of them, of ontological type and intimately connected, will be discussed in the present paper. I will do it in a conceptual way, avoiding many

---

[*] This paper has been produced under the framework of the research team directed by me in the UNGS (grant from the National Agency of Scientific and Technical Promotion) and in the UBA (grant from UBACYT). I am grateful to Mario Castagnino, Eduardo Izquierdo, Hernán Miguel, Alberto Moretti, Ricardo Page, Jorge Paruelo, Lilia Romanelli, and José Ure for comments to previous versions, which permitted to improve the contents of the paper. My greatest gratitude goes to two persons: Olimpia Lombardi, whose advice was of great help during the revision of the work. Her suggestions and indications were so important, that I can assert that her help was fundamental in order to avoid many errors. And Horacio Abeledo, who read and commented thoroughly my work in different versions, and discussed publicly one of them, thus allowing a development more free from errors, and inciting me to find the answers to the fundamental questions he posed. Abeledo helped me also to improve my English.

technical formulations, but trying to escape simplifications, which in my opinion could harm the arguments.

The first problem is related to the possibility that the probability distributions of initial conditions could be subject to restrictions ("extra" limitations) which are added to those normally accepted: boundary conditions, constraints, and constant energy. I shall try to show, independently from the theoretical approach used in each case, that the fact that isolated systems evolve towards equilibrium or maintain it requires probability distributions of initial conditions over phase space[1] that are clearly restrictive ("extra" limitations). Those "extra" limitations make it impossible to suppose arbitrary initial probability distributions, that is, any particular distribution (except for the accepted limitations: boundary conditions, constraints, constant energy). The task in section 3. will be to try to justify and explain the "extra" limitations.

The second problem refers to an apparently different situation (always from the ontological point of view) to the case of few particles ruled by classical mechanics. Here the "extra" limitations do not seem to exist; and arbitrariness seems to rule now with respect to successions of initial conditions, since we can fix the initial conditions in an arbitrary way in each repetition of the experiment (except for the normally accepted limitations). How many particles are needed for "extra" restrictions to "appear" or to "begin to function as such"? Starting with what number of particles does classical mechanics become statistical classical mechanics? A solution is looked for, trying to show that there is only one classical mechanics, namely classical statistical mechanics, and a solution is conjectured for the apparent contradiction presented; all that in section 4. Section 5. tackles in a synthetic way a collateral problem related with the ontological difference in the interpretation of probability, depending on whether the laws with which we deal are laws of evolution or laws of probability distribution of initial conditions.

---

[1] Phase space is the abstract space of the initial (or final) conditions of the system, and of its evolution. Each point represents the set of positions and impulses of all the particles of the system.

2. Introduction

I intend to conceptualize some aspects of particle classical statistical mechanics (henceforth "statistical mechanics") because of their explanatory interest, and also because of the astonishing situations to which are driven those who succumb to curiosity are driven, and to the pleasure of plunging into questions that are so complex but yet so attractive.

After a period of evolution, the state of an isolated system is fixed in a mechanical theory by:
(i) *the evolution laws of the system* and
(ii) *initial conditions, boundary conditions and constraints*.

Given the evolution laws of the system, the initial conditions, and the constraints, the state of the system is fixed in all later instants: we shall refer to this state as the "final conditions". Depending on the mechanical theory in question, the final conditions may be fixed in a probabilistic or in a deterministic way.[2] When we deal with statistical mechanics, a new element must be taken into account: the *initial ensemble*[3] or *probability distribution of initial conditions*. And for the state of

---

[2] In a work published a few years ago, Flichman (2001), I tried to show that it is nonsense to speak of mere determinism and indeterminism, as the two sole possible situations, one in the antipodes of the other. The extreme situations correspond to strong determinism (absence of any type or degree of indeterminism) and, at the other end, to strong indeterminism or "Greek chaos" (absence of any type or degree of determinism). But, in between, there is a whole gradation of determinisms and indeterminisms. As determinism is weakened, indeterminism is strengthened and viceversa. What we usually denote by the term "indeterminism" is in reality the absence of a strong determinism, but not strong indeterminism. Nevertheless, in order to avoid the use of an unusual nomenclature, which may produce confusion, I will use the term "determinism" in order to refer to strong determinism and the term "indeterminism" to refer to some degree of indeterminism. A similar problem appears with the consideration of the regions of validity of determinism. I think it is important to refer to situations of determinism because it could be held that there are regions or levels where there is determinism and others where there is not. For example, quantum physics is usually interpreted as a non-determinist theory in measurement situations. But in other situations it is interpreted usually as a determinist theory. Moreover, if we speak of the level of macroscopic physics, quantum indeterminism converges to a deterministic situation.
[3] I use here the term "ensemble" in a general way, in the sense used in Gibbs' approach.

the system in any later instant, the *final ensemble or probability distribution of final conditions is taken into account.*[4]

2.1. About what this paper will not treat

2.1.1. *The epistemic problem*

I will not deal in this paper with the problem concerning the possibility, in principle or in practice, of making predictions about either the evolution of a mechanical system, or of the probability distribution of its initial and/or final conditions. I will deal only with the ontological viewpoint of the system and of its evolution. So when I refer to probability or to probability distributions, it will refer to objective probabilities, and not to those related to ignorance. I will adopt as a definition of "determinism" of a theory that which indicates,[5] for the set of possible worlds or models of the theory (worlds ruled by the same laws), that their laws are such that there do not exist two worlds of that set exactly equal (referring to facts) in a given instant, and that differ in some other instant. Determinism is the determinism of the laws of evolution, which result from the articulation of dynamics[6] with force laws.

2.1.2. *Evolution equations*

The first point (i), concerning the evolution equations, will be not discussed here. I will only say in that respect, that statistical mechanics is considered a determinist theory if we make an exception, perhaps, of special situations in particle mechanics – which go over by extension to statistical mechanics – such as, for instance, the presence of certain types of singularities. Such cases have been thoroughly studied (see, for example, Earman 1986), and will not be discussed here. Thus, I shall consider that statistical mechanics is, in general – onto-

---

[4] We should consider one exception: in the case of "absolute chaos", discussed in section 3.1, the ensemble, even though it is a distribution of initial (or final) conditions, it is not a probabilistic distribution, as we shall see there.
[5] I follow here, in a simple way, definitions such as that of R. Montague. See Montague (1974).
[6] I will use "dynamics" to refer to the laws of mechanics, and "mechanics" to refer to the mechanical theory taken globally.

logically – deterministic, and particularly in the situations which will be used as the object of study of this paper.

2.2. About what this paper will indeed treat

I shall discuss instead the problem (ii) of the initial ensembles: probability distributions of initial conditions, always from the ontological point of view.

I want to tackle the following question: deterministic laws of evolution (dynamics plus laws of force) do not impose any restriction for initial ensembles. The sole limitations we should apparently consider (limitations normally accepted) are those derived from boundary conditions or, in general, from constraints (henceforth I will make no difference between boundary conditions and constraints: I will just say "boundary conditions").[7] Since we will deal with isolated systems, there is also one more normally accepted limitation: the – constant – value of the energy of the system. Anyhow, we will see immediately that this seemingly simple presentation shows two serious difficulties, which will be the motive of discussion of this paper.

3. First difficulty

We will see that if we want to explain random compensations, that is, the process through which a statistical mechanical isolated system evolves toward or stays in equilibrium, we cannot avoid considering certain "other" limitations ("extra" limitations) to the initial ensembles.

Henceforth, I will associate the expression "final" to some instant after the "initial instant", (final) instant in which the probability distribution of the (final) conditions should be those of – or, better, should have perceptibly reached a point near – equilibrium.[8] I will call

---

[7] Many of the simpler evolution equations of classical particle mechanics (and by extension, statistical mechanics) do not require differential equations with partial derivatives with respect to position, so we don't see in those cases what we strictly call boundary conditions. But there are more complex force laws which do require boundary conditions. For that reason we will not make any distinction between constraints and boundary conditions.

[8] I am referring to systems that evolve toward, or stay in, equilibrium. They are isolated systems. There are open systems that evolve into stable states, near or far from equilibrium. I am not referring to those types of systems, because we are deal-

the final ensemble, "product": probability distribution of final conditions. The product is fixed by the initial ensemble, the boundary conditions, the energy of the system, and the (deterministic) laws of evolution. The product (state of equilibrium or of quasi equilibrium) will be some type of more or less complex stochastic distribution, depending on the case and depending on the viewpoint (Bolzmann, Gibbs or other) from which it is studied.

From a Bolzmannian viewpoint, the simplest cases could be Gaussian or similar distributions on a base of macro-states, even though on a base of micro-states they would be equiprobable distributions. From a Gibbsian viewpoint, they will be distributions of equal density of probability (coarse-grained) in the phase space. But an example will soon show us (in *3.2.*) that if the initial conditions (for instance, the repeated beginning of the experiment) follow each other in an *arbitrary* way (except for boundary conditions and constant energy), that is, without "extra" limitations, then we cannot assure a product which accomplishes the *random* or *stochastic* distribution (that is, a state of equilibrium) to which we have just referred to.

3.1. Terminology and something more

I think it is important to make some terminological clarifications. It is very common to confuse notions that are almost opposite in meaning: "randomness", "stochasticity", "chance"; terms very similar in meaning (or having the same meaning) are usually confused with "arbitrariness", which has a radically different meaning.

I have already tried to clarify the use of several expressions, such as "determinism", "initial ensemble", and "final ensemble" or "product". I will try here to state with some degree of precision the difference between "randomness" and "arbitrariness". It is fundamental to clarify certain points in order to avoid fatal confusions. I will use a demarcation that is in some way related to that proposed by John Earman (see Earman 1986, Chap. VIII). We should take into account several dichotomies. I will consider "stochasticity" as a synonym of "randomness".

---

ing with isolated systems. There are also isolated systems that do not evolve toward equilibrium. I will deal with them in section 3.7.

(i)   probabilistic processes – probabilistic ensembles
(ii) probabilistic processes – absolutely chaotic processes[9]
(iii) probabilistic ensembles – "absolutely chaotic ensembles" – random ensembles –initial arbitrary ensembles

(i) The notion of probability can be applied to processes (probabilistic laws of evolution) or to initial (or final) conditions.

When we deal with *processes* ruled by probabilistic laws of evolution, there exist probabilistic bifurcations or multifurcations. In our (deterministic) case there is, in each case, a single possible process (once initiated).

On the other side, when we are concerned with *initial or final conditions,* there are probability distributions in them *(ensembles)*. In that case, the notion of *randomness* is strictly related with that of *probability. There is randomness if and only if a certain type of probability distribution exists: the distribution corresponding to equilibrium.*

We should clarify here what we understand by distributions of equilibrium (or quasi-equilibrium). They are the random or stochastic distributions, that are nothing other than probability distributions of initial or final conditions in which the system, macroscopically considered, maintains itself stable, that is, without any sensible modification of its macroscopic parameters. Statistical mechanical theories – Gibbsian, Bolzmannian or other – relate the macroscopic variables with the microscopic ones.

(ii) We shouldn't confuse a *probabilistic* process with an *absolutely chaotic* one. A world which "evolves" as an absolutely chaotic "process" is a world without laws of any type. Since there are no laws, not even probabilistic laws, there are no probabilities. Each moment of the evolution of such a world is not related in any way with its past or future. All possibilities are open. It is not the case that all possibilities have the same or different probabilities. There are no probabilities, neither zero, nor one, nor any value between zero and one. In such a world anything may happen in any moment. But it would have no sense to say that that would happen with equal probability for each

---

[9] We must not confuse them with the "physical chaos" processes, studied in present days physics. I refer here to what I called "Greek chaos" in note 2. Earman calls it "utter chaos".

possible situation. It is difficult to imagine an absolutely chaotic, strongly indeterministic world, and it needs to be proven that it is coherent to suppose it. But none of that concerns us here, because we are considering determinist processes.

(iii) We must also not confuse an initial or final ensemble, which is a *probability* distribution of initial or final conditions, with an *"absolutely chaotic"* one. The concept of an "absolutely chaotic ensemble" is, for one thing, a confusing notion. This does not imply any probability distribution (see note 4). It doesn't mean that each initial of final point (or cell) in phase space has some probability (zero or one or any other value between zero and one) or some probability density. On the contrary, there is not any probability distribution at all. What we can say in such a situation is that all the (initial or final) conditions are possible, without ascribing the category of probability to that possibility. In this case also it should be proven that it is coherent to suppose such a situation. Earman (1986) considers that such a situation could be impossible, even though he does not consider this supposition as a final conclusion. He only says that it "[...] *may not* be a coherent notion" (my italics). But he also adds: "I predict that the challenge cannot be met".

Nevertheless, I will not use this notion of absolute chaos. It can be seen as an idealization, but it will not be necessary for the discussion. Anyhow, what I will present as a possibility (which, as we shall see, will be finally abandoned) is an "arbitrary" initial ensemble. Such arbitrariness will correspond to probabilistic distributions of initial conditions, more limited than absolute chaos, but at the same time broader (compatible with the boundary conditions and the constant energy) than those that take us to the random product (equilibrium) which in fact happens. So instead of talking of absolute chaos, I will talk about arbitrariness. It is a (perfectly coherent) situation, intermediate between "randomness" and "absolute chaos", which includes the cases of randomness, but exceeds them. We will study now an example of this type.

3.2. An example

It is possible to find random compensations in cases where certain elements of the system are sufficiently large in size, while others sufficiently small and numerous. For instance, a sufficiently large disc, symmetric in size and weight, – similar to a coin – will fall down through the air inside a much larger container, and the molecular impacts on its sides will not displace it appreciably (small and numerous molecules).[10] The repetition of such macroscopic initial situation (most probably a different initial position in phase space) will not change the fact that "casual" compensations will occur.

Let us suppose now the initial conditions to be such that, in the final conditions, the molecules hit one side of the disc much more than the other, so that it jumps to one of the sides of the vessel. And let us suppose that the same or very similar initial conditions[11] occur in each repetition of the experiment. In such cases the product clearly does not satisfy randomness (equilibrium) and hence is inconsistent with what is in fact, usually observed. In such cases, the initial ensemble is *arbitrary* and, moreover, doesn't give rise to the random product that is normally observed. The initial conditions of our example (which is imaginary and anomalous and does not occur in reality) add up to a probability value of one. Those which, instead, take us to the usually observed product, add up (in our imaginary example) to probability zero.

Consequently, the product we actually observe, which is different, which is not that of the example, because the disc does not deviate sensibly, demands that we consider more restrictions ("extra" limitations") for the initial ensemble.

3.3. The questions[12]

The first question we ask ourselves is the following: how do we *justify* the fact that arbitrary initial ensembles (without "extra" limitations) are not possible? A pertinent answer is the following: the experi-

---

[10] It is clear also that a very small disk would appreciably undergo Brownian movement.
[11] Actually, it is sufficient for them to be such that in the final state the disc deviates from the trajectory that would have usually been observed.
[12] The problem was presented to me in a general manner (including both questions) by H. Abeledo (personal communication).

mental facts, the facts that are actually observed confirm[13] the initial ensemble from its consequences: the product. The product is random, it is the equilibrium, and it satisfies the expected casual compensations (expected because it is a fact that we can observe). The initial ensemble is calculated (when we can do it) so that, from it and from the evolution laws, the boundary conditions, and the value of the energy, we obtain the expected stochastic product: in our example, that the molecular impacts on the disc do not produce a sensitive deviation in its trajectory. The restriction to those initial ensembles eliminates any other (arbitrary) possible ensemble.

The first question has been responded, but not yet the second, which I present now: how do we *explain* such a probabilistic result about the distribution of initial conditions? *Why* do the results in that example compensate in such a way that practically half of the impacts happen to occur on one side of the disc, and the other half on the other side? *Why* is the probability distributed in such a way that the random compensations occur? The answer appears always as *statistical compensation*, as *chance*. But how is that *chance* to be explained? Why those statistical compensations are produced, apart from the immediate but not explained intuitive impression?

A possible explanatory hypothesis, based on arguments given by several researchers,[14] *consists basically in accepting the "natural" existence of such "other" restrictions on the initial ensembles.*

In many occasions, it is usual to postulate initial ensembles which fix equal (density of) probability for each initial condition (for each microstate: microcanonical distribution), compatible with the boundary conditions and with the energy of the system, *as if it were an arbitrary distribution*. But it is exactly the opposite: it is an extremely fixed and not arbitrary ensemble.

3.4. First explanatory assumption

There exist laws of chance (or stochastic laws, or laws of randomness) "for the product", and they are logically independent from the deterministic laws of evolu-

---

[13] That is, they allow making inferences, in a way that is obviously non deductive, but only conjectural.
[14] These types of conclusions have been presented by H. Reichenbach, A. Grünbaum and H. Mehlberg from diverse points of view.

tion "for the process". *This explains the need of introducing more restrictions in the initial ensemble.*

Under this supposition, the deterministic laws of evolution are not sufficient to complete the theoretical basis. We should add the probabilistic laws of chance, because all of them (deterministic laws of evolution for the process and probabilistic laws of chance for the product) play a role in the process we are studying. Thus, the initial ensemble cannot be arbitrary.

However, this supposition sounds uneconomic: on one hand we have the restrictions in the initial ensemble and on the other hand the probabilistic laws from which we infer (in the logical sense, not in the chronological one) the restrictions, in the product. That is why a second explanatory assumption has been deemed more acceptable.

3.5. Second explanatory supposition

Instead of supposing probabilistic laws, which postulate "extra" – in conjunction with boundary conditions and the constancy of energy – limitations for the initial ensembles, we may suppose the existence of the same "extra" restrictions as a natural basic founding fact for initial ensembles; as basic, as founding, and as natural as laws of nature are. Those restrictions will (now) allow the presence of stochastic *regularities* of chance in the product, which will not be considered laws within the new interpretation. They will be only consequences of the mentioned "extra" restrictions (plus those normally accepted, plus the evolution laws). Thus, the initial conditions cannot be arbitrary (we obtain the same result from the first supposition), which appears intuitively as surprising. Here we have, then, the second supposition:

There exists basic limitations for the initial ensembles, and those limitations are logically independent from the deterministic laws of evolution for the process.

If instead of considering it basic (as the laws of evolution are basic), we intended to explain such limitation (explanation of the explanation), we could realize a surprising move. I shall use the metaphor of the Big Bang. But afterwards I shall put it aside, because classical mechanics cannot presuppose it. The surprising move consists in going back to the Big Bang and accepting that in that moment the initial conditions were such that they prepared for the future the "extra" restrictions, that is, all casual compensations.[15] Finally, if we put the problem in a more correct way for classical mechanics, that is, without the Big Bang, time extends into the past, indefinitely. And the explanation of the explanation disappears. Of course, we could suppose[16] a beginning for a classical universe without Big Bang, in which the initial conditions were such that they would prepare the "extra" restrictions, that is, all the casual compensations for the future. But, even though logically and physically possible, it is a thesis that is very difficult to admit, because without eliminating the "extra" restrictions, which remain fixed in the initial instant of the universe, it adds in its turn a new absolutely unnecessary restriction: an initial instant for the classical universe. Another objection to the hypothesis of a beginning of the universe for the classical theory is that it would imply the cancellation of the determination into the past by the laws of evolution, something not contemplated in classical theory. Anyhow, the restrictions are basic, be it that we fix them at the beginning of time or that we fix them at the beginning of each statistical process. Randomness of the product will continue allowing certain initial ensembles and prohibiting others.

Thus, we see that, if we accept any of the two first explanatory suppositions, there would be ontological restrictions to the arbitrariness of the initial ensembles: ontological randomness of the product is the result of "extra" limitations of the possible initial ensembles, even though there is ontological determinism of the evolution laws. These are surprising conclusions. Could it be possible that there are no arbitrary initial ensembles existing in the classical deterministic world (compatible with the boundary conditions and the energy)? Is it possible that initial ensembles have intrinsic characteristics (essential chance), which express much more than the simple ignorance of initial conditions?

---

[15] This idea was suggested to me by H. Abeledo a long time ago. Many years after that I found it presented in Sklar (1993). I am not sure if it can be proven that the possibility exists.
[16] This idea was also presented by Abeledo (personal communication).

3.6. Articulation of the first and second suppositions

In the beginning, the first supposition may seem more interesting: to accept the adding (in the product) of laws of chance (equilibrium), which restrict the initial ensembles. But the second supposition seems to have the advantage of economy: it is sufficient to have the initial ensembles, restricted as mere funding facts, and it is possible to eliminate the stochastic laws, which result simply as a consequence of such restrictions, without a founding nomological autonomy.

But perhaps the view that the second supposition is more economic is illusory. Perhaps we could accept a mixed explanatory supposition: perhaps it is equivalent to suppose founding stochastic laws which determine restrictions in the initial ensembles, or founding initial ensembles which determine, together with the determinist laws of particle mechanics, stochastic regularities.

3.7. Third explanatory supposition

I will suggest now a completely different supposition. It tries to show that the resulting randomness of the product is derived ultimately from the deterministic mechanical system. So that, if it is correct we may forget about initial ensembles and accept that a deterministic mechanical statistical system evolves generating random products. If it were so, it could be expected at first glance that the initial ensembles could be *really arbitrary*. From the initial ensembles, the deterministic evolution equations would just carry out the system to its random products. The situation corresponding to this third supposition is fulfilled basically in mixing systems (a special type of ergodic systems). This third supposition presents some unsolved problems. I will not deal with them because they are not related to the difficulty that I intend to discuss here. I will only deal with what is related to the problem here discussed. Even if we suppose that all systems are mixing, "anomalous" systems exist that do not evolve into the randomness usually expected in isolated systems (mixing systems "which do not mix").[17] There are systems which initial conditions correspond to a finite probability (they are derived from the so called "KAM theorem"). There are other systems that do not tend towards the random-

---

[17] I use here the ideas of Sklar (1993).

ness usually expected, but to which initial conditions correspond to a probability of null measure.

Our concern *is not* to ask why we do not observe these kinds of systems in reality. The answer could be obvious: that we do not observe them because the probability of their occurrences (in both cases) is so low that an observation would be practically impossible. Even null measure probability cases are possible. But it is obvious that it would be almost miraculous to observe them.

Instead, our concern *is* to ask through what mechanism has been decided that such systems have finite probability (in one case) or null measure probability (in the other). What has been done is to *relate proportionally* the probability of the initial occurrence of one of those systems with its correspondent volume in the phase space. On the other hand, even in the "normal" cases (mixing system "which mix") their initial probability is also proportional to such volume. From this point of view it is supposed that all the points in the phase space (microstates) are equally probable, because only under such a supposition is it possible to calculate the probability "counting" (integrating) microstates. All the cells ("coarse grained" states) of the phase space in Gibbs's view or all the microstates in Bolzmann's view, occupy the same volume and they are conferred (it is postulated for them) equal probability. So, both for the "anomalous" cases which do not mix and for the "normal" cases which do mix, an initial distribution of probabilities on the phase space has been postulated that is absolutely restrictive, because it assumes *a priori* the equiprobability of all its points. Of course, that equiprobability is more than justified by the experimental results. But the only explanation of such a restriction[18] is, again, that which we have already pointed out for the first two suppositions.

For all the systems (whether "anomalous" or "normal") a previous postulation is required: a probability proportional to the corresponding volume. So the initial ensemble is restricted ("extra" limitation, besides the normally accepted limitations) and, consequently, it is not and it cannot be arbitrary.

---

[18] Horacio Abeledo's question about the "why" of such equiprobability was, perhaps, the central initial motive for the making of the present work.

3.8. Conclusion

The third explanatory supposition is reduced in the last instance to the two previous ones, or to the articulation of both of them (3.6.), which is the only explanation which we find in order to solve this first difficulty.

4. Second problem and my conjecture

4.1. The problem

A different, but related problem, is that of classical particle mechanics "becoming" particle statistical mechanics, in which a disturbing vagueness appears. How many particles are needed for the casual laws and/or the restrictions in the initial ensembles to "appear" or to "begin to function as such"? It seems self-evident that no extra postulation is needed when we deal with very few manipulable particles. It is sufficient with the deterministic laws of evolution and "any" initial conditions compatible with the boundary conditions and the energy. Curiously enough, in that "any", the hypothesis of the arbitrariness for few particles is hidden (let us suppose three manipulable small spheres; or two; or one). Nothing allows us to suppose that, apart from the restrictions determined by the boundary conditions and the energy, there are probabilistic restrictions for initial conditions. It is senseless to speak of the probability of each initial condition because it will depend on us to *choose* an initial condition in order to start the system.[19] Consequently, it seems that (in the repeated experiments) there are only deterministic laws of evolution and arbitrary successions of initial conditions. In each experiment, once the arbitrarily chosen (except for the normally accepted limitations) initial conditions take place, the system is left isolated, always with the same energy.

But, then, starting from what number of particles does mechanics becomes statistical mechanics? Or is a process for a few particles of

---

[19] I am not concerned with the errors in the implementation of those initial conditions. But we can always find examples (in classical mechanics) where they do not affect the argument. For the same reason, I don't take into account that we are not dealing with particles, but with bodies (small spheres) with sensible appreciable dimensions.

the same type as one as for many? If that were the case, there would be no particle mechanics, only statistical mechanics. Mechanics would have been reduced to statistical mechanics and not the other way around. This is a very delicate point, because, if this is true, then there is only one mechanics: statistical mechanics. And there would be, even for one particle, allowed and prohibited initial ensembles; and that result is (or seems to be) completely absurd if we take into account what was said in the previous paragraph.

I think that for the case of many particles – just our example in section (3.2.) – we could imagine a fantastic goblin who fixes the initial conditions in each experiment and leaves the system isolated, always with the same energy. The goblin (as we do in the case of few particles) neither adds energy into the system nor removes it. He fixes that energy in the desired value and closes the system. There would be no restrictions then, as in the case of the three (or two or one) manipulable balls. I believe, then, that there is only one mechanics (there is nothing to reduce). And the apparent absurd still stands.

4.2. The conjecture

I propose the following possible conjecture in order to solve this problem: *when the goblin (or we) choose arbitrarily the succession of initial conditions, that is, the initial ensemble, what we are doing is to add in each experiment more boundary conditions, so that there remains no more room for more restrictions ("extra"). So the initial conditions remain totally determined by the boundary conditions and the energy (normally accepted limitations), and the degrees of freedom that allow the "extra" restrictions over them, just disappear. We find only the probabilistic distributions of initial conditions that allow the random (equilibrium) product that is observed.*[20]

In this way, the existence of "extra" restrictions when we do not *choose* the initial conditions is made compatible with the absence of such restrictions when we do *choose* those conditions. The difference between mechanics and statistical mechanics is, thus, eliminated from the ontological field and is maintained only in the epistemic field: with few particles we can *choose* the initial conditions in each repetition of

---

[20] At most, there remain the degrees of freedom given by the error in the implementation of the initial conditions.

the experiment. With many particles (the case of air molecules, for instance) we cannot make such a choice (we are not omniscient goblins). Consequently, there remains certain degrees of freedom open for the functioning of the "extra" restrictions over them, so that only the probabilistic distributions of initial conditions which allow the observed random (equilibrium) product can occur.

5. Complementary note: two ontological notions of probability

The concept of *probability* changes completely (even though it satisfies formally the same axioms) when we deal – not in our case – with *probability in the laws of evolution* (probabilistic laws), and when we deal with the *distribution of probabilities in the initial conditions (initial ensembles)*. In the first case, which does not apply to classical statistical mechanics, it is the probability that the system *evolves* in one of the branches in the bifurcation (or multifurcation) points.

In the second case, it is the probability of *occurrence* of each *initial condition*. An ensemble is a distribution of probabilities of initial conditions. Each initial condition (point in the phase space) has a probability – or density of probability – of *occurrence*.

References

Batterman, R.W. (1998), "Why Equilibrium Statistical Mechanics Works: Universality and the Renormalization Group", *Philosophy of Science* 65: 183-208.

Earman, J. (1986), *A Primer on Determinism*, Dordrecht/Boston/Lancaster/Tokyo: Reidel.

Earman, J. & M. Rédei (1996), "Why Ergodic Theory Does Not Explain the Success of Equilibrium Statistical Mechanics", *British Journal of Philosophy of Science* 47: 63-78.

Flichman, E.H. (2002), "Grados de determinismo e indeterminismo", in Lorenzano, P. & F. Tula Molina (eds.), *Filosofía e Historia de la Ciencia en el Cono Sur*, Bernal: National University of Quilmes, pp. 155-160. (Also published in Secretaría de Investigación (ed.), *Problemas de investigación, ciencia y desarrollo*, Los Polvorines: National University of General Sarmiento, 2001, pp. 419-424.)

Friedman, K.S. (1976), "A Partial Vindication of Ergodic Theory", *Philosophy of Science* 43: 151-162.

Grünbaum, A. (1973), *Philosophical Problems of Space and Time*, Dordrecht/Boston: Reidel. (Second edition, enlarged. It is the XII Volume of the Boston Studies in the Philosophy of Science.)

Krylov, N. (1979), *Works on the Foundations of Statistical Physics*, Princeton: Princeton University Press.

Lebowitz, J.L. & Penrose, O. (1973), "Modern Ergodic Theory", *Physics Today*: 23-29.

Malament, D.B. & Zabell, S.L. (1980), "Why Gibbs Phase Averages Work – The Role of Ergodic Theory", *Philosophy of Science* 47: 339-349.

Mehlberg, H. (1980), *Time, Causality and the Quantum Theory*, Dordrecht: Reidel.

Montague, R. (1974), "Deterministic Theories", in Thomason, R.H. (ed.), *Formal Philosophy*, New Haven, Connecticut: Yale University Press.

Quay, S.J., P.M. (1978), "A Philosophical Explanation of the Explanatory Functions of Ergodic Theory", *Philosophy of Science* 45: 47-59.

Reichenbach, H. (1956), *The Direction of Time*, Berkeley: University of California Press.

Sklar, L. (1973), "Statistical Explanation and Ergodic Theory", *Philosophy of Science* 40: 194-21.

Sklar, L. (1993), *Physics and Chance – Philosophical Issues in the Foundations of Statistical Mechanics*, Cambridge/New York/Melbourne: Cambridge University Press.

Tolman, R. (1938), *The Principles of Statistical Mechanics*, Oxford: Oxford University Press.

Vranas, P.B.M. (1998), "Epsilon-Ergodicity and the Success of Equilibrium Statistical Mechanics", *Philosophy of Science* 65: 688-708.

www.ingramcontent.com/pod-product-compliance
Lightning Source LLC
Chambersburg PA
CBHW070738160426
43192CB00009B/1482